ANGLING
IN THE
BAILIWICK OF GUERNSEY

BY
LEN LE PAGE

peterprint limited

Published by: L.R. Le Page, Guernsey

First published: April 1999

                         ISBN 978-0-9509360-7-9

Second edition: September 2007

                         ISBN 978-0-9556523-0-1

Third edition: Oct 2011

                         ISBN 978-0-9569841-0-4

Printed by: Peter Print Limited, Guernsey,
                         Channel Islands

Cover pictures by: Brian Green

Front Cover: An early morning angling session for Daryl Butcher
                         and Joe Gomez at Havelet Bay

Back Cover: Your author!

CONTENTS

About the Author

The book's author Len Le Page was born in Guernsey and was educated at the Vale School and the Boy's Intermediate School, as the Grammar School was then known.

He joined Guernsey Telecoms just before his sixteenth birthday and retired in January 1997 after 44 years service, during which he rose to the post of Network Services Director. He married Joy in 1960, has a son and daughter and four grandchildren.

As a young man he pursued many sports, with, it must be said, very little success! However he soon realised that angling was to be his favourite sport and so began a long and successful angling career.

He has held three British Records, nine Channel Island Records, 19 Bailiwick Records and numerous Club Records. He has been the Guernsey Sea Anglers Club Champion on three occasions and Telephone Angling Club Champion 14 times.

He has won a number of top prizes in open competitions, including the Guernsey Bass Anglers Sportfishing Society's Bass Festival, as well as awards in the Fish of the Month Competition.

He has taken an active role in angling administration, including being the secretary of the Bailiwick of Guernsey Record (Rod-Caught) Fish Committee for the 44 years since its inception in 1966, chairman of the Telephone Angling Club for 30 years, a member of the Guernsey Sea Anglers Club Committee for 36 years, during which he was competition secretary for 14 years and president for 19 years, and secretary of the 30 Fathom Club for two years during his 28 year membership.

He is a member of the Guernsey Mullet Club, the Guernsey Freshwater Angling Society and the Bailiwick Bass Club and was a member of the Shark Angling Club of Great Britain for 11 years.

He wrote the weekly angling reports in the Guernsey Press for over 30 years, between 1980 and 2010 producing 1580 columns. He had articles published in the Angling Mail and was the Guernsey angling columnist for the now defunct Channel Island Sunday News.

He also taught "Sea Angling for Beginners" at the Guernsey College of Further Education for a four year period.

Thanks

The author wishes to acknowledge with gratitude the friendly and generous help that was so freely given by so many people when he was collecting information and material for this book.

In particular he expresses his most sincere thanks to the late Peter Witterick who gave so many hours of his time giving advice and constructive criticism, proof-reading the initial script of the first edition to ensure the author's grammatical errors and spelling mistakes did not go unnoticed and providing many photographs from the earlier years, and all this at a time when he was suffering indifferent health.

Similarly thanks go to the Guernsey Press and photographer Brian Green who so readily allowed the use of some of their pictures in this publication.

Sincere thanks are also given to Sean Johnson from PeterPrint for his enthusiastic support and expertise on the production of the second and third editions.

Dedication

To my wife Joy, who has always given positive support to my enthusiasm for angling.

It has been her understanding and help over the years that has made my achievements possible, my disappointments more bearable and my enjoyment of such a great sport even more complete.

ENGLISH CHANNEL

The Bailiwick of Guernsey

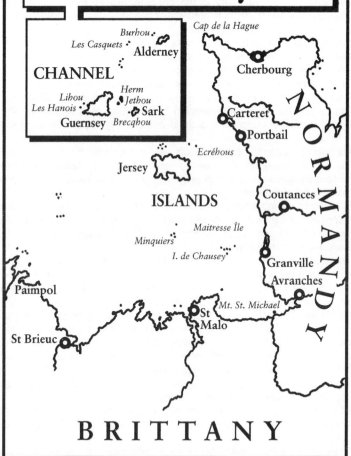

CHANNEL

Burhou
Les Casquets
Alderney

Cap de la Hague

Cherbourg

NORMANDY

Herm
Lihou
Les Hanois
Jethou
Sark
Guernsey
Brecqhou

Carteret

Portbail

Ecréhous

Jersey

Coutances

ISLANDS

Maitresse Île

Minquiers

I. de Chausey

Granville

Avranches

Paimpol

St Malo

Mt. St. Michael

St Brieuc

BRITTANY

Chapter 1 - Introduction

The Bailiwick of Guernsey comprises the islands of Guernsey, Alderney and Sark, including Brecqhou, Herm, Jethou, Lihou and the large number of uninhabited islands including Burhou.

The Bailiwick is so-called as it is under the jurisdiction of a Bailiff, who is the Island's chief citizen.

The Bailiff is appointed by the Sovereign and has many duties and responsibilities including the Presiding Officer of the States of Deliberation (Guernsey's Parliament), President of the Royal Court and President of the Court of Appeal.

The Bailiwick of Guernsey is the northern half of the Channel Islands archipelago. The southern half consists of the Bailiwick of Jersey, which is completely separate and independent.

The islands that form the Bailiwick of Guernsey are surrounded by a wonderful marine environment. The strong tidal flows, the interminable number of reefs and sandbanks and the clean, clear waters have produced an area that is rich in marine life, including a great variety of different species of fish.

It is hardly surprising that sea angling has become one of the Bailiwick's most popular participant sports. It is enjoyed by hundreds of local anglers and an increasing number of visitors who come over especially to experience the fishing it has to offer.

Although it doesn't seem to be officially recognised, the huge amount of angling activity has become a positive contributor to the Bailiwick's economy, providing a source of income and employment for many people across a wide spectrum of the community.

In spite of angling's enormous growth over the 63 years up to 2010, very little has been recorded of its development and history. The first book produced in that time was a 40 page publication "Angling in the Channel Islands" written by Peter Witterick and published way back in 1957.

The Guernsey Press and the Guernsey Star (until it ceased publication in October 1965) have given excellent coverage of the sport. A weekly angling column has been running for over 60 years and has ensured that anglers were always kept up to date with the latest news and gossip.

In addition, from 1992 to 1999, an annual sea angling guide was produced on behalf of Visit Guernsey (States Tourist Board) which gave both local and visiting anglers information that includes details of good fishing spots, open competitions, local legal fish size limits and the names and details of the tackle dealers and commercial angling boat skippers. Finally, in 2003 "Fishing in Guernsey" written by Peter Perrio was published. This 54 page book was a guide to shore fishing in the islands of the Bailiwick.

All this effort has been appreciated by the local angling community and there is no doubt that it has greatly helped the development of the sport in the Bailiwick.

However there has never been a publication that has set out to provide a complete overview of Bailiwick angling.

As your author I feel that I'm in a good position to try and remedy that omission. I have been active in angling administration for over 45 years, which has included being President of two clubs and the secretary of the Bailiwick of Guernsey Record (Rod-Caught) Fish committee since its inception in 1966. In addition I was the Guernsey Press angling columnist for over 30 years.

Consequently I have access to many records, photographs and press cuttings which contain much of the information that has helped me to investigate, record and describe the many happenings that have occurred in one of the most dynamic, yet fragmented sports in the Bailiwick.

The book includes information on where to fish, bait, tackle, competitions and records. This will be of great value to visitors to the island, newcomers to the sport and the less experienced local anglers who are seeking help and advice.

Anglers with extensive local knowledge may consider that the information is a little basic for their needs, but it is hoped that they will find it interesting.

There is also a great emphasis on the Bailiwick's angling history. The need for this became obvious as this book was being researched. Many of the anglers who were responsible for the forming of the present clubs, or who started the competitions that are still being enjoyed by the local angling community, have either died or have forgotten many of the facts and details – simply because it was so long ago.

If it is not recorded now, the true history of Bailiwick angling will be lost to posterity for ever.

There were many problems in the compilation of the book, due mainly to the great amount of information that was available. It included hundreds of club competition result sheets, over 700 record claim forms and detailed results, not only from 42 years of the Fish of the Month and Bass Competitions, but also from nearly 280 open events.

Obviously it was not possible to use every detail from this mass of information. Hopefully readers will understand, if they find details of their most memorable fishing achievement has been excluded.

One final point – weights. We should all be rushing to use metric weights these days, but in angling the affection for the avoirdupois (or imperial) system lives on! After all, everyone wants to catch a 10lb bass, catching a 4.535kg bass, just doesn't seem the same!

Consequently, all weights quoted will be in pounds, ounces and drams. To save the inclusion of lbs. ozs. drms. each time, the weights will be shown in abbreviated form i.e. 6lbs 15ozs 13 drams will become 6-15-13. It's a format that has been used in the angling column of the Guernsey Press for many years and seems to have been accepted without complaint by Bailiwick anglers.

Chapter 2 - Bailiwick Sea Fish

In December 2010 the Bailiwick's boat and shore rod-caught record fish lists contained no fewer than 68 different species with a further 25 species appearing on the 'mini' list, which is for fish weighing less than 1-0-0. What's more the lists are by no means finite, for new species have continued to be added on a regular basis over the years and there is no doubt that this trend will carry on into the future.

Why is there such a profusion of different species in Bailiwick waters? The main reason is the Bailiwick's geographical position. It is generally accepted that it is situated on the northern edge of the range of the "warm water" species and on the southern edge of the range of many of the "cold water" species. The ecology is further affected by the mild climate and the oceanic currents that sweep into the western English Channel.

These factors, coupled with the normal unpredictable patterns of fish behaviour, make it an exciting and fascinating area for anglers.

There are always fluctuations in the size of the population and movement of the various species of fish. No two years will be the same, many different conditions including water temperature and the success or failure of the fishes' breeding cycle will mean that each season one or two species will be more dominant than usual, while other species will appear to decline. This uncertainty is one of the intriguing aspects of angling in the islands.

Fish Gluts!

In Bailiwick waters these fluctuations have sometimes been quite dramatic and have produced quite a number of remarkable events, not least the mackerel glut of 1953.

In June of that year millions of mackerel came inshore chasing the white bait, i.e. the young fry of various fishes, usually herrings and sprats.

There were so many mackerel and they came so close into the shore that they were even being washed up on the beaches.

The sea walls, piers, slipways and rocks were packed with people, who were catching them on rod and line, handlines, scooping them up in buckets and in a few suitable spots even grabbing some in their bare hands!

It got so bad that a swimming gala, organised by the Guernsey Swimming Club at the tidal pools at La Vallette was in danger of being cancelled as the pool contained a mass of white bait and thousands of mackerel. There had to be a special effort to clear the pool of hundredweights of fish before the gala could go ahead!

Although society was not so conservation minded in those days there was concern expressed on the number of mackerel that were being caught and just left to rot. After all there were so many that it was impossible to give them away, let alone sell them.

It got to the stage that the Guernsey Press made an appeal for common sense in their comment column.

The bonanza was only to last a few days and although there was another short occurrence of the mackerel shoals in July, things soon returned to normal and those remarkable scenes have never been repeated.

A final mackerel story. In the late 1940's and 1950's housewives believed that as mackerel died their bodies initially, went into a curved shape.

It was considered that if 'straight' mackerel appeared on the market stalls they were stale and not that day's catch.

Of course, it was nonsense, but to placate the customers and ensure a good sale fishermen would methodically pack their catch in very narrow boxes, which forced the mackerel into the required curve. Needless to say it's a practice that has long since died out!

John Martel packing mackerel into narrow boxes which ensured they went to market in a curved state.

Much later in December 1988 and January 1989 there was a coalfish glut!

This is a 'cold-water' species and is normally fairly rare in Bailiwick waters, to the point where many local anglers had never caught one.

Suddenly they appeared in their thousands, particularly in the harbours. They were all takeable fish, averaging just under 1-0-0 in weight.

It was quite incredible. In one Telephone Angling Club evening shore competition in January 1989 I caught 134 weighing 110-6-0 on the Albert Pier slipway by the bus terminus and I only finished third! Roy Smith won the match with 159 for a weight of 132-12-0! The actual fishing time in the competition was about 180 minutes, which meant that Roy was landing a coalfish at a rate of nearly one a minute!

The coalfish made a mockery of club competitions. In December 1988 Peter Frise went into the Guernsey Sea Anglers Club's last competition of the year at the top of the club's championship list with an almost unassailable lead over his nearest rival. Richard Seager was way back in seventh place. Although Peter returned at the end of the match with a respectable catch of seven pollack and nine garfish, he was completely overwhelmed when Richard returned with 114 coalfish for 101-11-0, enough to take him through to win the club championship by a huge margin.

Club members who had not attended that TAC competition found that they were so far behind with no chance of catching up the leaders in the championship race, that they took no further part in club activities for the rest of the year.

Clubs were appalled not only by the adverse effect on their club competitions but also on the sheer numbers of fish being taken. Size limits for coalfish were raised considerably to ensure such a happening could not be repeated. They needn't have bothered for the coalfish disappeared in days, never to return!

Abnormal Fish Patterns

Other species have fared differently, disappearing after being prolific in Bailiwick waters over a long period.

In the mid-1960's Frank Le Page, a commercial fisherman, asked members of the 30 Fathom Club if they had ever caught a spurdog. The members had never seen one, let alone caught one, so they were intrigued when they were informed that for many years, professional fishermen had been catching huge quantities on longlines (trots) on marks north of Guernsey, in the early Spring. They weren't huge, the average weight being 3-0-0 to 5-0-0, but they would give good sport, particularly at the time of the year when anglers catches are normally at a low ebb. An angling trip with Frank was hastily arranged, but when they got to the area, the spurdog had completely disappeared and except for a few isolated specimens they have not been seen since!

During the late 1960's and 1970's red bream figured highly in Bailiwick anglers' catches. They were caught in considerable numbers on both deep-sea and inshore boat marks, as well as providing sport for the shore angler. Personal records confirm that I caught two in 1965, this rose to 73 in 1969 and 103 in 1972. In the 1960's the average weight per fish, particularly those from the inshore marks, was modest, certainly less than 1-0-0. In the 1970's the average weight increased, but the number of fish declined. In the early 1980's they finally vanished. The last one I caught at that time was a solitary 3-6-0 specimen in the Big Russel in 1984. (It would be 22 years before I caught another red, an 0-4-0 fish in 2006.) Black bream followed a similar pattern, catches steadily shrinking until they became almost a rarity in anglers catches.

The reason for the breams disappearance has caused much speculation~ Many anglers considered it was due to over-fishing by foreign fishing boats to the south of Guernsey where the biggest shoals were known to exist, but it is more likely that it was due to the natural movement of fish due to changes in their food chain. However in the mid 1990's black bream started to reappear, their numbers increasing until they were even more prolific than before.

Red bream were much more reluctant to return. Finally in the early 2000's small numbers began to crop up on a variety of marks, including an outstanding fish of 4-12-15 caught by Terry Lawrence in 2006. (see page 58)

These catches seemed to bode well for the future but, to date, their return has not been up to expectations.

Rare Fish

Confirmation of the Bailiwick's unique geographical position at the northern edge of the range of many warm water species has been the periodic appearance of fish that are considered rare visitors to the area.

Bearing in mind the amount of fishing done by the Bailiwick's commercial fishermen it's not surprising that they have been responsible for the capture of a number of strange piscatorial visitors over the years.

One of the most striking examples was the sturgeon caught by Peter Williams-Yeagers on his boat, the Rachel B in January 1977. It was trawled up on a mark southwest of Sark and weighed 79-0-0. The sturgeon is known as a "Fish Royal". Each one that is caught should be offered to the reigning monarch. This situation goes back to 1307, when a statute stated, "The King (or Queen) shall have, throughout the realm, whales and great sturgeons taken in the seas or elsewhere within the realm".

Ian Shell (left) and Gary Wilkins with the 79-0-0 sturgeon caught by Peter Williams-Yeagers.

The position of Guernsey as regards this statute may be unclear but the 79-0-0 fish was duly offered to the Queen, through the official channels, Her Majesty declined the offer with thanks and sent good wishes to the captors. There have been a few other sturgeon landed over the years but one has yet to fall to an angler's rod.

In December 1982 a 1-14-8 saupe was caught in a net that had been set off the Salerie by Phil Ryan. The saupe is a member of the bream family, whose normal habitat is the Mediterranean and the Atlantic up to the southern end of the Bay of Biscay. The only other time this species had been recorded in the English Channel was back in 1932. What this fish was doing in the Little Russel in the middle of winter was a complete mystery! The saupe was presented to the National History Museum in London for their fish collection.

In October 1996 Dave Markwick found a moray eel in one of his crabpots. Previously, this species had only been recorded in the English Channel on four occasions between 1834 and 1937. The eel, estimated to weigh 12-0-0, was presented to the Guernsey Aquarium where it quickly settled in to its new surroundings and where it lived happily until it died in June 2011.

In June 2010 Stuart Exall and Casey Brehaut had a bizarre catch. They found a strange brown fish in their gillnet which had been set off Lihou Island in 20ft of water.

The 1-7-11 specimen proved to be a cornish blackfish, a deepwater, oceanic species normally found in depths in excess of 200 metres. (see page 141)

Anglers have also been involved in the capture of fish that have strayed into Bailiwick waters.

In August 1972 Peter Jones was sorting through his catch at the conclusion of the annual Telephone Angling Club match against their Jersey colleagues that had been fished afloat south of Guernsey.

He noticed that one of the 28 mackerel in his catch looked different to the others.

The 1-0-6 specimen was later confirmed as a Spanish mackerel which is an extremely rare fish for the area. It went on to become the first Bailiwick and British boat-caught record for the species.

Its rarity was confirmed by the fact that the local record stood for 29 years and the national record was not broken for 23 years.

In 1980 Dave Samman and his party of anglers were fishing at the Casquets. Gannets were diving into the sea and gorging themselves on small silvery fish.

The anglers managed to net one that a gannet dropped. It proved to be a blue whiting (or poutassou) which are normally found in deep water in excess of 150 fathoms. What they were doing on the surface at the Casquets was a mystery. Curiously a small number were caught on other marks that year and Sam Clyde established the mini record with a 0-4-0 fish from the Great Bank. None have been seen or caught since.

The saga of the Couch's sea bream was even more astonishing. In August 1993 Bill Le Billon caught a small red-coloured bream while shore-fishing in Soldiers Bay. He realised it was not a red bream and took the 0-13-8 fish to the Bailiwick Record Committee for further investigation. .

It was finally identified as a Couch's sea bream, a species that had not been recorded in the Channel since the 1890's.

Bill's catch was accepted as the first ever Couch's sea bream on both the Bailiwick and British record lists, but his record status was not to last long, for they began to be caught regularly both afloat and off the shore. Dave Fox-Reilly established the first boat record with a 1-10-4 fish caught at Gabriel, off Guernsey's east coast in September 1995. By April 2007 the shore records would be broken 12 times and the boat records seven times. The shore best was pushed up to 3-4-7 a fish caught by Simon Newton at Belgrave Bay in July 2008 and the boat records had reached a remarkable 6-9-7 a specimen caught at the Susanne reef, off Guernsey's west coast by Raymond Fallaize in April 2007. (see pages 223 & 225)

The Bailiwick had temporarily lost its monopoly on the national records for the species in late October 1997 when a fish of 4-12-9 was caught by an angler boat fishing off Cornwall.

In the midst of the furore over the Couch's sea bream John Breedijk caught a small pinkish bream that clearly wasn't a red bream or a Couch's! The 0-8-6 fish which had been caught over a wreck south-west of Guernsey, proved to be an axillary bream. The saga of strange bream visitors was not yet over, for in September 1998 Carl Shrigley caught a 2-12-13 fish off Guernsey's Belgrave Bay.

It proved to be a pandora, the third species of bream to be a rare vagrant from southern climes.Yet more bream species were to follow. Andy Marquis caught an 0-2-5 white bream at the Salerie in July 2009, another first for the Bailiwick. A 2-13-3 specimen was caught soon after on a long-line (trot) in Belgrave Bay, so there must be a good chance Andy's record will be short-lived.

Finally a two-banded bream was netted by a commercial fisherman north of Guernsey.

George Staples added to the list of unusual visitors when he caught a 1-6-10 Guinean amberjack at Noir Pute in September 2000. This was the first time this species had been recorded in the British Isles.

A 1-7-12 almaco jack was caught by Colin Torode off Grange Rocques in August 2007, yet another first for local waters both fish went on to become both the local and national records.

George Staples witha very rare fish, his 1-6-10 Guinean amberjack.

Trigger fish are another warm water immigrant, although they have become less rare over the years, and a number of specimens are now reported nearly every year.

However, if there was a prize for the strangest fish ever to be caught by an angler in Bailiwick waters it would surely go to Robert McCracken. In July 1977 he landed a 1-8-1 fish while shore fishing near Petit Port. He had no idea what he had caught and took it to the Bailiwick Fish Record Committee for advice. They were equally puzzled. It had a fleshy adipose fin which suggested it was a member of the trout or salmon family, but it didn't seem to comply with any of the identification details in the books that were available to the committee's members. It was finally sent to Alwyne Wheeler at the Natural History Museum in London, who was the consultant marine biologist to the British Record Fish Committee and was acknowledged as one of the leading experts on fish biology in Europe.

It's not surprising that it completely confused the local anglers for it was finally identified as a coho salmon, a native of the Pacific coast of North America!

Apparently the French Fisheries Authorities had been rearing this species in cages in the Brest area. Some escaped into the open sea and Robert's fish was obviously one of them. It was formally approved as the Bailiwick and British records and although a few more were caught in the Channel in the following months, the record has never been beaten.

To date they do not appear to have established themselves as an indigenous species, for no further captures have been reported.

Another rare fish was caught on 21st November 2010 when Peter Merrien netted a 3-12-8 bonito at the Hanois. This is at least the second recorded in local waters for commercial fisherman Dougal Lane caught one weighing 2-14-15 east of Sark in July 2007. However it has never been recorded locally on rod and line.

There are British rod caught records for this species 8-13-4 boat caught in Torbay in 1969 and 2-10-5 shore caught in South Wales in 1996. What are the chances of one being caught locally on rod and line in the future?

There are encouraging signs that this is a possiblilty. Besides the two reported here, two have been netted in Jersey, one in 2000 and the other in 2004 and reports have confirmed that they were unusually common around the south west coast of England during the summer of 2010 with some being landed from commercial fishing boats.

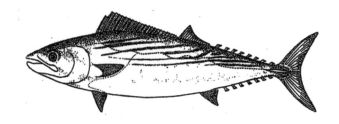

Bonito

Common Species

Although the capture of the more unusual and exotic fish is always an exciting event, Bailiwick anglers know that they have to rely on the more mundane common, species to provide their sport. What are the different kinds of fish that the Bailiwick angler can expect to find?

The Bailiwick's boat and shore record lists (which are covered in detail in Chapter 9) show that 68 species have been recorded on rod and line locally.

However, in practice the number of different species caught by an angler during the course of a year is quite modest.

Using my own records as an example. I find that the most I've caught in a year, not counting those of less than 1-0-0 that appear on the mini record list, was 22 in 1967. Even in that year the bulk of my yearly haul came from just 10 species.

In fact in an angling career spanning more than 55 years, I've managed to catch just 41.

No doubt many anglers will be able to better that total, but it all confirms that there are many species in local waters that while not considered rare, do not occur in sufficient numbers to be an important factor in the angler's day to day catches.

One factor that seems to be common to nearly all species in Bailiwick waters is the poor fishing that is experienced in the early months of the year.

January through to April is normally a comparitively slack time. It is a period where in spite of a lot of effort and time, the angler usually experiences poor catches.

Visitors who are planning to come to the Bailiwick to enjoy the fishing should avoid the early part of the year.

The timing of this quiet fishing period has another rather unfortunate aspect. Newcomers to angling will often receive their new rods and reels as Christmas presents and will naturally be keen to try them out.

In spite of the winter weather, they will get some bait and rush down to the Breakwater or a rock mark. They become very disillusioned when they struggle to make even a modest catch. As they make their way home, usually cold and wet, their keenness for their new hobby rapidly vanishes and as a result many put their tackle in the cupboard and never go fishing again!

The moral is, "if you get fishing tackle for Christmas wait until the early summer months before you try it out!"

The best time for shore fishing in the Bailiwick is May through to December, although in Alderney it tends to be a little later, July to February. The boat fishing season can be considered April to November.

These periods should not be taken too categorically, for the unpredictability of fish behaviour will sometimes mean that fish will be caught "off-season". However they can be considered a good general guide to the best times of the year.

If the boat and shore record lists are analysed, the species they contain can be listed under three different categories;

A.   Common species that are normally caught on a regular basis by anglers engaged in "general fishing" either afloat or ashore.
B.   Species that can be deliberately targeted by the angler.
C.   Species that are only caught very occasionally and cannot normally be specifically targeted.

Due to the unpredictable pattern of fish behaviour there is no doubt that the make-up of the three categories will change in the future. However, they give a good indication, particularly to visiting anglers and the sports newcomers, on what type of catches can be anticipated.

In the descriptions that follow, the specimen weights quoted are quite arbitrary. They are merely an indication of what is considered a "good" fish in local waters. The "seasons" quoted are the periods considered the best times for that species. Obviously they are not finite and specimens will almost certainly be caught at other times. Readers should note that "bait" is discussed in detail in Chapter 4.

Category A - Common species

Species	BLACK BREAM	Local Names	-
Bailiwick Record Weights	Boat 6-10-8		Shore 6-8-6
Specimen Weights	Boat 3-8-0		Shore 3-0-0
Average Weights	Boat 2-0-0		Shore 1-4-0
Seasons	Boat July - December		Shore August- January
Bait	Squid, cuttlefish, ragworm, scallop frills, sandeel		

(see page 219)

Comment:

This species has made a dramatic come back after years of decline.

Can be caught from numerous marks both afloat and ashore. A shoaling fish so if you're lucky enough to locate a shoal it's possible to make an excellent catch.

Usually caught by shore anglers bottom fishing on sandy ground particularly in areas of green grass-like weed, but can also be found over rough ground, and at times can even be taken on float gear. One consistent hot-spot in recent years has been St. Peter Port Breakwater.

Boat anglers will come across them almost anywhere on the more inshore marks in the late summer and autumn months.

Boat skippers who have the necessary knowledge can go out to a number of deep water marks where big shoals are known to congregate.

Species	BREAM, COUCH'S SEA	Local Names	-
Bailiwick Record Weights	Boat 6-9-7		Shore 3-4-7
Specimen Weights	Boat 3-0-0		Shore 2-0-0
Average Weights	Boat 2-0-0		Shore 1-8-0
Seasons	Boat July - November		Shore August- November
Bait	Verm, ragworm, scallop frills, sandeel, squid, cuttlefish		

Comment:

A species that first appeared in local waters in 1993. Numbers caught each year are modest, and are usually taken by anglers after black bream.

Shore anglers will find the odd specimen on sandy or mixed ground. Boat anglers will find them on the more inshore marks that also produce black bream.

This species appear to prefer the shallower inshore waters, rather than the deep water bream marks. (see pages 223 and 225)

(As the book went to print a 9-4-5 record specimen was caught off the west coast of Guernsey)

Species	COD	Local Names	-
Bailiwick Record Weights	Boat 39-0-0	Shore 29-0-0	
Specimen Weights	Boat 6-0-0 (over wrecks 15-0-0)	Shore 4-0-0	
Average Weights	Boat 3-8-0 (over wrecks 10-0-0)	Shore 1-8-0	
Seasons	Boat All Year Round	Shore September - February	

Bait   Mackerel, squid, cuttlefish, ragworm. Artificials (pirks etc) for boat fishing over wrecks

Comment:

This cold water species is only an irregular visitor to inshore Bailiwick waters. They are certainly not present in the numbers found in the United Kingdom and some years miss Bailiwick waters completely. When they do make an appearance both shore and boat anglers catch them while bottom fishing over mixed or sandy ground. A few are caught by boat anglers using spinning tackle.

To find and catch good-sized specimens, anglers usually go to the more distant wreck marks.

Otto Envoldsen with the 24-2-0 Cod he caught in January 1972.
Otto was a professional fisherman who enjoyed rod fishing in his retirement.

12

Species DOGFISH, LESSER SPOTTED	Local Names DOGGIE, LSD	
Bailiwick **Record Weights**	Boat 3-2-11	Shore 2-13-11
Specimen Weights	Boat 2-8-0	Shore 2-4-0
Average Weights	Boat 1-12-0	Shore 1-8-0
Seasons	Boat July - November	Shore September January
Bait Squid, cuttlefish, sandeel, mackerel, garfish, ragworm.		

Comment:

A species held in very low esteem. Can be a nuisance taking baits meant for other species. Taken on bottom gear both afloat and ashore. Can turn up anywhere on a sandy sea-bed.

Often very prolific in the late autumn. (In a WCSAC all night competition two anglers caught 102 on St Peter Port Breakwater!)

Species GARFISH	Local Names Longnose	
Bailiwick **Record Weights**	Boat 2-12-5	Shore 2-11-11
Specimen Weights	Boat 1-8-0	Shore 1-4-0
Average Weights	Boat 0-12-0	Shore 0-10-0
Seasons	Boat July - December	Shore All Year Round
Bait Small sandeels, small strips of garfish or mackerel		

Comment:

A very prolific species which are caught in some numbers, especially by shore anglers. Behavioural patterns have changed in recent years, with some now being caught in nearly every month of the year.

Can be taken on spinning gear, for they will chase small sandeel bait or a lure, but the vast majority are caught on float tackle with the bait usually being presented within 15 feet of the surface.

Can be found on most inshore marks afloat, and on-shore, particularly where there is a tide run.

A shoal fish, whoch can be attracted by the use of shirvy (Groundbait). Catches in excess of 30 a common occurance.

13

Species	GURNARD, RED	Local Names	-
Bailiwick Record Weights	Boat 2-13-11		Shore 2-4-6
Specimen Weights	Boat 2-0-0		Shore 1-4-0
Average Weights	Boat 1-4-0		Shore 0-12-0
Seasons	Boat July - November		Shore August- December
Bait Sandeel, ragworm, mackerel.			

Comment:
Usually caught by boat anglers using bottom gear on sandy ground for other species.
Predominately a boat-caught fish, but each autumn a few get caught from shore marks.

Species	LING	Local Names	-
Bailiwick Record Weights	Boat 36-14-0		Shore 14-2-8
Specimen Weights	Boat 20-0-0		Shore 7-0-0
Average Weights	Boat 12-0-0		Shore 4-0-0
Seasons	Boat All Year Round		Shore August - December
Bait Fish (mackerel, garfish etc.), sandeels, squid.			

Comment:
Almost a rare fish from the shore. Boat anglers catch them on deep water wrecks and reefs. Only occasionally from inshore marks.

Chris Carter with his 36-4-0 ling caught in February 2004. The ling was only 10 ounces under the Bailiwick boat caught record.

Species MACKEREL		Local Names Joeys (small specimens)	
		Ground mackerel (big fish)	
Bailiwick **Record Weights**	Boat 4-2-10		Shore 2-13-0
Specimen Weights	Boat 2-8-0		Shore 1-8-0
Average Weights	Boat 0-8-0		Shore 0-8-0
Seasons	Boat May - October		Shore June - October
Bait Feathers, spinners, fish strips			

Comment:

Shoals usually arrive in May or early June. If a shoal is located by the boat angler, catches in excess of 100 can be made on feathers.

Tend to occur on the same marks each year, the southern end of the Great Bank, off Guernsey's east coast being a prime example.

Late in July the shoals seem to scatter and it's possible to catch some on many marks both afloat and ashore. The boat angler will still get some on feathers, but will also catch them on bottom gear on sandy ground or while spinning for bass or pollack.

The shore angler will usually catch them on float gear, while after garfish, or on spinning tackle, using either a small lure or a string of feathers.

Species MULLET, GOLDEN GREY	Local Names	-
Bailiwick **Record Weights**	Boat 2-8-3	Shore 3-0-4
Specimen Weights	Boat 1-12-0	Shore 2-0-0
Average Weights	Boat 1-4-0	Shore 1-8-0
Seasons	Boat August - October	Shore May - December
Bait Verm, ragworm, catbait (white ragworm), bread, sandeel.		

Comment:

Almost exclusively a shore anglers fish, very few are caught by boat anglers.

Normally taken on bottom gear, but have also been caught using float tackle. Will occasionally become the anglers prime quarry if it becomes known they are present at a particular mark. They have been more prolific in recent years.

Species	MULLET, RED		Local Names	-
Bailiwick Record Weights	Boat 3-7-0		Shore 3-15-0	
Specimen Weights	Boat 1-8-0		Shore 2-0-0	
Average Weights	Boat 1-4-0		Shore 1-4-0	
Seasons	Boat August - December		Shore August - December	

Bait   Verm, ragworm, scallop frills, catbait (white ragworm).

Comment:
Very few are caught by boat anglers. Usually taken on bottom gear by shore anglers fishing on sandy or mixed ground.

Species	POLLACK		Local Names	Guernsey Whiting
Bailiwick Record Weights	Boat 25-12-0		Shore 16-1-6	
Specimen Weights	Boat 10-0-0		Shore 5-0-0	
Average Weights	Boat 2-4-0		Shore 0-12-0	
Seasons	Boat May - November		Shore June - December	

Bait   Sandeel, ragworm, catbait (white ragworm), redgill and similar artificial lures.

Comment:
As far as boat anglers are concerned, one of the most common and prolific fish in Bailiwick waters. It has often been said "take away pollack and there wouldn't be much left", although this statement has become less true in recent years. Taken on a wide variety of marks, more common over reefs and rocky ground, but also caught on sandbanks. Mostly caught by anglers spinning with sandeels or artificial lures, but are also taken on bottom gear. Wreck marks produce the heavier fish.

The shore angler has to be satisfied with a much smaller run of fish, and are sometimes plagued with immature specimens. Taken on both spinning tackle and float gear, and also on bottom tackle cast out by anglers chasing other species.

Ernie Baker, who was one of Guernsey's leading tackle dealers with a typical Bailiwick pollack.

Species	POUT		Local Names	Flobber
Bailiwick				
Record Weights	Boat 3-8-13		Shore 4-9-0	
Specimen Weights	Boat 2-8-0		Shore 1-8-0	
Average Weights	Boat 1-0-0		Shore 0-10-0	
Seasons	Boat June - December		Shore June - January	

Bait   Sandeel, squid, cuttlefish, ragworm, mackerel strip, verm, lugworm, garfish strip.

Comment:
A species treated with disdain by most anglers. This is due to their small size, and their habit of seizing baits meant for more sought after species.

Afloat, tend to be taken on isolated marks that became known as "pout-holes" or over inshore wrecks, the so-called "cement wreck" in the Little Russel being a good example. Seem to be more active just on dusk.

Shore anglers tend to catch them on sandy or mixed ground, mostly after dark.

Species	SCAD		Local Names	Horse mackerel
Bailiwick				
Record Weights	Boat 2-1-13		Shore 2-5-12	
Specimen Weights	Boat 1-0-0		Shore 1-0-0	
Average Weights	Boat 0-10-0		Shore 0-8-0	
Seasons	Boat July - September		Shore August - November	

Bait   Feathers, sandeel, catbait (white ragworm), ragworm.

Comment:
Another unpopular species, afloat they are caught by anglers feathering for mackerel, or spinning for pollack or bass.

Shore anglers can catch them in some numbers in August through to November under the lights at the harbour entrance, usually on float or spinning tackle.

Will take shore anglers baits meant for garfish, mackerel or even grey mullet.

Species	WHITING	Local Names	-
Bailiwick Record Weights	Boat 5-4-0		Shore 2-3-12
Specimen Weights	Boat 2-8-0		Shore 1-0-0
Average Weights	Boat 1-8-0		Shore 0-8-0
Seasons	Boat January - June		Shore October - February

Bait Sandeel, ragworm, mackerel strip, squid/cuttlefish.

Comment:
This species has become almost rare in recent years, and tends to put in only spasmodic appearances.

Caught by boat anglers over sandbanks. Very few get caught by shore anglers.

Species	WRASSE, BALLAN	Local Names	Rockfish, rockie
Bailiwick Record Weights	Boat 8-1-0		Shore 8-10-13
Specimen Weights	Boat 5-0-0		Shore 5-0-0
Average Weights	Boat 3-8-0		Shore 2-0-0
Seasons	Boat May- November		Shore June - February

Bait Green crab, hardback or peeler, verm, ragworm, lugworm, scallop frills, sandeel.

Comment:
A very popular fish particularly for the shore angler for they can be found on most marks where there are rocks and weed.
Big specimens can be caught very close in, often is quite shallow water.
The bigger fish will put up a strong fight and have a habit of diving into the nearest weed or under the rocks when hooked. It follows that robust tackle is required.
Although a few boat anglers deliberately go for the wrasse on some occasions, the majority caught afloat are taken by anglers spinning with sandeel or ragworm for other species.

One of the Bailiwick's woman anglers, Sue Le Cras with a 6-9-2 ballan wrasse.

(see pages 59 and 220)

18

Species WRASSE, CUCKOO		Local Names	-
Bailiwick Record Weights	Boat 2-1-11	Shore 1-12-9	
Specimen Weights	Boat 1-8-0	Shore 1-0-0	
Average Weights	Boat 1-0-0	Shore 0-12-0	
Seasons	Boat May - November	Shore July - November	
Bait Verm, ragworm, sandeel, mackerel.			

(see page 142, 220 and 223)

Comment:
Considered a nuisance fish. Favours deeper water than the ballan wrasse and as a result is very uncommon from shore marks.

Caught by boat anglers who are presenting a sandeel or ragworm bait near the bottom over rough ground.

Will accept a "fish" bait more readily than the ballan wrasse. Unusual species for the male and female have completely different colouration.

The males have vivid blue heads and backs, while the belly dorsal and anal fins are yellow or orange.

Females are orange/pink with three dark spots on the back.

Category B - Species that are deliberately targeted by the angler.

Species	BASS		Local Names	Schoolies (small species)
Bailiwick **Record Weights**		Boat 18-6-12		Shore 18-6-5
Specimen Weights		Boat 10-0-0		Shore 10-0-0
Average Weights		Boat 4-8-0		Shore 2-8-0
Seasons		Boat All year round		Shore All year round

Bait   Sandeel, peeler crab, verm, ragworm, artificial lures and plugs.

Comment:
A cult species! No doubt due to its sporting prowess and its monetary value it is the most prized and sought after fish in the Bailiwick. It is the only indigenous fish that has resulted in the formation of two specialist clubs, consisting of like minded enthusiasts, three annual Open Festivals and a year long specimen competition.

With so much interest in this game fish it's not surprising that angling methods have developed and changed considerably. The accepted method for the shore angler was to cast out a bait from a surf covered beach. Although this will still produce bass, the majority of anglers now tend to fish gullies or small areas of sandy or mixed ground, often over the low water. In addition spinning with lures or plugs, or just freelining the bait has become extremely popular and has proved to be very successful. The majority of bass landed by boat anglers used to be those caught while bottom fishing over sandbanks for other species, a method that still produces a fair number of fish. However, anglers began to realise that the bass' love of fast running water that races through and over the reefs and rocks, particularly on spring tides could be exploited successfully.

These areas were sought out, and good catches have been made mostly on spinning gear using plugs or sandeels.

In addition new areas have been discovered where bass tend to congregate in large numbers.

Marks to the north and east of Sark and Herm have produced superb catches, with anglers using bottom gear with very long flowing traces.

Another such area is the Boue Blondel off Guernsey's west coast where gigantic shoals of spawning bass have been located.

(see pages 223 and 224)

In the early months of each year thousands of bass, many over 10-0-0 have been caught by both professional and sport fisherman on rod and line.

The situation has caused controversy and heated debate concerning the ethics of targeting spawning fish.

However, in spite of the heavy exploitation of the bass both at this venue and generally in the English Channel the British Department of the Environment, Food and Rural Affairs has confirmed that the fishing effort was sustainable and bass stocks remained at a healthy level.

A superb shore-caught bass. Mark Amies with his 12-5-7 specimen - caught in October 2001.

Species	BRILL	Local Names	-
Bailiwick Record Weights	Boat 13-9-0	Shore 4-13-8	
Specimen Weights	Boat 8-0-0	Shore 2-0-0	
Average Weights	Boat 4-0-0	Shore 1-8-0	
Seasons	Boat March - November	Shore August - October	

Bait Sandeel, garfish strip, mackerel strip.

Comment:

A much sought after flatfish, but it is an almost exclusively boat anglers quarry.

Shore-caught brill are very rare. Usually caught afloat by drifting with a sandeel (or fish bait) on a long flowing trace on offshore sandbanks.

In recent years they have moved in to the Bailiwick's sandbanks earlier in the year, with good catches starting as early as March.

Nicholas Hannah with a 11-5-8 brill.

22

Species	BULL HUSS	Local Names	HUSS
(Greater Spotted Dogfish)			

Bailiwick		
Record Weights	Boat 16-5-0	Shore 13-14-0
Specimen Weights	Boat 10-0-0	Shore 10-0-0
Average Weights	Boat 9-0-0	Shore 7-0-0
Seasons	Boat June - September	Shore August - December
Bait	Squid, cuttlefish, mackerel, garfish	

Comment:
Being caught in increasing numbers in recent years. Marks have been discovered both afloat and ashore, and good catches have been the outcome.

As a result this species has now joined the "deliberately targeted list!"

Usually caught over sandy or mixed ground.

Boat anglers prefer to fish at anchor for this species, and at one mark east of Sark literally hundreds have been caught, although the shoal only congregates at this spot for a short time each year. Shore anglers usually enjoy the best sport and success in the hours of darkness.

Three anglers who hit the bull huss off Sark in June 2005. Shane Bentley (left) 12-10-1, Tim Froome 14-5-0 and Paul McLaren 13-12-9.

(see page 225)

Species	CONGER	Local Names	Whip (small specimens)

Bailiwick		
Record Weights	Boat 108-0-6	Shore 65-14-10
Specimen Weights	Boat 35-0-0	Shore 25-0-0
Average Weights	Boat 15-0-0	Shore 8-0-0
Seasons	Boat May - January	Shore June - January

Bait   Mackerel, squid, cuttlefish, pout, garfish.

Comment: (see page 219)

Found over rough ground, both ashore and afloat. Very much a nocturnal feeder, although a few specimens are caught during daylight hours, especially on the deeper boat marks.

The more distant deep water wreck marks produce the biggest specimens, and seem able to provide the angler with a catch almost at any time of the year.

A very strong and resilient fish, so it is essential that robust tackle is used. Traces should be wire or a very heavy monofilament to combat the conger's powerful teeth which can cut through light line very easily.

A typical wreck caught conger - Phillip Dunne with a 78-12-0 fish caught over the wreck of the Radiant Med, south of Guernsey in May 1996.

Congering in the old days! Two well dressed fisherman show off their shore-caught fish. They were obviously caught on hand lines but surprisingly during daylight hours, the conger is normally a nocturnal feeder!

Species	EEL, COMMON	Local Names	
Bailiwick **Record Weights**	Boat 3-11-8	Shore 3-15-4	
Specimen Weights	Boat 2-0-0	Shore 2-0-0	
Average Weights	Boat 1-0-0	Shore 0-12-0	
Seasons	Boat June - October	Shore June - October	
Bait	Sandeel, squid, ragworm, catbait, fish strips.		

Comment:

A species that has fallen out of favour with anglers in recent years.

A good fish for the young angler or newcomer to the sport for they are comparatively easy to catch and a big specimen gives a good fight on light tackle.

Nearly all are caught in St Peter Port Harbour, either from a boat or from piers in the inner harbour.

(They are also found in many of the fresh water sites in the Bailiwick - to the point where the fresh water record is substanially higher than the sea records - a 6-1-6 fish caught by Greg Whitehead in La Lande Quarry in May 2011)

Species	MULLET, GREY THICK LIPPED	Local Names	-
Bailiwick Record Weights	Boat 8-7-6	Shore 11-14-6	
Specimen Weights	Boat 4-0-0	Shore 5-0-0	
Average Weights	Boat 3-0-0	Shore 2-8-0	
Seasons	Boat June - October	Shore All year round	
Bait	Bread, pieces of fish, meat.		

Comment:
A shy species that can be found by the shore angler over a great variety of venues, including shallow beaches, harbours and rock marks.

It has proved such a fascination and challenge to some anglers that they fish for little else!

Enthusiasts have formed a specialist club, which targets three species of mullet, golden grey, thick-lipped grey and thin-lipped grey. Each year the club holds an open competition.

It is a scavenging fish, which can be brought into the anglers' reach by the use of ground-bait.

A few are caught from boats, usually when anchored in the shallow waters in the harbour or bays.

How it used to be! Alderney anglers Mr and Mrs Henry Slade with a catch of 33 grey mullet in 1960. Note the long bamboo rods and multiplier reels. In those days they didn't use floats - they just lowered the bait into the shoal of feeding mullet.

Can be caught on bottom gear, but the vast majority are taken on float gear, or a bait carefully lowered down into mullet's feeding position. It is considered that fishing for mullet is the nearest the sea anglers get to freshwater coarse fishing. This certainly seems to have been confirmed in recent years as anglers have refined their mullet tackle and now use waggler floats, lead shot and light lines and trace down to 3lb BS or less, all tackle more usually seen on lakes and rivers. (See page 142 & 145)

Species	PLAICE	Local Names	-

Bailiwick Record Weights	Boat 8-11-9	Shore 8-3-4
Specimen Weights	Boat 4-0-0	Shore 3-0-0
Average Weights	Boat 1-8-0	Shore 0-12-0
Seasons	Boat May - October	Shore March - November

Bait Ragworm, catbait, lugworm, verm, baited spoon.

(see page 58)

Comment:

A species that has declined dramatically in recent years to the point where it's almost a rare catch.

More a shore anglers fish. It used to be one of the first species to be targeted early in the year.

Obviously fished for, on sandy areas with bottom tackle. Boat catches are at best spasmodic. In fact a plaice caught afloat can almost be considered a fluke event.

Catches would almost certainly improve from a boat, if a spoon baited with a worm was slowly trolled along the bottom.

Species	RAY, BLONDE	Local Names	-

Bailiwick		
Record Weights	Boat 36-2-7	Shore 32-8-0
Specimen Weights	Boat 15-0-0	Shore 10-0-0
Average Weights	Boat 8-0-0	Shore 5-0-0
Seasons	Boat July - November	Shore August - December

Bait Sandeel, squid, cuttlefish, mackerel.

Comment:

The number of rays caught by Bailiwick anglers is extremely modest, yet they are there in some quantity as catches by the commercial fisherman will confirm.

To target rays, the boat angler MUST anchor over sandy or mixed ground, even if the spring tides will necessitate the use of heavy leads to keep the tackle on the sea bed. Drifting will never be successful for rays as they do not like to chase a fast moving bait.

Shore marks facing into fairly deep water and a sandy bottom is the spot to try for ray.

These comments apply to all the rays in the Bailiwick, although the blonde ray is by far the most common.

(see page 138)

Species	SHARK, BLUE	Local Names	-
Bailiwick **Record Weights**	Boat 132-13-3	Shore	-
Specimen Weights	Boat 75-0-0	Shore	-
Average Weights	Boat 40-0-0	Shore	-
Seasons	Boat July - October	Shore	-

Bait Whole mackerel

General comment for both species: (blue and porbeagle)

Exclusively boat angler's fish. Favourite areas are south of Guernsey, or well north of the island almost in the Channel shipping lanes. The bait is presented on float tackle, the biggest difficulty is deciding on what depth to present the bait, as the shark can be at any depth in the 30 fathoms deep water. Most anglers will position their bait within 60 feet of the surface. Long wire traces, usually in excess of 20 feet must be used, in order to combat the shark's powerful teeth and rough skin. The sharks are attracted to the baits by the use of rubby-dubby. This is minced, or mashed up, fish offal which is hung over the side of the boat in a mesh sack. It produces a trail of fishy bits that drifts away down-tide of the boat. It goes without saying that the anglers gear must be robust with the reel holding at least 250 to 300 yards of braided line. The use of monofilament lines is not recommended. The tight compaction of the line on the reel during a long fight with a shark produces compression forces that can completely destroy the reel. It has happened in the Bailiwick — many times! One final point — many anglers consider that the sharks come much closer inshore than is generally realised. A concentrated effort just a mile or so off Guernsey's south coast may produce surprising results. It could well prove there is no need to go out seven or eight miles!

Sadly, interest in shark fishing has declined dramatically over the last 10 to 20 years.

Yet they are still out there, and will give superb sport for the anglers who will make the effort to give it a try.

(see pages 221 and 222)

Species SHARK, PORBEAGLE	Local Names	
Bailiwick Record Weights	Boat 295-8-6	Shore -
Specimen Weights	Boat 100-0-0	Shore -
Average Weights	Boat 75-0-0	Shore -
Seasons	Boat July - October	Shore -
Bait Whole mackerel		

As it was in the 1960's. Ernie Baker (left), Jim Ikeringill, Mike Dew and Peter Witterick with their shark catch.

Species	SOLE	Local Names	-
Bailiwick Record Weights	Boat 4-1-12	Shore 6-8-10	
Specimen Weights	Boat 3-0-0	Shore 4-0-0	
Average Weights	Boat 2-0-0	Shore 2-0-0	
Seasons	Boat May - September	Shore July - December	

Bait   Ragworm, verm, lugworm, catbait, sandeel.

Comment:

Very much a shore anglers fish, a nocturnal feeder, so the majority are caught after dark.

Occasionally an angler fishing for plaice during the day will be suprised to catch a sole.

Caught on bottom gear cast out over sand.

Sole from a boat are uncommon and are usually caught by anglers drifting over sand with a sandeel bait intended for other species.

An unusual catch, a boat caught sole Marc Eppelein with his 4-1-12 fish caught on the Great Bank in June 1993.
It was the British record for 12 years and is still the Bailiwick record.

Species	TOPE	Local Names	-
Bailiwick Record Weights	Boat 55-12-0		Shore 50-14-13
Specimen Weights	Boat 30-0-0		Shore 20-0-0
Average Weights	Boat 20-0-0		Shore 15-0-0
Seasons	Boat June - September		Shore August - November
Bait	Squid / cuttlefish, mackerel or other fish baits		

(see page 143)

Comment:
Predominately a boat anglers fish they have been caught on widespread marks, but in recent years a number of "hot-spots" have been found east of Sark and up near Alderney.

Anglers usually fish from an anchored boat.

Tope prefer sandy or mixed ground.

Fairly rare for the shore angler, although large numbers have been caught from beaches in Alderney, including the 50-14-13 record caught in 2004.

Species	TURBOT	Local Names	Tubbies
Bailiwick Record Weights	Boat 30-4-0		Shore 22-3-0
Specimen Weights	Boat 15-0-0		Shore 5-0-0
Average Weights	Boat 7-0-0		Shore 2-8-0
Seasons	Boat March - November		Shore August - November
Bait	Sandeel, mackerel strip, garfish strip		

Comment:
This is a much sought after prime flatfish and is very much a boat anglers quarry.

Usually caught by drifting with a sandeel bait on bottom gear on offshore sandbanks.

Like the brill it appears to be moving into the Bailiwick's sandbanks, earlier in the year, with anglers making catches as early as March.

Very occasionally shore anglers are surprised to catch a turbot, but they are usually the smaller specimens.

(see page 219)

Category C - Species that are only caught occasionally

One of the delights of angling is that it is not an exact science, it's the sheer unpredictability that makes it so exciting. Basically you never know what you are going to catch next.

However methodically you prepare and however precise you try to be when targeting a specific fish, other species will come along and spoil your efforts by grabbing your carefully selected and presented bait. Usually it will be one of the common species referred to in Category A, but it could be one of the much more

Sark angler Glyn Williams with a trigger fish, a comparitively rare visitor to our shores.
Usually caught in the late summer or autumn months.

uncommon fish. These species can crop up at any time anywhere but do not occur regularly enough to warrant more than a passing mention. The following list contains all of the more uncommon species that have been caught by anglers and have been formally identified and weighed and appear on the Bailiwick's boat or shore record lists.

Almaco Jack
Angler Fish
Amberjack, Guinean
Bogue
Bream, Gilthead (page 143)
Bream, Pandora
Bream, Red (page 58)
Coalfish
Dab
Dogfish, Spur
Flounder
Gurnard Grey
Gurnard Tub (page 224 and 225)
Haddock
Hake
John Dory (page 220)
Lumpsucker
Mackerel, Spanish
Megrim (page 145)

Monkfish
Mullet, Grey Thin-Lipped
Ray, Marbled Electric (page 59)
Ray, Smalleyed
Ray, Spotted
Ray, Sting
Ray, Thornback
Ray, Undulate (page 58)
Rockling, Shore
Rockling, Three Bearded (page 220)
Salmon (see page 224)
Salmon, Coho
Sea Trout
Shad, Twaite
Smooth Hound
Smooth Hound, Starry
Sunfish
Trigger fish (page 219)
Weever, Greater (page 59)

One of the strangest fish in local waters, the sunfish

Mini Fish

In addition to the species discussed so far, there are the 25 that appear on the mini record list (see chapter 9).

Many anglers feel that this list is incidental. They consider that there is no angling skill or satisfaction in catching a fish that only weighs a few ounces and consequently have no interest.

A basket full of roselet!

34

This is a valid argument, but they tend to ignore the fact that the sole aim of the record lists is to formally record the heaviest fish of each species, caught fairly on rod and line. The level of skill and expertise to catch the fish is completely irrelevant as far as the record lists are concerned.

Nevertheless it is accepted that normally anglers will not set out deliberately to catch any of the mini species, and usually will not get too excited if they do hook one!

There is however, one exception. This is the atherine smelt, or roselet as it is known locally. The word roselet is an anglicized version of the Guernsey French word for smelt, ross'let.

This little silver fish occurs in vast numbers in the harbours and on rocky shore marks in the autumn and early winter months. Many anglers enjoy fishing for them using multi-hook traces, baited with catbait (white ragworm).

There has even been open fishing competitions for roselet (see chapter 8). However there is one mini-fish that cannot be ignored, although the lesser weever only grows to 2-4 ounces it is dangerous for it has venomous glands in the first dorsal fin and on the gill cover. If handled, the wounds caused by contact with the poisonous glands can be extremely painful, with the discomfort spreading to the whole arm.

Bathers are particularly vunerable for the weever buries itself in the sand with just the black dorsal fin showing. When stepped on the pain in the foot can be excruciating. (It's bigger cousin the greater weever is just as dangerous, but as it normally frequents deeper water, its contact with humans is rare.)

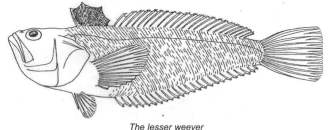

The lesser weever

Fish Identification

With such a great variety of fish that are indigenous to local waters and with so many unusual piscatorial visitors, it's essential that every angler should own a good comprehensive book on fish identification.

It will not only confirm the identity of any strange catches but will also provide interesting details on the habitat, biology, feeding habits and range of all the different species in Bailiwick waters. Correct identification of your catch is a basic requirement if you intend to enter one of the many competitions open to all anglers in the Bailiwick, or if you intend to claim a record (see chapters 8&9).

Sadly there is a snag! Have you ever gone into a bookshop and searched for such a book?

If you're a bird-watcher (feathered variety!) there are usually shelves of suitable publications. You will also find titles on everything from bats to butterflies and spiders to snakes, but good books on fish are very sparse indeed.

There is no point in acquiring one of the smaller, cheaper books. You will find that they only cover the more common fish and ignore the more unusual species which more often than not are the very fish that you are trying to identify.

My own favourite and in my opinion one of the best books ever compiled on fish identification is "The Fishes of the British Isles and North West Europe" by Alwyne Wheeler, published in 1969. An excellent book that has been my main source of reference for nearly 42 years, but sadly, like so many good publications of the past, it's long since out of print and is no longer available.

Enquries during 2006 and 2007 confirmed that many fish books that have been published since 1969, some from quite recent years, have also become unavailable, so the problems in finding suitable worthwhile publications remain.

One comprehensive book published in 1997 was available at the time the enquiries were made. This was 'Collins Pocket Guide, Fish of Britain and Europe' - highly recommended.

Other books will undoubtedly be published in the future, it's purely a question of making regular enquiries at your favourite bookshop to ensure you don't miss out.

Fish Conservation

There is no doubt that Bailiwick anglers have always enjoyed superb fishing with a steady stream of specimen fish and heavy catches. However in recent times there has been a growing realisation that the sea will not always be able to provide an infinite supply of quality fish, especially if the fishing is exploited to such an extent that the stocks are severely decimated.

There have already been some early warning signs. Catches of some species have fallen dramatically, while the average fish size in other species has shown a noticeable decline.

As a result Bailiwick anglers have tended to become more conservation minded. They realise that although their catches make up only a small percentage of the total fish landed, they must do all they can to ensure that fish are not wasted and are not killed unnecessarily.

Some anglers may not be aware that there are legal size limits for many species.

These are listed in "The Fishing (Minimum Size and Prescribed Species) Order, 1997" which states that it is an offence to land, import, export, take, buy, sell or have in possession any fish which is of a size less than the minimum size. The legal 'size' of the fish is the distance measured in centimetres from the tip of the snout to the end of the tail fin, except for Skates/Rays which are measured between the two most distant extremities measured across the broadest part of the back.

The size limits that stood in 2010 were:

Bass	36	Mackerel	20
Bream, black	23	Megrim	25
Bream, red	25	Mullet, grey	20
Brill	30	Mullet, red	15
Coalfish	35	Plaice	25
Cod	35	Pollack	30
Conger	58	Scad	15
Dab	15	Shad	30
Flounder	25	Skate/Ray	36
Haddock	30	Sole	24
Hake	30	Turbot	30
Herring	20	Whiting	23
Lemon Sole	25	Witch	28

As we will discover later, angling clubs and open competition organisers support conservation measures in a number of ways, not least by setting size limits above those required by law.

It follows that all unwanted fish and certainly those below club competition or legal size limits, should be carefully unhooked and returned alive whenever possible.

Fish must never be wasted. If they are over size limits they should only be kept if they are to be used as bait (for either crab pots or the angler's future trips) are wanted for the table, or need to be formally weighed and identified for competition or record claim purposes.

Food fish

It is a sad reflection of our times that the majority of the different species caught in local waters are completely ignored as a food source.

Bailiwick residents are extremely fortunate to have access to a ready supply of a great variety of fresh fish and yet they show little enthusiasm for all but a few of the more well known or "accepted" species.

They seem to increasingly prefer pre-packed imported fish or products such as fish fingers! Preparing fresh fish for the table is considered by some to be just too much trouble and effort.

There is a good demand for the so-called prime fish such as bass, brill and turbot, from both the housewife and the hotel and restaurant trade and for a few other species such as mackerel when they are available, but interest in many other fish seems to be negligible.

Even pollack (or Guernsey whiting, as it was known) which has been popular in the islands for generations is rapidly falling out of favour.

This is a pity, for nearly all of the 68 fish that appear on the boat and shore record fish lists can make an excellent, nutritious meal.

True there are some that are not very appealing! Lumpsucker marbled electric ray, trigger fish and sunfish cannot be considered gastronomic delights, while cuckoo wrasse, three bearded rockling and scad may be just a little too bony and modest in size to be worthwhile.

Nevertheless it's a great mystery why there just isn't a sale for many of the species.

Our professional fishermen must get very frustrated when parts of their catch, which consist of perfectly good edible fish such as ling, has to be sold at a pittance to be used as crabpot bait.

There is a lot of ill-informed nonsense and prejudice concerning the culinary aspects of fish. Some top national angling magazines have even stated on a number of occasions that ballan wrasse are completely inedible. Absolute rubbish! Fillets from a big wrasse, correctly prepared, seasoned and cooked are absolutely delicious.

Garfish is another species that causes problems; many people refuse to even consider eating it, just because it has got green bones!

It is understandable that the appearance of some species can put some people off and yet there is a saying "that in general, the uglier the fish, the tastier it is!" This is certainly true when you consider gurnard, angler fish, monkfish and John Dory.

The moral for all anglers should be "don't waste your catch, try each species, you will almost certainly be pleasantly surprised".

Sometimes Bailiwick anglers will catch an edible crustacea, for chancre and spider crabs, lobster and even crayfish have all been caught by local anglers on occasions.

This is a real bonus for they make a great meal. However, anglers must remember that there are legal size limits for crustacea.

Chancre and spider crabs, including their size limits are discussed under the "crab section" in chapter 4.

The size limit for crayfish is 23 centimetres measured from the tip of the beak to the extreme end of the tail.

Lobsters have to be at least 8.7 centimetres measured from the rear of either eye socket to the rear end of the carapace.

Chapter 3 Tackle/Methods

Angling visitors will find that tackle and angling methods used in the Bailiwick are similar to those used elsewhere.

This is not surprising for as there are no tackle manufacturers in the islands, local anglers have had to rely completely on imported tackle and accept the changes to design as they occurred.

The more venerable anglers will remember how it all started with bamboo rods, each with a crosspiece of wood attached to the butt end on which the 'string' line was wound!

It's no wonder that anglers were delighted as things progressed to cane, split cane, greenheart, solid fibre glass, hollow fibre glass and on to carbon and kevlar in numerous blends and configurations.

Reels followed a similar pattern, with wooden centre-pin reels giving way to fixed spools and multipliers that have progressively become easier to use and more reliable, as technology along with new materials gave rise to many innovations that greatly helped their performance.

Lines have gone from string or cord, through to monofilament and on to braided or wire line.

Local anglers more than matched their UK colleagues in their keenness to use the latest tackle, the main difference being the Bailiwick anglers trend towards the use of lighter gear.

The majority of island anglers have been scaling down their gear for many years, going for lighter rods, smaller reels and lower breaking strain lines. Even the humble float saw dramatic changes. Out went those huge bulbous models that could have been mistaken as mooring buoys, and in came thin pencil shaped floats that were a lot more sensitive and consequently indicated the bites much more clearly.

Some anglers, particularly the mullet enthusiasts, even started to use small freshwater coarse fishing floats.

Visiting anglers who are aware of the strong tides in the islands may well anticipate the need to use heavy weights when boat fishing. After all, in many other areas the use of one pound or even heavier leads is quite commonplace.

Local anglers fish much lighter and many do not even own weights over eight ounces and normally use no heavier than four to six ounces!

How is this possible? In the UK and Jersey, boats normally fish at anchor, which means that in strong tidal conditions heavy weights are essential, in order to get the bait down to the bottom.

In the Bailiwick boat fishing is nearly always done on the drift and as a consequence the weights used can be a lot lighter.

It is certain that this trend to lighter tackle has produced better catches and has given the local angler better sport and greater satisfaction from his fishing.

Bailiwick anglers do have one problem! Due to the great variety of the different types of fishing, they need a wide range of tackle, far greater than that used by anglers who live in an area where just one type of angling predominates.

For the Bailiwick angler to enjoy the full range of fishing on offer he needs a wide selection of tackle.

Beach casters, spinning rods, boat rods, light gear for mullet and rods for float fishing, all with their associated reels are required. If the angler participates in the local freshwater coarse or trout fishing as well, the list becomes almost endless.

Visitors coming over for an angling holiday may see this as a problem. They may not own such a range of gear and in any case there is a limit on what can sensibly be brought over, particularly if travelling by air.

Most visitors compromise for they realise that some tackle can be used for more than one type of fishing. Not an ideal solution but one that gets over the difficulties.

Another answer is to hire tackle. It is possible from local tackle shops and charter boat skippers, but it will probably be wise to contact them in advance to confirm what is available.

The Bailiwick is well served by tackle dealers. They have kept abreast of the new trends, are aware of the anglers' needs and have a very comprehensive stock. Another advantage to the visitor, it's VAT free!

Visitors will find them a good source of information and friendly advice.

Those operating in Guernsey in 2010 were:-

Boatworks+, Castle Emplacement, St Peter Port	726071
Boat Exchange, Orion House, Bridge Avenue, Vale	242576
	07781 111889
Mick's Fishing Supplies, Les Canus, St Peter Port	700390
Quayside Marine and Leisure, Northside, Vale	245881
Tackle and Accessories c/o Thompson Motors	
Rue de L'eglise, Castel	254383
Tackle Direct, Lowlands Industrial Estate, St Sampsons	244665

Up in Alderney the tackle dealer is:-

Alderney Angling and Sports, 32 Victoria Street	824028

In Sark the tackle dealers are:-

Gallery Stores, The Avenue	832078
Glyn Williams, La Grange, Clos du Menage	832273
Harbour Cafe	832396

There are a number of fundamental differences in the way that Bailiwick anglers make up their terminal tackle.

They tend to use fewer booms, clips and other propriety items than their UK colleagues.

Obviously there will be slight differences in the way that each angler puts together his terminal gear; the breaking strain and length of traces, the hook and swivel sizes and the choice of weight will all differ with each individual.

However, the trend in the Bailiwick certainly seems to be "keep it as simple, yet effective as possible".

Diagrams of typical Bailiwick terminal tackle configurations follow.

Running Leger
(Boat fishing over sandbanks)

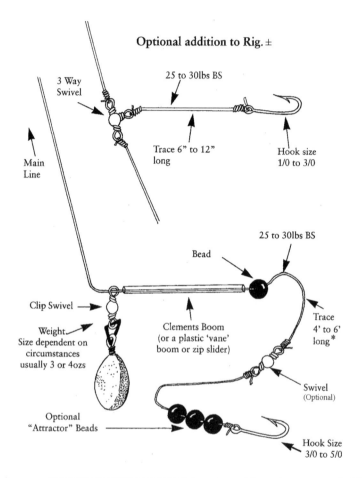

Optional addition to Rig. ±

3 Way Swivel

25 to 30lbs BS

Trace 6" to 12" long

Hook size 1/0 to 3/0

Main Line

25 to 30lbs BS

Bead

Clip Swivel

Trace 4' to 6' long *

Weight.
Size dependent on circumstances usually 3 or 4ozs

Clements Boom (or a plastic 'vane' boom or zip slider)

Swivel
(Optional)

Optional "Attractor" Beads

Hook Size 3/0 to 5/0

*   The trend amongst bass anglers is to use a much longer trace, even up to 15' to 20' in length. In this arrangment a straight swivel should be inserted half way along the trace which help to combat twist and tangling.

±   This allows a second flyer hook to be added. This is usually positioned 2' up the main line.

Running Leger
(Shore Fishing)

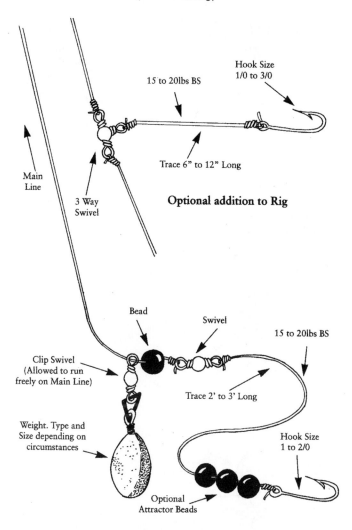

Hook Size
1/0 to 3/0

15 to 20lbs BS

Main
Line

Trace 6" to 12" Long

3 Way
Swivel

Optional addition to Rig

Bead

Swivel

15 to 20lbs BS

Clip Swivel
(Allowed to run
freely on Main Line)

Trace 2' to 3' Long

Weight. Type and
Size depending on
circumstances

Hook Size
1 to 2/0

Optional
Attractor Beads

*   This allows a second flyer hook to be added. Its postion up the main line,
must be at a distance from the swivel at the main trace, greater than the
aggregate lengths of the two traces. If this is not done, tangling between
the two traces will occur.

Paternoster Rig

(Used for Bream fishing ashore or afloat. Number of hooks optional)

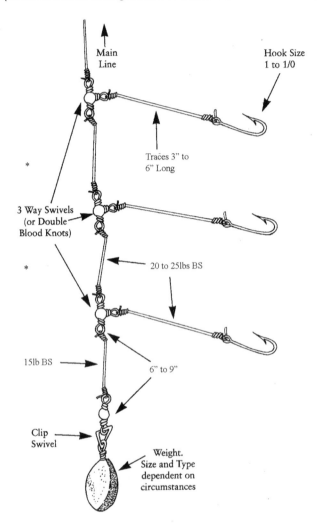

Main
Line

Hook Size
1 to 1/0

Traces 3" to
6" Long

*

3 Way Swivels
(or Double
Blood Knots)

*

20 to 25lbs BS

15lb BS

6" to 9"

Clip
Swivel

Weight.
Size and Type
dependent on
circumstances

*   Distance between three way swivels must be greater than the combined
length of two hook traces, otherwise tangling will occur.

Ballan Wrasse Trace
(Shore Fishing)

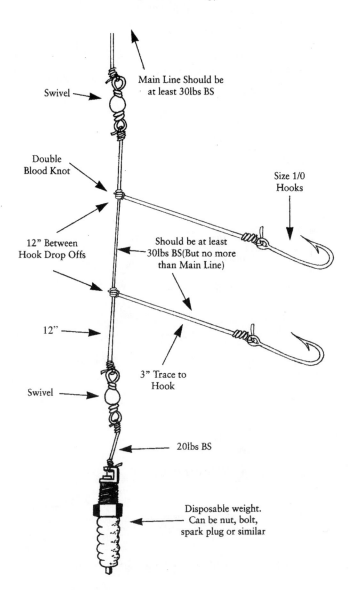

Swivel

Main Line Should be
at least 30lbs BS

Double
Blood Knot

Size 1/0
Hooks

12" Between
Hook Drop Offs

Should be at least
30lbs BS(But no more
than Main Line)

12"

3" Trace to
Hook

Swivel

20lbs BS

Disposable weight.
Can be nut, bolt,
spark plug or similar

Conger Tackle
(For fishing boat or shore in rough ground)

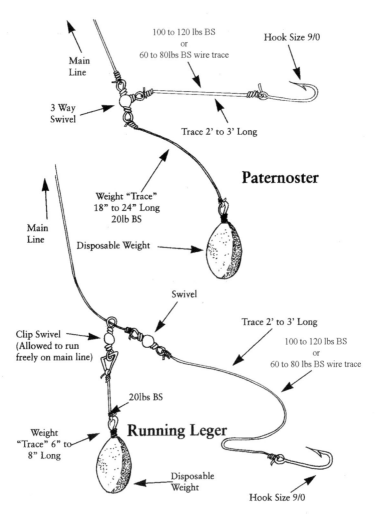

Main line should ideally be in excess of 50lbs.

General Spinning Trace
(Boat or Shore)

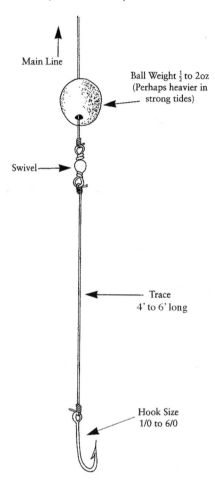

Main Line

Ball Weight $\frac{1}{2}$ to 2oz
(Perhaps heavier in strong tides)

Swivel

Trace
4' to 6' long

Hook Size
1/0 to 6/0

Note: Breaking strain of main line and trace and weight of lead will depend on where the trace is used. Generally shore anglers can use 12 to 15 lbs BS mainline, 1 oz weight 8 to 10 lbs BS trace and 1/0 to 2/0 hook. Boat anglers 15 to 20 lbs BS mainline, 2oz weight 12 to 15 lbs BS trace 3/0 to 6/0 hook. Boat anglers fishing over rough ground in fairly shallow water may well have to use higher breaking strain line and trace.

Boat anglers in deep water or strong tides will often use a heavier weight (4 oz or bigger) on a clip swivel or zip slider, instead of a ball weight.

Roselet Trace

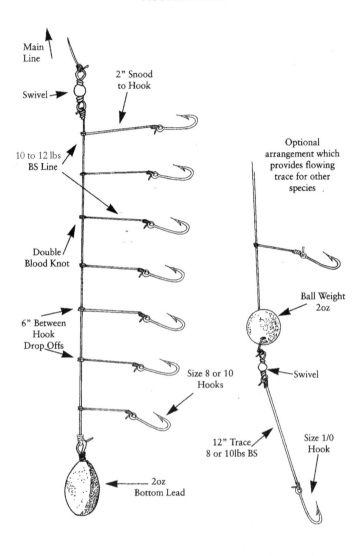

Main Line

Swivel →

2" Snood to Hook

10 to 12 lbs BS Line

Double Blood Knot

6" Between Hook Drop Offs

Size 8 or 10 Hooks

2oz Bottom Lead

Optional arrangement which provides flowing trace for other species .

Ball Weight 2oz

Swivel

12" Trace 8 or 10lbs BS

Size 1/0 Hook

Note: Number of hook optional, between 5 and 10 is the normal preferred number.

Float Tackle
(For Garfish, Mackerel, Scad etc)

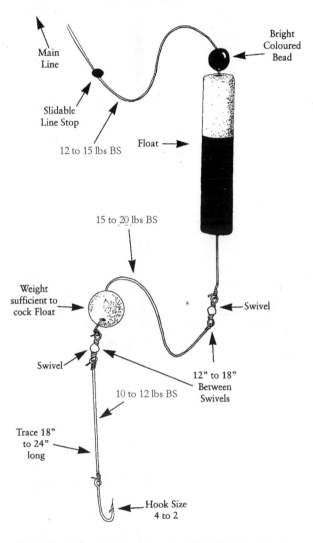

Main
Line

Bright
Coloured
Bead

Slidable
Line Stop

12 to 15 lbs BS

Float →

15 to 20 lbs BS

Weight
sufficient to
cock Float

Swivel

Swivel

←Swivel

12" to 18"
Between
Swivels

10 to 12 lbs BS

Trace 18"
to 24"
long

Hook Size
4 to 2

*   The addition of the second swivel and the 12" to 18" of line helps to overcome the trace tangling with the float when being cast.

48

Mullet Float Tackle

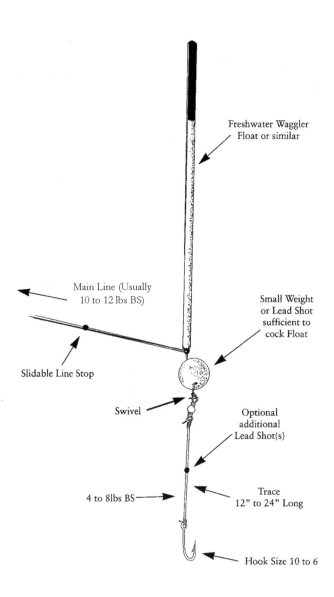

Freshwater Waggler Float or similar

Main Line (Usually 10 to 12 lbs BS)

Small Weight or Lead Shot sufficient to cock Float

Slidable Line Stop

Swivel

Optional additional Lead Shot(s)

4 to 8lbs BS

Trace 12" to 24" Long

Hook Size 10 to 6

Chapter 4 - Bait

The Inter Tidal Zone

The islands have one of the biggest tidal ranges in the world. On a spring tide, the range, which is the vertical distance between the heights of low and high water, often exceeds 10 metres.

In fact in 2010 the biggest range achieved in Guernsey was the 10.2 metres, or nearly 33 1/2 feet, which occurred on 2 March!

This enormous tidal range coupled with the comparatively flat foreshore found in many parts of the islands, produces an enormous inter-tidal zone.

It is a quite fantastic area. It doesn't just consist of a series of sandy beaches, but an incredible mixture of sand, mud, shingle, stones, boulders and rock.

This uneven terrain means, that as the tide ebbs it leaves behind rock pools and larger areas of water.

The result is an environment that is absolutely teeming with an abundant variety of both plant and animal life.

Seaweeds abound in a great profusion of different colours and shapes, the rocks are covered with limpets and winkles, the pools are home to anemones and small fish, crabs scuttle and hide under the stones and boulders, while the sand, mud and shingle hide razorfish, sandeels and many different types of worm.

Many island residents have become adept shore-gatherers. Over the years some have built up a comprehensive knowledge of the geography of the foreshore, and when the low spring tides uncover the lower limits of the inter-tidal zone they set out to see what they can find.

They are usually after inhabitants of the foreshore that will supply an excellent meal. Careful searching, coupled with their knowledge of the area, can produce, depending on the season, chancre, spider and lady crabs, or if they are extremely lucky the occasional lobster. Even the odd conger can sometimes be extricated from its lair in the rocks.

It's probably a sign of the sophistication of our times that much of the available food on the foreshore that was harvested by our ancestors is now largely ignored.

Limpets and winkles are usually left untouched by the majority of the modern shore gatherers even though they can be collected on any low tide, even on the smallest neaps when the tidal range can be as little as nine feet.

Some of the local Portuguese community have no such qualms.

They know that they make a delicious meal and are pleased to take full advantage of the abundance of these molluscs on the Bailiwick's beaches.

Ormers

However it's the ormer that is the most sought after prize by all the shore-gatherers. It is so much in demand that it has become almost an island tradition that when the tides and the season are right, hundreds of islanders take time off work and flock down to the beaches, or take a boat out to the offshore islets and reefs that become exposed with the falling tide, in order to search for this great delicacy.

Newcomers, or visitors to the island will probably not have a clue what an ormer is, or what the fuss is all about.

It is known as an abalone in other parts of the world. It is an earshaped gastropod that sticks to the underside of boulders, or in rock crevices, in the same manner as a limpet.

They are only found at the extreme lower limit of the inter-tidal zone that is uncovered by the biggest spring tides.

Not only do they make absolutely superb eating, but their shells are also much sought after. The underside of the shell is covered in an iridescent layer of mother of pearl and are often used for house decoration or ornaments. (see page 61)

They are at the northern edge of their range in the Channel Islands, and consequently are not found in the United Kingdom.

In local waters they could almost be considered an endangered species, and in a bid to safeguard their future, ormer farming has been tried with some success.

The ormer's breeding cycle and well being is very dependent on the right water temperatures. A series of very cold winters could reduce their future number considerably.

It is obvious that the ormer is a very vulnerable species. After all, it "just sits there" and can be picked off the rocks with very little effort. If unlimited access was permitted for both divers and shore gatherers it would not be very long before the species was extinct in local waters.

In order to protect the ormer stocks from such an eventuality there are quite strict laws governing the methods that can be used to collect them and the times of the year they can be taken.

The laws state:

"It is only permitted to take ormers between the 1st January and the 30th April and then only on the day of each new or full moon and on the two days following. It is an offence to take ormers at any other time. It is not permitted to take ormers by diving, which includes using masks, flippers, diving suits, any breathing apparatus or being submerged to any extent.

Ormers may only be taken between sunrise and sunset. It is only permitted to possess, buy or sell wild ormers on the days when they can be taken and the two days following, unless they are preserved. This includes cooked or pickled but not deep frozen.

Ormers taken must be at least 8 centimetres across the broadest part of the back".

As the regulations indicate they can only be gathered in the winter months, but this does not deter the dedicated ormer hunters! Fully clothed, they will often wade, waist deep in the icy waters as they grope under the rocks in an attempt to find their elusive prize!

In the distant past catches in excess of five or six dozen were not unusual.

51

Nowadays a dozen is considered a fair haul, which is quite sufficient for an excellent family meal.

Very occasionally there are freak catches. The ormerer's dream conditions are a calm day with no swell, a big spring tide, and high barometric pressure which has the effect of pushing the tide down just a little further than usual.

On one occasion in 1996 all three conditions came together with perfection. The tide dropped considerably more than expected, uncovering areas of the sea-bed that hadn't dried out for years.

Quite phenomenal catches were the result. Many gatherers were seen carrying home bags well in excess of 10 dozen and the fishmongers stalls were piled high with ormers for sale, a most rare and unusual sight.

For the angler, the ormer means more than just a good meal, for ormer guts make an excellent bait for bass!

Sadly, there is a snag. The law concerning the taking and keeping of ormers naturally applies to their innards as well. This means that the angler has to use his bait almost immediately, while it is still legal to have them in his possession!

Bait

To the angler that huge inter-tidal zone means something much more important than food. It means bait!

Bailiwick anglers are in a virtual utopia as far as bait is concerned. There are not many other angling venues where the angler has almost unlimited access to such a fantastic variety and abundance of bait and all virtually on their doorstep.

Local anglers have no need to travel dozens of miles to search for bait, or visit a number of scattered, different areas in order to obtain a varied selection, or be forced to pay considerable sums to get bait they cannot collect themselves. Here it's a few minutes drive, and a short stroll down the beach where there is a profusion of different bait waiting to be found!

There are very few restrictions on collecting bait in the islands. Some years back there was a law which prevented ragworm being dug on Guernsey's east coast in the spring months but this has long since been revoked.

However, one problem the bait digger does face is boats and their moorings, which are present in large numbers in nearly all the bays.

Digging for bait leaves very soft areas of sand which can take a considerable time to recompact and harden. Many boats have side legs fitted to ensure that they stay upright when dried out at low water. If a leg comes to rest on a recently dug area that has not fully recompacted the leg can sink into the soft sand and the boat could topple over with disastrous results. Alternatively, excavations sometimes cause stones or small rocks to come to the surface. If a boat settles on the falling tide on top of a sharp piece of rock it could well become holed. It is therefore obvious that anglers should use their common sense and keep well clear of boats and their moorings. Sadly some don't and as a consequence some Parish Constables have already introduced a bait digging ban in the proximity of boat moorings.

It will be no surprise that bait digging in St Peter Port and St Sampson's

Harbours is strictly controlled. For a time it was completely banned, but the authorities relaxed their total prohibition and it is now possible to obtain a bait digger's licence for St Peter Port Harbour.

It is issued by the States Harbourmaster under the "Harbours (Prohibition of Bait Digging) (Guernsey) Regulations 1994, Section 2" and costs £5 per annum.

It stipulates that digging is not allowed within 30 metres of any quay or harbour wall, or within 10 metres of any mooring area or temporarily moored vessel. Digging in St Sampsons Harbour is prohibited. In spite of the restrictions, it is well worth obtaining the annual licence, for the harbour bed contain large numbers of big ragworm.

It is impossible to consider the collection and storage of all the various types of bait under one communal heading.

Each has its own unique range of demands and problems. Consequently each type is now discussed and considered in the following seperate sections.

Sandeels

Sandeels are the most popular bait in the Bailiwick. Both boat and shore anglers favour sandeels as THE bait for a multitude of species.

In many angling centres fresh sand eels are very difficult to obtain. Anglers have to be satisfied with small packets of preserved or frozen sandeels sold by tackle dealers.

There has been no such problem for Bailiwick anglers, as sandeels are very prolific and easy to obtain locally.

There are at least five different species of sandeels in Bailiwick waters, although it's the two main species which interest the angler. There are the greater sandeel, which is also known as the launce, and the lesser or red, sandeel.

Very few anglers in the Bailiwick bother to collect, or catch their own sandeels.

The vast majority, probably as high as 98% of those used for bait by both the commercial and sport fishermen, are purchased from the professional fishermen who trawl up the sandeels mostly from the Great Bank, which is situated just off Guernsey's east coast. The sandeels usually move in to the Bank in March/April of each year and stay until September. Many tons are trawled up and landed during this period. (see page 61)

Local anglers strongly favour the use of live sandeels, and go to great lengths to ensure the sandeels stay alive and in pristine condition until they are needed. The most popular method of achieving this aim is the use of a courge.

This is basically a basket of cylindrical design with pointed ends. Traditionally they were made with willows, but in recent times they are invariably constructed from lengths of plastic tubing! The willows or plastic tubing are woven close enough to prevent the sandeels escaping, but the small gaps between the weave permit sea water to flow through freely, which ensures that the sandeels stay alive. When the sandeels are collected from the trawler they are placed in the courge as quickly as possible. The courge is then moored alongside the fisherman's boat, until he leaves for his planned fishing trip.

Fishermen who have their boat moored away from the harbour carry the sandeels across the island in tubs of sea water, as quickly as they can! In those situations an aerator is sometimes used to ensure that the sandeels don't expire on the journey!

In the past, the common practice was to tow the courge containing the live sandeels, behind the boat on the way out to the fishing grounds. As boats got more powerful and faster this method proved to be unsatisfactory. Now the majority of boats, both commercial and angling craft, have purpose-built sandeel tanks on board. Fresh sea water is continually pumped through the tank to make certain the sandeels stay alive for the duration of the trip.

Shore anglers who wish to use live sandeels usually use a bucket with an aerator attached.

There is always good humoured argument and debate on the merits of the use of live as against dead sandeels.

Is all the bother of keeping the sandeels alive worth it? It does appear that live bait has the edge, particularly when fishing in areas on times of slack water or minimal tidal flow. It may not be so important when fishing in tide race when the fish has little time to see whether the sandeel bait is alive or dead!

Courges on Maurice Down's trawler, waiting to be filled with sandeels. (see also page 61)

One thing is certain, the supporters of live sandeels clearly outnumber those who use dead sandeels by choice! In fact some anglers will not bother to go out if live sandeels are not available!

Obviously there are times when dead sandeels have to be used. In the early spring, autumn and winter frozen sandeels are all that are available. The majority of anglers realise this will be the case and stock up their deep freezers accordingly. Many anglers ensure they have a supply of "melvie", which is the local name for very small sandeels, some only matchstick size. These make an ideal bait when float-fishing for garfish and other species in the autumn and winter months.

Should anglers prefer to catch their own sandeels there are a number of ways open to them to achieve their aim.

They can be caught in seine nets, but this assumes the angler has access to such equipment, and has the knowledge, not only to work the net, but also of the areas where it should be set, and at what state of tide.

Sandeels, usually the launce or greater sandeel are regularly caught on rod and line or handlines. Normally this is when the angler is feathering for mackerel. However in recent years anglers have been deliberately targeting sandeels which can be found on many of the offshore sandbanks, including Godine, south of Sark, the Great Bank, Banc de la Schole and Banc au Nord.

Sandeel hunters use purposely made traces of sandeel feathers which are similar to those used for mackerel, but have smaller hooks and feathers.

Amazingly greater sandeels are sometimes caught when they take a bait meant for a very much larger species. They even appear on the fish record lists! On 23 June, 1979 Guernsey angler Bryan Le Breton was fishing on the Amfroque Bank, east of Herm, when his sandeel bait was grabbed by a sandeel!!

It weighed 239 grammes or 8 ounces 7 drams and became the Bailiwick, Channel Island and British record for the species, records that still stood in December 2010. Just a little further afield, off Jersey's north coast, an angler caught a Corbin's sandeel, which weighed 4 ounces 9 drams, which also attained Channel Island and national record status.

Sandeels can also be collected by shore gatherers. A few are found by anglers who are digging for worm baits.

However the best method is to go after dark down to the low water mark on a big spring tide. If you are lucky and have chosen the right spot you will find many sandeels by raking through the shingly sand in which they have buried themselves. On a number of occasions anglers on all night fishing sessions in Herm have picked up literally buckets full with their bare hands at both Belvoir and Shell beaches.

In Guernsey the west coast bays are good places to try, with Cobo probably being one of the favourites. In Alderney try Longy and Braye bays. It is clear that all anglers, including visitors and newcomers to the sport will have no problem in getting sandeels. Supplies in the smaller islands may at times be a little uncertain, so anglers intending to visit Alderney and Sark, and more particularly Herm, are advised to take sandeels with them from Guernsey, to make absolutely certain they do not find themselves without this most versatile of baits!

In the summer months freshly caught sandeels are available daily from local fishmongers and frozen sandeels can be obtained from tackle dealers throughout the year.

Storage of live sandeels is a problem. In spite of all the best efforts of anglers including leaving them in a courge, four or five days appears to be the limit.

Dead sandeels are no problem, for they can be kept in a deep freeze for months. The secret to good frozen sandeels is to get them to the freezer as quickly as possible after they are caught. The longer they are left dead, but unfrozen, the less satisfactory they will be when they come to be used.

One word of warning, sandeels once frozen and thawed for a second time tend to go soft and mushy and are useless as bait.

It is therefore advisable to store the sandeels in small separate packets. This will enable the right quantity to be taken for the planned fishing trip and keep waste down to a minimum.

An old friend used to freeze his sandeels singly by laying them out in rows on a tray! If you have the time, and the patience, this is the best way of all!

The importance of the sandeel to the continued success of the Bailiwick's fishing effort both from the commercial and sporting aspects is obvious.

If they were ever out-fished, or if they disappeared from our local waters it would have an extremely detrimental effect on the local fishing industry.

In some parts of northern Europe this has begun to occur, with sandeel stocks in some areas coming under extreme threat due to over-exploitation.

In an attempt to safeguard local stocks and prevent overfishing, all the various Fishing Ordinances covering Guernsey, Alderney, Sark and Herm, place a complete ban on the export of sandeels.

One final point. Most anglers look upon the humble sandeel purely as bait. However it must not be forgotten that they make a delicious meal in their own right.

Try some, you will be pleasantly surprised!

Cephalopods

These are members of the mollusc family and include octopus, squid and cuttlefish, all of which make excellent baits for a number of different species. The octopus used to be extremely common in Bailiwick waters until 1962.

However, in the winter of 1962/63 the islands, in common with the United Kingdom and most of Europe suffered an extremely long spell of bitterly cold weather.

In January 1963 local temperatures dropped to a record low of - 7.8°C, while February was only a little better with a low of -5.0°C.

The abnormally cold conditions completely decimated the local octopus stocks. They have never recovered and to see an octopus in Bailiwick waters is now quite a rare event.

Kevin Symphorien with a squid caught behind the Signal Station on the White Rock

There is better news for bait-seeking anglers as regards squid and cuttlefish. The members of these two species seem to increase every year to the point that they are almost becoming a nuisance. In the autumn and early winter months both boat and shore anglers get increasingly frustrated as their baits are pinched by the squid and cuttlefish before the fish get a chance!

There really is no need for anglers to catch their own squid or cuttlefish for bait, for they are easily obtainable in deep frozen packs from both fishmongers and tackle dealers at reasonable prices. They are available in boxes of small squid, also known as calamari, packs of squid or cuttlefish strips, or whole larger specimens.

Nevertheless many anglers set out to deliberately catch squid or cuttlefish for it can be good sport and a lot of fun, and more to the point they make good eating!

Catching them on a single hook, baited with a fish or sandeel can be both difficult and frustrating. They grab and hang on to the bait as the angler plays up his catch to the boat or pier. When the squid or cuttlefish get near the surface they have the infuriating habit of just letting go, and sinking back down to the depths. On a few occasions you may be lucky by carefully placing a landing net behind the squid/cuttlefish.

As it lets go of the bait it shoots backwards and if the net is in place in time, it's yours! Well that's the theory, in practice it usually lets go just out of reach of the proffered net!

To be successful you must use a squid jig. (see page 61) This is basically a brightly coloured lure, with a series of small upturned spikes or pins around the base. When this is grabbed the squid/cuttlefish tentacles get caught up and tangled with the spikes and it cannot let go. To tempt the squid/cuttlefish the jig is either spun slowly through the water, or suspended below a float at the required depth. Some anglers add a small piece of fish or sandeel to the base of the jig as an added attraction.

In the autumn, usually when a high tide occurs just on dusk, anglers go down to the harbours and often land squid over two feet long and weighing in excess of four pounds.

This is becoming a very popular pasttime to the point where favoured spots, including the end of St Peter Port Breakwater or Havelet Bay slipway by Castle Cornet become very congested with anglers enjoying the action, for a big squid on a rod and line will give the angler quite an exciting battle before it is safely landed.

There is no problem in storing squid or cuttlefish for future use.

A rare sight in Guernsey, a brace of undulate ray. Tony Ozard (left) with his 11-4-1 fish and Sam Ellis with one of 11-2-10.

After an absence of many years, red bream have started to make a very modest comeback. Most are small, but Terry Lawrence caught this 4-12-15 specimen over a reef mark south-east of Guernsey.

Plaice have become scarce in recent times, but Len Hall is pleased with his 7-8-4 specimen caught in Herm in October 1995.

Peter Frise surely the Bailiwicks most successful match angler.
Up to 2010, he won the GSAC senior championship and incredible 23 times in a 28 year period.

One of the Bailiwicks rarer species,
Dave Vaudin with his 7-10-12 shore-
caught marbled electric ray, hooked
while he was participating in the 2006
Specimen Fish Hunt

Veteran angler, Fred Ferbrache with a
ballan wrasse of 7-3-0 caught in
December 1997 on St Peter Port
Breakwater

A very rare fish as far as Bailiwick anglers are concerned. Australian visitor Paul
Berry with the smallest fish on the Bailiwick and Channel Island boat-caught
record lists, a 1-0-5 greater weever caught on the Casquets SW bank in July 2004

A view of Belgrave Bay (taken from the Salerie) showing the varied terrain at low water, a bait diggers paradise.

St Peter Port Breakwater, the most popular shore fishing mark in Guernsey. Picture by Brian Green

Ormer shells

Trawler skipper Maurice Down pours part of his sandeel catch into a customers courge

Squid jigs, note the absence of hooks which are replaced by a series of small spikes.

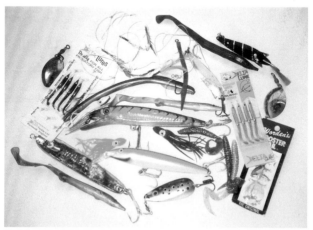

A selection of artifical lures, including a redgill, a pirk (bottom left) and two Rapala type lures (centre)

61

We get very few cod in Bailiwick waters, but Mark Page is delighted with this double figure specimen.

Dennis McKane with his 16-4-3 boat-caught bass. The top fish in the GBASS festival 2007 and the biggest bass ever caught in any of the local bass festivals.

Caroline Froome one of only two female anglers to win a Bailiwick Open Bass Festival. Seen here with her 11-10-1 winning bass in the 2007 Bailiwick Bass Challenge boat section.

The Bailiwick is a great place for junior anglers to enjoy their sport.

GSAC Junior Section secretary John Davey
helps the youngsters to sort out a tangle
during a club match on St Peter Port
Breakwater in 2006

GSAC youngsters enjoying the competition on the breakwater.

Even the very young can enjoy good sport, Martin (left) Ross, Lee and Jemma, the authors grandchildren with part of their bass and mackerel catch in August 1996.

Ben Brouard in August 1991 with a superb red gurnard of 2-4-12

One of the smaller record fish Ryan Thomson with his 0-13-8 Bailiwick, Channel Island and British record common topknot, caught at Grandes Rocques in August 1998.

Young anglers at the 2009 Bailiwick Bass Club Childrens Open which was held on St Peter Port Breakwater.

Two juniors took the top two section awards at The Bailiwick Bass Clubs 2010 Open Festival. Brandon La Touche (left) 9-1-1 boat caught fish and Callum McLaren 8-1-8 shore caught specimen the first time this had ever been achieved.

Once they have been gutted and cleaned they can be kept in a deep freeze for a considerable time. It can even be taken out for a fishing session, with the remaining unused portions put back and re-frozen to be used at a later date.

One word of warning! All three species of cephalopods eject copious amounts of black inky fluid when they are caught and/or when you attempt to gut and clean them. The fluid stains everything and is very, very difficult to remove. So it's not very wise to take it home and clean it on the kitchen table!

A short true story to illustrate the point. Some years back a professional fisherman had stored a few spider crabs intended for his own consumption in a store pot on the bed of St Peter Port Harbour. When he raised it to get the crabs he found that an octopus had got in, killed the crabs, and sucked out all the meat. His language was indescribable! In a blind rage he yanked the octopus out of the pot, whereupon it squirted ink all over his face! The fate of the octopus is best left to the imagination!

Crabs

The common green shore crab is much sought after as a bait by Bailiwick anglers, particularly those after wrasse. They can be easily found by searching under the stones or amongst the fronds of growing seaweed (or vraic as it is known locally) on any of the numerous stony or rocky beaches throughout the islands. The smaller specimens two to three centimetres across are the favoured size. Many anglers will also take the larger crabs. These can be cut in portions to be used as hook bait, or crushed into small particles to be used as ground bait. The real prize for the crab collector is the peeler or soft crab, for they are a superb bait for many species, including bass. As the crab grows, its shell becomes too small and it needs to form a bigger one. During this process a new soft skin forms over the crab's flesh. The old outer shell becomes unwanted and the crab gets ready to shed it. At this stage it is known as a 'peeler'. Once the old shell has been discarded, the crab's new soft skin will swell and harden into its new shell. During this period it is known as a 'soft' crab.

Many angling books and magazines will blithely advise the angler to go and collect a quantity of peeler or soft crabs for bait. It's not that easy! Hard back green crabs are not difficult to find, especially in the summer months, but peeler or soft crabs can be a little more elusive. Nevertheless, they are there to be found and with some effort Bailiwick anglers can usually get enough to satisfy their requirements. As far as peelers are concerned the winter months can be forgotten, March through to October/November being the usual season. In their soft state crabs are very vulnerable creatures and consequently tend to hide under stones or amongst the weed much higher up the beach than the hard back crabs, where there is less chance of them being discovered by predators.

As peelers or soft crabs always seek a safe refuge, a piece of guttering or a ridge tile placed upside down in an appropriate place on the beach will become a focal point for crabs both hard back and peeler. One snag with this idea? Someone else may see your piece of guttering, lift it and remove the crabs from underneath. You must ensure you get there first as the tide falls! There is no 'best place' for peelers, or for that matter hard backs. One just has to find the beaches that contain their favourite habitat. However, two likely spots in Guernsey are Grande Havre and the beaches at the back of Bulwer Avenue.

One plea to all crab gatherers. When you turn over stones and boulders in your search for crabs, ALWAYS replace them as you found them, do not leave them overturned. This will ensure that any marine life that is attached to the underside of the stone or boulder will not be left exposed. As it's replaced it will hopefully settle back roughly into it's original position and will continue to provide a refuge for more crabs that you may well wish to collect at a later date.

Care must be taken while collecting shore crabs, not to take undersize specimens of the three edible species, the chancre, spider and lady crabs. How do you recognise them? Telling them apart from the shore crab is not a problem. The shore crab is the only one that is green! The chancre is oval in shape and brown, the spider is a pale red or pink, covered in spines and is roughly triangular in shape, while the lady crab which is known as the velvet swimming crab elsewhere is brown and appears to have a 'hairy' back!

The chancre and spider crabs play a very important part in the Bailiwick's commercial fishing industry, so it's very important that immature crabs are not taken from the beaches.

In fact, the taking of undersize edible crabs is strictly against the law and is an offence. The Fishing (Minimum Size and Prescribed Species) Order 1997 confirms that no-one is allowed to take, land or possess any chancre which is less than 14 centimetres measured across the broadest part of the back, any spider which is less than 13 centimetres measured from between the two spikes protecting the eye sockets to the rear of the back, along the centre line of the back, and any lady crab less than 6.5 centimetres measured across the broadest part of the back.

Once collected hard back green crabs can quite easily be kept alive for some weeks. They must be kept in a cool place, even in the 'fridge'!

They should be kept in a container where they have some room to move around and are not piled too deeply on top of each other. A small amount of damp seaweed, bladder vraic is ideal and can be included in their temporary home. Every two or three days they should be checked and any dead crabs or decaying seaweed removed.

While this is being done the crabs should be placed in a bucket of fresh sea water for 15-30 minutes, which will freshen them up and help to keep their bodies moist and in good condition.

On no account should they be kept permanently in water. Even if there is only a very small amount of water left in the container in which they are housed, the water quickly goes stagnant and the result is a lot of dead smelly crabs.

One word of warning. Make absolutely certain that the container used to keep the crabs has a secure lid, and is escape proof. The crabs must be allowed some air holes but beware, the green shore crab is a very resilient and resourceful creature. It can live out of water for a long time, and can climb and escape through a surprisingly small aperture.

One angler kept his crabs in the boot of the car, but forgot to tell his wife. They all escaped when the container fell over and the lid came off.

The first that his wife knew of their presence was when some crabs crawled over her feet when she was driving the car. The result? - a highly hysterical woman, who in the midst of her terror somehow managed to bring the car to a shuddering halt without writing it off!

What happened to the angler when his stressed wife finally returned home is thankfully not recorded!

Live hardback green crabs are not usually available from tackle shops so it really is a case of gathering your own. There is no doubt that they can be deep frozen, but whether they make a good bait when thawed is open to conjecture. This doubt is simply due to the fact that so few anglers have bothered to deep freeze their crabs, as new supplies are so easy to find.

Theoretically a thawed crab should be no different to a fresh dead specimen which has been proved to be a successful bait.

Local tackle shops usually have peeler crabs for sale but they can be rather expensive. One trick with peelers is to freeze them with a hook already inserted but with its eye protruding.

This enables the bait to be tied to the trace and cast out while still frozen. This ensures the bait stays on the hook when it is cast. Unfrozen peelers and soft crabs are fairly fragile and have to be tied onto the hook, particularly when long casting is involved.

Casting a frozen bait does away for the need for any ties.

Obviously the sea water quickly thaws the crab, which is then in the right place, and in a good condition to hopefully attract the fish.

Another crustacean that makes an excellent bait is the hermit crab. This crab, which looks a little like a very tiny lobster, has a soft tail, and probably as a result they usually find a permanent home in a discarded whelk shell, which gives their soft rear end protection!

They are not found in the inter-tidal zone in any great numbers; as they usually frequent much deeper water.

Commercial fishermen catch them quite regularly in their trawl nets and crab pots, but as they have no commercial value they are usually discarded.

It would seem the only way to obtain this bait is to find a friendly professional fishermen who may be persuaded to keep some for you!

Catbait

This rather strangely named bait is the white ragworm. Why the name 'cat' has been applied to a marine worm has always been rather obscure. Suffice to say, at least one marine biological text book refers to it as the 'catworm'.

In the United Kingdom it is a highly prized bait, but it is extremely difficult to obtain, being almost rare in many parts of the country. Here in the Bailiwick there are no such problems. It can be found in abundance, the only restriction on its collection being the state of the tide.

Catbait (or white ragworm).

It is found in firm, clean sand or in areas where there is fine surface gravel. They are located well down in the inter tidal-zone the lower the spring tide, the better the chances of finding the catbait.

As a general guide, it is probably not worth attempting to dig for catbait if the height of the low water is 1.5 metres or more.

Unlike some of the other marine worms that leave 'casts' or 'holes' on the surface of the sand, the catbait gives no indications of its whereabouts. It follows that finding the worms can be a little 'hit and miss' until you have discovered by experience the best places to try.

The catbait is a relatively shallow burrowing worm, usually found in the top 12 inches of the sand. The best tool to use when digging for the worms is a flat pronged fork, a spade will almost invariably cut some worms in half, making them virtually useless.

Once dug, they should be kept in a clean plastic container of sea water. They must be stored in a cool place, the bottom of the fridge is ideal. Every couple of days they should be checked, suspect or dying worms discarded, and the sea water changed. If this is done conscientiously the worms will live for weeks rather than days! One word of advice, be careful where you collect the sea water. At some bays, Cobo is a good example, there are outfalls that pour large quantities of fresh water out on to the beach. As the tide recedes, some of the pools left behind are highly 'contaminated' by fresh water. This can also apply at the water's edge, where the freshwater stream meets the sea.

If water from these areas is inadvertently used for the catbait it will have disastrous results, which has been confirmed by personal experience. A back-breaking hour of digging to collect over 70 catbait, became a completely pointless waste of time and effort when all the worms died within a few hours.

Where should you go to get catbait? It's worth trying any beach, where there are areas of clean sand at the spring tide low water mark.

Cobo, Grande Havre and Perelle are popular spots that give quite well. On Guernsey's east coast Havelet is worth trying but its potential seems to have declined a little in recent years.

Up in Alderney, Braye and Longy bays are the spots favoured by the locals; while in Sark, Dixcart and Derrible bays are worth a try.

Lugworm

In the United Kingdom anglers will travel many miles to dig lugworm, or be prepared to pay quite considerable sums in order to guarantee a supply if they can't get their own.

Some UK anglers will not even contemplate going fishing unless they have sufficient lugworm for their planned session.

At times the demand exceeds supply, and the price at some angling venues sometimes rise to over £4 for 20 worms. In the Bailiwick there are no such problems. Lugworm is abundant and very easy to dig. In the past one of the most prolific spots used to be the area where the North Beach car park at St. Peter Port Harbour is now situated. It was a lugworm mecca where it was possible to dig 200 worms an hour! Present day anglers need not be worried that progress buried the lugworm beds under millions of tons of soil and tarmac, for there are still many other spots around the coastline where 100 lugworm per hour is still easily attainable!

In spite of the huge numbers of lugworm available locally and the ease of its collection, it has almost been ignored by Bailiwick anglers who considered it a second rate bait. In the past, bait diggers after ragworm would find the occasional lugworm, but would discard it with disdain saying "it's only a slug"!

Why this attitude existed was a mystery, for there is no doubt that it's an excellent bait attractive to many species. In the late 1960's a personal experience should have proved, beyond doubt the lugworm's true potential. A friend's father came over to Guernsey on holiday. A boat fishing trip was planned and the father said "leave the bait to me, I'll get enough for all of us". We decided to try a mark off Fermain on the edge of the "gutter" a deep offshore gully that drops down to 150 ft or more. As we anchored up the friend's father unpacked the bait. Our hearts sank, it was all lugworm. In England that was all he used and no-one had thought of telling him that this certainly wasn't the case in Guernsey.

Anyway, we were stuck with it. There wasn't time to go back to the harbour to try to get an alternative bait. In any case in those days it wouldn't have been easy, for sandeels and ragworm were not so readily available as they are today.

Without much enthusiasm lugworm baited hooks were lowered over the side.

To our amazement bites were experienced immediately and pout, pollack, bream, whiting and the occasional cuckoo wrasse were soon coming aboard in a steady stream. It was to prove to be a great day's sport. Even after this successful trip, our completely unjustified mental block against the use of lugworm remained. We considered the catch was a one-off, a fluke and we were still not convinced. It goes without saying we didn't use lugworm on future trips.

Why was lugworm so underrated in the Bailiwick? There are probably two main reasons. One was the easy availability of other baits, including ragworm, catbait (white ragworm), verm (see next section) and sandeels. Anglers considered these were all much superior and consequently the humble lugworm was relegated to the bottom of the wanted list. The other reason was the type of fishing that was done locally. In the years prior to the 1980's spinning and float-fishing were the predominant methods used from the shore, while spinning or drifting over the sandbanks was the favourite pastimes for boat anglers, none of which favoured or needed the use of lugworm.

However, the last two decades has seen a great increase in bottom fishing from shore marks, for bream, plaice, red mullet and bass and as a consequence, lugworm has finally become a bait that the local shore angler is taking seriously.

There are two main species of lugworm in the Bailiwick. The common lugworm which is often known as "blowlug" and the much larger black lugworm.

Unlike the catbait (white ragworm) which leaves no marks on the sand to reveal its whereabouts, the lugworm advertises its presence quite clearly. It lives in a U-shaped burrow in the sand. The entrances of the burrow are marked at one end by a cast of sand and the other by a depression or blow hole, through which the worm gets its food, which is mixed with the sand. The worm digests any organic matter and excretes the unwanted sand, thereby forming the cast. A flat pronged fork is the ideal tool to dig for the lugworm. A spade is useless as it will cause considerable damage to the worms making them unusable. Where to dig? The simple answer is "anywhere you see the tell-tale casts and depressions". The lugworm does not favour the clean firm sand, which is liked by the catbait. Softer more muddy, almost stagnant sandy areas are best. In the United Kingdom river estuaries are considered good areas for lugworm, which gives a clue to the type of environment that they prefer. Unlike the catbait, which is only found well down the inter-tidal zone, lugworm can be found and dug comparatively high up the beach. Places to try in Guernsey include Grande Havre, Belgrave, Cobo, Perelle, just below the reservoir outfall pipe, and Rocquaine. In Alderney, Braye and Longy are favoured spots.

How do you store lug? As soon as they are dug wash them in clean sea water, in order to remove all the surplus sand. They should be carefully sorted through and any damaged worms immediately discarded. Finally lay them out on clean, dry newspaper which must be at least five or six pages thick.

The worms must not be piled too deeply on top of each other.

For storage a flat box or tray is preferred to a deep jar or bowl. A sheet of newspaper should be placed over the top of the worms.

They must be stored in a cool place, otherwise they will quickly die. Unless they are kept cool, their life span particularly during summer months could be as short as 24 to 36 hours.

The ideal place is in the fridge as long as the temperature is not set too low. Periodically, at least every two days, although daily is better, the worms should be checked and the wet newspaper replaced with dry. Any dead worms should be removed. If all these precautions are taken, lugworm can be kept in good condition for up to a week.

Common lugworm cannot be deep frozen successfully. However this doesn't apply to the big black lug. If you don't wish to use the black lug within a few days, they can be kept for future use. The innards should be squeezed out through the head end, following which the worms should be rolled without touching each other in newspaper and placed in the deep freeze.

In the United Kingdom enormous quantities of lugworms are sold every day by tackle dealers.

Due to the fact that they were so readily available, and they have not been a very popular bait in the islands, they were not stocked or sold locally. .

However this situation has changed and supplies of frozen lugworm can now be obtained from Guernsey tackle dealers.

Verm

What is verm? To Bailiwick anglers it's a large fleshy worm, which is considered the king of all the worms, a superb bait that is second to none.

To United Kingdom anglers it's an unknown. They probably have never heard of the word 'verm' and wouldn't know what it is. They certainly never get the chance to experience its terrific potential as a bait.

Where does the name 'verm' originate? It is the Guernsey French (or Guernsey patios) word for 'lug-worm or rock-worm'.

Although it will not mean very much to the majority of anglers the worm's scientific latin name is marphysia sanguinea. It is only found in the Channel Islands and in a very few small areas, on the coasts of Devon and Cornwall where it is known as 'rock-worm'.

Verm is found well down in the lower regions of the inter-tidal zone, and consequently you will need quite a big spring tide when you decide to search for it.

Some anglers reckon that you need a quarrying licence to get verm! There is no doubt that searching for verm is hard work. It burrows deeper than ragworm and tends to frequent much harder ground which invariably consists of soft rock and compacted stones. To make matters worse it usually favours extremely wet areas, which is usually being caused by the drainage of water from the higher inter tidal zone levels.

To find the worm the angler needs a strong trenching tool, as he needs to get down 12 inches or more into the rock and stones and a small bailer to remove the water that will continue to flood his digging area.

The worms can grow up to a length of 12 inches and will disappear deeper into the rock fissures at a quite remarkable speed if disturbed. They break quite easily and it is very difficult to get the worms out of the rock in one piece. The best technique is to select a suitable rock and stone filled gully well down in the lower level of the inter-tidal zone and dig a small trench across its base. You can then work inwards, knocking down the up-side of the trench and hopefully the verm will fall down with the dislodged spoil.

Great in theory, but it takes a lot of hard graft and sometimes difficult to achieve in practice. Although verm is a very prolific species it is not possible to accurately predict the anglers likely collection rate. This will be dependent on it being a good spot, for verm quantities can vary quite considerably from place to place.

Once collected whole worms and sections with the head intact should be sorted and separated from all the other broken pieces, which should be stored in a separate container and used first.

They must be kept dry and cool. On no account leave them in an unlined metal or plastic container. A wooden box or plastic tub lined with seven or eight layers of newspaper is ideal. The worms should be kept in either coarse sawdust, fine wood shavings or granulated vermiculite and placed in the fridge.

Every couple of days they should be checked and any dead or decaying worms removed. If these precautions are taken it is possible to keep the verm alive and available for use for well over a week.

Verm is not available from tackle dealers, so in spite of the necessary hard work, the angler has no alternative other than to collect his own.

Places to try for verm in Guernsey include Grande Havre, beaches on the east coast north of Bordeaux and the foreshore south of the reclamation site in Bulwer Avenue. In Alderney, Clonque and Braye are considered good areas. However, it is worth having a try wherever there are suitable rock and stony areas down near the spring tide low water mark.

Verm

Joe Gomez digging for verm.

Ragworm

Up to the 1960's ragworm was undoubtedly the most popular local bait. Many anglers used little else, whether they were fishing afloat or on shore.

However, over the last four decades the ragworm's popularity seems to have slightly declined.

As we have already noted sandeels became easy to obtain, 'new' baits such as scallop frills became available, the value of lugworm as a good bait began to be recognised and spinning with artificial plugs and lures rather than worms became very popular.

Anglers have become more knowledgeable and have exploited the greater variety of available bait with increasing success.

Nevertheless ragworm still remains high on the angler's bait list and it is still the most used worm bait in the Bailiwick.

Although there are a number of varieties of ragworm on local shores, as far as the angler is concerned there are just two, the large ragworm which can grow up to 18" which is known as kingrag, and the smaller worm usually up to 6" in length which is called rockbait.

The king rag is a comparative newcomer to the Bailiwick. For many years tackle dealers had been importing kingrag into Guernsey. Sometimes a number of the worms remained unsold, and these were tipped into the harbour where they quickly became established. When the harbour bed was excavated and levelled during reconstruction works for the marina loads of spoil were carted away and dumped on a number of beaches, in particular in Belgrave Bay opposite the Longstore. This obviously had the effect of spreading the kingrag out into new locations.

74

As a consequence it is now possible for the Guernsey angler to obtain his own kingrag, although he must remember that if he wishes to dig in the harbours, he must get a licence from the Harbourmaster's Office. Care must be taken at the Longstore to avoid the boat moorings.

As the king rag is usually found in muddy sand the best tool to use to dig for them is a flat pronged fork. They tend to burrow fairly deep so it may be necessary to dig down more than one fork's depth.

In spite of greatly increased angling activity, the continued importation of kingrag and the greater use of other baits, has meant that there has been reducing pressure on the Bailiwick's ragworm stocks. In the United Kingdom ragworm can be difficult to obtain in some areas and on occasions the purchase price has risen to over £4 for 20!. For most of the year there are no such problems for Bailiwick anglers. Rockbait is comparatively easy to locate, and provided a good spot is found, anglers can usually manage to collect at least 60 an hour. However, there is an annual short interruption to this halcyon situation. For a period in the Spring the ragworm goes through its spawning cycle. During this process they go very soft and 'milky' and are completely useless for bait purposes.

Where do you go to dig for ragworm? There are very few beaches around the Bailiwick that don't have suitable areas consisting of stones and coarse gravel, that is the ragworm's ideal habitat. However, recommended places to try for rock bait in Guernsey include Rousse at Grande Havre, La Rocque to the west of Perelle, beaches between Bordeaux and Beaucette Marina, Cobo and Belgrave Bay. In Alderney, Raz Island causeway, Longy, Braye and Clonque are worth a try. In Sark go to Havre Gosselin and in Herm the beaches between the harbour and Rosaire Steps. Rockbait can be found much higher up the intertidal zone than catbait or verm but it can be difficult to find a good spot on the smallest neap tides. Unlike verm they do not seem to favour areas that are very wet, nor do they like places where there is a predominance of black sand or gravel. They do not live very far below the surface and in some locations they can even be found by merely turning over the surface stones.

The bait diggers tools, a flat pronged fork and a trenching tool.

75

However, it is nearly always necessary to do some excavating to get to the rock bait. In some spots, surface stones can be cleared from an area and the rock bait dug out with a fork.

It is more likely though, that the angler will find his rock bait in stone and gravel filled gullies, or in stony areas amongst the rock, and in such cases a trenching tool is the best implement to use.

Stored in the right conditions rock bait can usually be kept for up to five or six days and kingrag up to 10 to 12 days. It is essential that both types of ragworm must be kept dry and cool. A wooden or plastic container heavily lined with newspaper and kept in the fridge is ideal.

Some anglers keep their rockbait in damp green seaweed, but a small amount of clean dry gravel is probably just as good.

If you purchase kingrag from a tackle dealer it is usually in a black peaty material, which is quite satisfactory for it to be kept in, for its subsequent storage.

Every couple of days check the worms, discard any dead or dying specimens and replace the wet newspaper.

Scallop Frills

Scallop frills are a comparatively recent addition to the angler's bait selection. They have proved attractive to a number of different species, but particularly to bream and wrasse.

Most anglers will be aware that the scallop is part of the mollusc family and makes delicious eatingl

Scallop frills are actually the scallop's mantle, an outer layer of tissue in which the scallop's body is contained. The mantle also secretes the material which makes the scallop's familiar fan-shaped, two hinged shells.

The frills are part of the discarded material, when the scallop is cleaned and prepared for the table.

Scallops live on the sea-bed in comparatively deep water and are not found in the inter-tidal zone.

There is a quite active scallop fishery in the Bailiwick. They are caught by the commercial fisherman using scallop dredges, or collected by divers.

It follows that the normal angler will not be able to obtain his own scallop frills.

Unless you can scrounge some from a friendly commercial fisherman, the angler's only source of supply is from tackle dealers, who sell them in deep-frozen packs.

Once obtained they can be kept for long periods in the freezer, and seem to be quite usable even if they are unfrozen and re-frozen for future use.

Artificials (see page 61)

There's an old saying that artificial lures catch more anglers than fish!

There is such a variety of lures, that the angler, particularly the less experienced, will often be tempted to purchase those with the brightest, most garish colours, in the sadly mistaken belief that a bright object will be easily seen and attractive to the fish.

Highly coloured, bright lures are not always the answer. Anglers fishing over the wrecks will often make excellent catches using black or other dark coloured lures, even though the very deep water means that the light levels near the sea bed must be very low indeed.

Nevertheless it's a fact that there is an almost infinite selection of artificial lures, with pirks, spinners, spoons, feathers, flies, plugs, rubber or plastic eels, imitation worms, muppets and wobblers all available in a vast multitude of shapes, colours and designs.

It's not surprising that anglers new to the sport find it quite daunting to try and select those that will give him success in making a good catch. The tackle dealers or fellow anglers are usually very helpful and give advice, but in the end, it's the angler himself that has to make the final choice.

The angler must remember that the whole object of artificial lures is to try and trick the fish into believing that it is not a chunk of metal or plastic but a live fish or worm that would make a good meal!

He must appreciate that it's not necessarily the colour that will do the trick, but what the lure will look like to the fish as it moves through the water. It is the movement that the angler gives to the lure that will make the difference between success or failure, the speed of the lure through the water and the depth that it is presented, being the main factors that will ensure the best results.

An artificial lure, cast out and left motionless is a pointless exercise which will not produce any fish.

Artificial baits are not new, they have been used in the Bailiwick with great success for years, the most common in use being feathers and rubber eels.

On a rod, feathers are usually fished in a set of seven. As long as they are kept continually on the move by letting them drop quickly down to the bottom and immediately retrieved, or 'jigged' at the correct depth, they can be deadly lures and account for many different species. Mackerel are usually the main target when using feathers, not just by anglers but also by commercial fisherman who usually use a set of 15 on a handline. They do, however, tempt other fish with scad (horse mackerel), pollack, coalfish, John Dory, herring, pilchard, cod and garfish being just a few of the species that have fallen to this popular lure.

As we have already noted, sandeels are a good bait in themselves and are also caught on feathers, with special sets being made with smaller hooks.

Ironically many anglers do not consider the use of feathers to be an acceptable angling technique. They will use them to make a quick catch of mackerel or sandeels for bait, or to take home a few mackerel for tea, but do not consider that their use is 'real' angling!

However there is no doubt that feathers used correctly in the right place at the right time of the year, can account for quite superb catches of mixed species.

Rubber eels, which were designed to imitate sandeels, were originally used by the professional fishermen using handlines and regularly accounted for heavy catches of pollack. In more recent years the introduction of plastics have allowed the rubber eel to evolve into a much more realistic lure. Anglers (and professionals) now have a selection of upmarket imitation sandeels in various sizes.

They are usually referred to by their brand names, including Redgills (which are not necessarily red) and Deltas which are the smaller size lure of this type.

From the late 1940's through to the 1960's spinning was the most popular angling method in the Bailiwick both ashore and afloat. This was mostly done with natural baits such as ragworms, but its popularity particularly amongst shore anglers seemed to wane, and float fishing became the vogue.

However, in recent years there has been a big revival in spinning, along with a much greater interest in the use of lures.

Good catches of pollack and bass have been made both afloat and ashore, using both the imitation plastic sandeels and worms of varied sizes and types as well as with metal lures and spinners.

There are two other types of lure that have become increasingly popular in the Bailiwick, the plug and the pirk.

Locally, the plug is usually referred to as a Rapala, which is one of the more popular brand names. They have been used both afloat and ashore with quite incredible success accounting for enormous catches of quality bass.

Pirks are self weighted metal lures, usually silver or chrome in colour. They are mainly used over the deep water wrecks, where they are lowered down to the wreck and jigged sharply up and down. They have been responsible for big catches of pollack and cod.

One lure that is not very widely used in the Bailiwick is the baited spoon. The spoon is usually spun very slowly over a sandy sea bed, its fluttering action proving to be a great attraction to flatfish, especially plaice. It's certain that if this technique was more widely used, catches of plaice would greatly improve.

In conclusion, artificial baits come down to a small number of basic categories.

Pirks, plugs (or wobblers), rubber/plastic sandeels/worms, feathers, spoons and flies.

Artificial flies do catch sea fish but to date it's a little used method in Baliwick waters.

Some anglers do find an interest in making their own lures. There is a great satisfaction in catching a fish on a lure you've made yourself.

However, there is no real need to make your own, for the local tackle shops stock a great profusion. The only snag, some can be relatively expensive.

Fish

Probably due to the abundance of sandeels, fish baits are not used so widely in the Bailiwick as elsewhere, even though they can give excellent results.

Conger, shark, tope, turbot, brill, ray, ling, cod, dogfish, gurnard, whiting and even bass have all been tempted by a fish bait at one time or another, and there is no doubt that anglers will confirm from their own personal experience that many more species can be added to that list.

Mackerel, herring, pilchard, garfish, pout, and roselet (atherine smelts) are just a few fish that have given anglers good catches when used as bait.

Where do you get the necessary fish? Anglers cannot rely on fishmongers as a reliable source. This is not being disparaging to the Bailiwick's fishmongers.

They do a great job and provide a remarkable array of good fresh fish, but the species that the anglers require are not usually those in demand from customers seeking a tasty meal. As a result the availability of the species wanted by the angler can be a little uncertain at times and cannot be guaranteed.

Tackle dealers do sell fish baits, but their selection is normally quite restricted. Often deep-frozen mackerel is all that is available.

It really comes down to the angler catching his own bait, which is best used just after it has been caught. In years past surplus bait, or bait which was deliberately obtained to be used at a later date would have been salted down, but obviously in these modern times it is usually deep-frozen.

One small tip, whatever fish you are freezing down, put them in several lots in separate packets. This makes it easy to take out the right amount needed for the planned fishing trip. If the fish had been frozen in one large lump it's almost certainly too much for one session and wastage will occur. Most fish baits cannot be successfully re-frozen once they have been thawed out. They go soft and unusable.

Razor Fish

Although this member of the mollusc family is commonly called razor fish, its correct name is razor shell.

As the name suggests they are similar in shape to a cut throat razor, their 'body' being contained within two long slim shells which are hinged together.

They live in deep tube-like vertical holes which they dig in the sand. They are found in similar sandy areas that are frequented by catbait so it follows that it requires a big spring tide in order to search for them, for they are found well down in the lower levels of the inter-tidal zone.

They often confirm their presence by shooting a jet of water out of their hole.

Some angling books state that razor fish can be lured to the surface by pouring coarse salt down their hole, while some anglers in the United Kingdom collect their razors by pushing an iron rod with a pointed tip into the hole, and pull out the razor fish impaled on the end.

In the Bailiwick these methods have not found great favour and the local anglers usually obtain their razorfish by simply digging them out with a fork.

Razorfish can quite successfully be deep-frozen for future use, either in a whole state in their shells, or with the shells removed.

It doesn't appear to make any difference to the texture of the razor fish when it is refrozen for use, the only snag in leaving the shells on, they take up more room!

Incidentally this is another bait that has recently become available from local tackle dealers.

However if you wish to dig your own, try the areas that have been suggested for catbait.

Shirvy

Shirvy is a word that will not be familiar to visiting anglers to the Bailiwick or for that matter, to local newcomers to the sport. Quite simply, it's the local name for groundbait or cloud bait. But why shirvy?

Originally local anglers, particularly those after mullet, would use a specially prepared prawn or shrimp net to obtain their groundbait.

They would take a large shrimp net and ensure that it was made up with as fine a net as possible, muslin was considered ideal. Two small wheels were then fixed, one to each end of the front flat wooden bar of the net. The completed outfit was then pushed along over the sand in waist deep water.

The quarry was tiny shrimps, prawns or microscopic animal plankton.

The resultant mush was then spooned into the sea at the chosen mark which apparently drove the mullet into a feeding frenzy! If the angler was in the happy state of having too much ground bait for his mullet session the remainder was put into jars and salted down to be used at a later date.

The Guernsey-French (or Guernsey patois) word for small shrimp is chervin, which was gradually bastardised into chervie, and much later into shirvy.

The use of the word is spreading. It has been used in Jersey for years, but it is occasionally used now on the English south coast. This is undoubtedly due to the increasing number of United Kingdom anglers coming over to fish in the Bailiwick, who hear the word used, when in discussion with the local anglers or tackle dealers.

No one bothers to net the small shrimps and plankton these days. Modern shirvy is usually a concoction of mashed up or boiled fish, bread, catfood, fish oil, bran or anything else the angler believes would attract the fish.

Up in Alderney, the main ingredient for many years was minced meat. Apparently the instigator was the local butcher who found it was very attractive to the mullet shoals and he even used a tiny piece of meat for his hook bait. The mullet certainly seemed to get quite a taste for meat, but the Alderney anglers have always wondered whether it had been a deliberate ploy by the butcher to increase his sales! In recent years the use of minced meat as a shirvy additive seems to be going out of fashion in the northern isle and its use is rapidly declining.

There is a definite advantage in using shirvy when angling from the shore to the point that many anglers will not go to a rock or pier mark without it. Although it was originally used almost exclusively by the mullet angler it soon became clear that it attracted other fish. Catches of garfish, mackerel, pollack, bream, scad, roselet (atherine smelts) and many other species will be greatly enhanced if the angler spoons a small quantity of shirvy into the sea at his chosen mark at regular intervals throughout his fishing session.

One small tip, always make sure that fish or vegetable oil is added to the shirvy mix. The oil will rise and produce an oil slick which will smooth the sea's surface. Without the ripples and chop caused by the wind and tide the angler has much improved visibility to see down into the depths, enabling him to observe the presence of fish. The recipe for the shirvy can be varied depending on the chosen quarry. For example, if the target species are wrasse, crushed up crabs should be added to the mix.

One cardinal rule when using shirvy, put in just enough to tempt the fish but not enough to satisfy their appetites!

Groundbait can also be used when afloat. Rubby dubby (yet another name for groundbait) is a mixture of mashed up fish and is used to produce a slick or trail down-tide of the boat to tempt shark. This is usually achieved by hanging a mesh sack containing the rubby dubby over the side of the boat. If the sack is fixed so that it is just in the water, the rolling of the boat will ensure that the rubby dubby is slowly washed out of the sack, producing a continuous trail.

In order to attract bottom feeding species the mesh sack containing the fish offal can be tied to the anchor rope just a few feet clear of the sea-bed.

Whatever ground bait you need you will have to make and prepare your own.

The local tackle shops sell specially prepared ground bait for the freshwater anglers, but there is nothing ready made up that is available for the sea angler.

Miscellaneous Baits

There are many other miscellaneous baits that can be used by the sea angler, which are available locally, either by the angler collecting his own, or by purchase.

Mussels, clams, whelks, limpets, prawns, shrimps and even garden worms have all proved successful at one time or another.

If one considers bait for mullet the list almost becomes infinite, for they have been taken on bread, hard boiled egg white, maggots, cheese, bacon rind, cake, meat, sand hoppers and even white toilet soap to name just a few.

Incidentally, an interesting way to collect sandhoppers is to sink a bowl into the sand until the tip of the bowl is level with the sand's surface. This should be done just above the last high tide mark where the sand is dry. As it gets dusk place a light in the bowl. This attracts the sand hopper which will jump into the bowl! It doesn't take long before there is enough not just for the hook bait but to become an ingredient of the shirvy as well.

Chapter 5 — Where to Fish

Due to the Bailiwick's extremely varied marine environment the number of different places or marks where the angler can enjoy his sport both afloat and ashore is quite incredible.

The angler is really spoilt for choice and it's not just the quantity, but also the almost infinitesimal variety of the fishing spots. Ashore there are surf covered beaches, quiet bays and gullies, piers and rocky outcrops, while afloat there are reefs, wrecks and sandbanks.

Shore Angling

Shore anglers are greatly helped by the huge tidal range, for as the tide falls it uncovers an increasing number of rocks or reefs for the angler to visit.

One of the Bailiwick's bass enthusiasts has recorded nearly 100 shore fishing marks around Guernsey alone, where he has caught bass. There is no doubt that many other anglers can match that figure for more general fishing spots.

It's obvious that this all presents quite a big challenge to the angler. He has to learn the best time to fish each mark, not just from the weather and tidal aspects, but also the fishes normal feeding pattern at each spot. This problem is further compounded by the fact that each species may well feed at different times during the tidal range.

It confirms that for an angler to become really successful in the Bailiwick he has a lot to learn, which will only be achieved through experience gained over a period of time.

The sport's newcomers, or visitors, could well become over-awed by the size of the problem.

They may well not get very much advice from the more experienced local anglers who can be very secretive about the best spots to fish. This is quite understandable in such small islands. If an angler has found a mark that produces exceptional sport, he is naturally reluctant to share the knowledge with other anglers, for as the word gets around, very soon the spot becomes overcrowded and overfished!

In spite of all these problems, newcomers or visitors should not despair for there are many well known shore marks where good fishing can be had at the right time of the year.

However, a few words of warning and advice are necessary. Shore anglers have very few restrictions on where to fish but there are a number of places in the Bailiwick where shore angling is not permitted. These are the Fisherman's Quay, the enclosed customs area on the New Jetty and the marina pontoons in St. Peter Port and St Sampson Harbours, the White Rock and the container berth, the oil tanker berth at St. Sampson's Harbour and the Beaucette Marina property. There can also be restricted access to the north pier at the St. Sampson's Harbour entrance, if ships are being loaded / unloaded.

In Alderney there is restricted access to the Commercial Quay during shipping operations, but no problems at other times. If you intend to fish overnight in Herm, you must leave your name and address at the Mermaid Tavern on arrival. Anglers are requested to avoid Herm's south coast cliffs from February 14 - July 14 due to nesting sea birds. No access is permitted to Brecqhou or Jethou as they are private islands.

Burhou off Alderney's west coast is closed from 15 March to 27 July due to nesting sea birds. There are no restrictions on access to Burhou at other times, but if you wish to stay overnight and rent the hut accommodation that is sited on the island, you must contact the Alderney Harbourmaster's Office.

Angling on Lihou Island is permitted, but the islets of Lihoumel and Lissroy off Lihou's west coast are closed from 1 January to 31 August due to nesting birds.

Although the tides can be a great advantage to the shore angler, both as regards fishing spots and bait collection they can also be really dangerous, particularly on big spring tides.

The angler must always be aware of the prevailing tidal conditions. It's all too easy to fish a low water mark, or go to get bait, become completely engrossed in what you are doing and fail to see that you are surrounded by the rising tide.

For their own safety shore anglers should make themselves fully aware of the so-called "Twelfth Rule" concerning the tides.

The tide rises (or falls) very approximately over a six hour period. However, during the six hours it does not rise (or fall) at a regular rate.

It rises (or falls) 1/12 of its range in the first hour, 2/12 in the second hour, 3/12 in each of the third and fourth hours over the half-tide, 2/12 in the fifth hour and 1/12 in the sixth hour. This pattern holds true whether it's a spring tide or the smaller neap tides.

It follows that the tide rises (or falls) half of its range in the middle two hours.

If it's a spring tide with a 10 metre range, it means the tide will rise (or fall) 5 metres, or nearly 16 1/2 feet in the middle two hours, or if you prefer 8 1/4 feet per hour, or over two feet every 15 minutes.

It will be appreciated that such a rapid rise in water levels can swiftly cut off an angler's retreat and soon cover any low-lying rocks he's standing on. Anglers should always be aware of their route back to safe ground.

There's no excuse for an angler not knowing the state of the tide. Each year the Guernsey Marine Traders Association produce an excellent tide table booklet which is available from all GMTA members, including fishing tackle shops.

Although it is a free publication a donation to the Royal National Lifeboat Institution and/or the Channel Island Air Search is greatly appreciated.

In Alderney the tide tables are produced by the States of Alderney Marketing Department and are available as a free anglers guide.

In addition the current tidal information is published each day from Monday to Saturday in the Guernsey Press and is also available on various websites.

Detailed information on a selection of the Bailiwick's shore fishing marks is listed a little later in this chapter.

Deciding which to include out of the hundreds of available spots was quite difficult, but it was a decision that had to be made for it was obviously impossible to describe all of them!

Hopefully those chosen will give anglers, including visitors, a good choice of a variety of marks that have given good sport in the past.

When the species that can be caught at each mark are being considered, the time of year and time of day must be taken into account. It must be remembered that some species are nocturnal feeders, while many species only come into the shore marks for a few months each year. The information given in chapter two will give good indication on what you can expect from your chosen mark.

The information provided includes details on the type of venue. This is listed as 'beach', 'rock' and/or 'pier'. In this context 'pier' means any man-made landing stage, breakwater or steps as opposed to natural rock formations.

Although there are many good fishing spots on the cliffs in all the islands, readers will find that very few of these marks are included.

This is quite deliberate, for the cliffs can be very dangerous, particularly if you stray off the recognised paths and access routes.

It is strongly recommended that newcomers to angling, and visitors, do not attempt to climb down to likely fishing spots on their own, but join experienced local anglers who know the marks and how to get down to them safely.

Although it is unwise for newcomers or visitors to venture down the cliffs, they are by no means restricted only to the marks listed in this publication.

One delight of the Bailiwick, is that within reason, wherever you cast a baited hook you have a chance of making a catch.

It is highly recommended that readers try many other spots that can be fished in complete safety.

Good examples are the beaches around the islands. The north beach in Herm, Alderney's Braye Bay and Douglas Quay. Vazon and Cobo Bays on Guernsey's west coast and some of the inner piers and quays of the harbours are all worth a try.

One plea to all anglers — please take all your rubbish home with you at the end of your fishing session. All too often rocks and piers are left covered with discarded line, plastic bags, drink cans, rotting piles of bait or even worse, unwanted fish.

Such actions will mean that angling will come under severe criticism, and in the case of the piers and breakwaters a possible ban on angling.

Make certain your fishing spot is cleared of your rubbish before you leave.

One final point, in order to assist newcomers and visitors to locate the shore marks, map references from the 2010 Perry's Official Channel Island Guide to Guernsey, Alderney, Sark and Herm are quoted. This publication is widely available at local shops, priced at £5.95 (An A4 commercial version is also available priced at £9.95.)

84

Seals

One final point of interest - Some shore anglers have recently experienced a problem that had previously been unknown in the Bailiwick, the presence of seals!!

In the last few years a group of seals have become established on the rocky islets North of Herm.

Anglers fishing on Herm's east coast have been startled when they have suddenly surfaced only a few feet out from the rocks. On a few occasions they have even ripped fish off the anglers tackle as they reeled in their catch.

They have also been sighted further afield on Guernseys east coast, and on the Casquets reef.

As the seals are a recent edition to local waters they have been the subject of much curiosity and excitement when they are seen. As they were so few they have not caused any major problems to date but the situation is going to change for their numbers are steadily increasing. It is now considered that the colony north of Herm is in excess of 30!

They could become a real nuisance to both commercial and sport fisherman and will almost certainly have an adverse affect on fish stocks.

Guernsey Shore Fishing Marks

GUERNSEY	
PLACE	Queen Elizabeth II Marina
PERRY MAP REF.	Page 19
TYPE OF VENUE	Pier
ASPECT FACES	East
SHELTERED FROM	Winds from south-west through to north-west.
ACCESS	Parking at fishing spot.
BEST STATE OF TIDE	Half tide up to two hours down
SPECIES	Grey mullet, golden grey mullet, plaice, pout, ballan wrasse, red mullet, garfish, conger, sole, lesser-spotted dogfish, black bream.
METHODS	Float Bottom fishing - leger or paternoster

GENERAL INFORMATION

East arm bottom is nearly all sand. The pier is built on a rubble mound, so it can be awkward to land a fish over the boulders.

The most favourite fishing area is the last 125 metres of the pier.

Grey mullet are caught from the boulders at the extreme north end of the pier, including on the pier's west side in the approach channel to the marina entrance. It's a very busy marina particularly in the summer, so be aware of the heavy boat traffic. Similarly mullet can be caught from the boulders on the west (Salerie) side of the approach channel and along as far as the small Salerie Harbour.

Grey mullet, and occasional bass can be caught inside the marina, but fishing from the pontoons is not permitted.

In recent years golden grey mullet have been caught with some regularity in the marina's south west corner.

You can't fish there anymore! Anglers fishing for mullet in 1968, where the North Beach car park is now situated. This spot used to be called the 'RAC' for that organisation's office used to be sited nearby.

GUERNSEY	
PLACE	White Rock Pier
PERRY MAP REF.	Page 19
TYPE OF VENUE	Pier
ASPECT FACES	East
SHELTERED FROM	Winds from south-west through to north.
ACCESS	450 metre walk from North Beach car park. Only route is to go along the top walk to avoid harbour working areas.
BEST STATE OF TIDE	Half tide up to two hours down
SPECIES	Pollack, garfish, mackerel, roselet, conger, black bream, lesser-spotted dogfish, scad, ballan wrasse, grey mullet, pout, red mullet.
METHODS	Spinning, worm bait, sandeel or lure. Float Bottom fishing - leger or paternoster

GENERAL INFORMATION

A Number of different spots used to be fished at this venue.
(a) Harbour mouth. Spin for pollack, scad and mackerel, but bear in mind it's a busy harbour, so extreme care must be taken when casting.
(b) Top walk, the 100 metre stretch north from the lighthouse. There is rock and weed close in, sand further out. A cast of 50 metres plus can produce pout, black bream, dogfish, conger. Close in ballan wrasse. Float for garfish, pollack and mackerel.
(c) Small square at the back of the watchhouse. Same as (b) but also spin for pollack etc.

Note:
Due to health and safety concerns caused by unsafe structural problems on the pier access to the area is no longer permitted.
An exception is a short section of the top walk behind the custom sheds from the QE2 east arm to the locked gate on the top walk.
At the time of going to print it is not known when, or if, access will be restored.

GUERNSEY	
PLACE	St Peter Port Breakwater (see page 60)
PERRY MAP REF.	Page 18
TYPE OF VENUE	Pier
ASPECT FACES	East
SHELTERED FROM	Winds from south-west through to north-west.
ACCESS	350 metre walk along the pier from the nearest car park
BEST STATE OF TIDE	Half tide up through to half tide down
SPECIES	Garfish, mackerel, black bream, pollack, red mullet, conger, lesser-spotted dogfish, ballan wrasse, scad, pout
METHODS	Spinning with worm baits, sandeel or lures. Float Bottom fishing - leger or paternoster.

GENERAL INFORMATION

Due to its ease of access and above average catches probably the most popular angling shore mark in the Bailiwick. Most of the angling done in the deeper water at the end of the Breakwater. Between 1966 and 2010 no fewer than 47 Bailiwick shore records covering 21 different species were caught on the Breakwater, four of which were also British records. In addition nine mini records (fish under 1-0-0) were caught covering six different species, of which three also became British mini records. Can get very crowded at times, both as regards the number of anglers and sightseers.

St Peter Port Harbour is a very busy port. Anglers <u>must</u> excercise great care in casting so as not to interfere with passing shipping and must be prepared at times to reel in gear to avoid vessels.

Problems have occured in recent years including cast out weights hitting passing boats. This resulted in warning from the harbour authorities that unless things improve, fishing from the pier could be banned.

Anglers cooperation is important, not only on this matter but also to eliminate the problem of litter and discarded bait being left on the pier. Unless anglers comply with these requests the popular mark could be lost.

The bottom is rock and weed close in and to the south of the breakwater, but sand to north and east. Should **not** be fished in strong or gale force southerly winds, as waves can wash right over the structure.

GUERNSEY	
PLACE	Castle Cornet Rocks
PERRY MAP REF.	Page 18
TYPE OF VENUE	Rocks
ASPECT FACES	West and South
SHELTERED FROM	Winds from north through to east.
ACCESS	200 metre walk across rocks from the car park on the pier.
BEST STATE OF TIDE	Two hours up to three hours down.
SPECIES	Garfish, pollack, ballan wrasse, conger, pout, black bream, grey mullet, plaice.
METHODS	Spinning with worm baits, sandeel or lures. Float Bottom fishing - leger or paternoster.

GENERAL INFORMATION

Best fishing around the south side of the rocks. The south end can be approached from either side of the Castle, but the west side rocks are very much easier to cross. In fact after the first 100 yds or so, just after you cross a disused sewer pipe, you can climb up to the grass plateaus at the base of the Castle wall, after which it's a simple walk to your fishing spot.

Access back to the pier is cut off for up to two hours either side of the high water depending on the tide. On the smaller neaps access back to the pier is available at all states of tide. However it is quite safe to stay on the rocks over this period.

Bottom is rock and weed close in, and to the south-east.

Casting towards the bathing pools and to the south-west will find sand.

GUERNSEY	
PLACE	Havelet Bay
PERRY MAP REF.	18 and 25 - H1, 2 and 3
TYPE OF VENUE	Rock & Pier
ASPECT FACES	North, East, South
SHELTERED FROM	Depends on which side of bay fished.
ACCESS	Car parking available in road alongside mark (can be difficult to find a space in business hours).
BEST STATE OF TIDE	Sea wall by South Esplanade, four hours up to two hours down. Various marks on the south side of the bay, low water through high to two hours down. Main Harbour wall, north side of bay half tide up to two hours down.
SPECIES	Ballan wrasse, bass, grey mullet, black bream, red mullet, garfish, pollack, conger, plaice.
METHODS	Spinning with worm baits, sandeel or lures. Float Bottom fishing - leger or paternoster.

GENERAL INFORMATION

Sea wall by South Esplanade, bottom mostly sand, best for grey mullet and bass. Sheltered from winds from northwest through west to south.

There are numerous rock ledges that can be fished between the Half Moon Cafe and the Ladies Bathing Pool (furthest pool to the east) - but the angler is forced off some of the spots by half tide up. One exception is the Ladies Pool itself where fishing is possible on small spring or neap tides, from the north west corner. Whole area is mainly sand. Sheltered from winds from south west and south.

Main harbour wall north side of bay comfortable fishing from "top walk". Mostly sand but areas of rock abreast of the fishermans vivier (square concrete building) up to Castle Cornet. Sheltered from winds from north west through north to north east.

Slipway by Castle Cornet can be good spot for garfish and mullet.

GUERNSEY	
PLACE	Les Terres Point
	(Cowhorn) (see page 98)
PERRY MAP REF.	25-H3
TYPE OF VENUE	Rocks
ASPECT FACES	South
SHELTERED FROM	Winds from west through to north to north east.
ACCESS	Car parking available along La Vallette, near bathing pools (can be difficult to find a space during business hours). Walk up steps by aquarium. Turn off to the left and go down along Fort wall.
BEST STATE OF TIDE	One hour before low to half tide up
SPECIES	Black bream, pout, conger, lesser-spotted dogfish, plaice, sole, grey mullet, garfish, pollack.
METHODS	Spinning with worm baits, sandeel or lures. Float Bottom fishing - leger or paternoster.

GENERAL INFORMATION

Rock and weed close in, sand can be found with a short cast. Fishing is from the south side of the point.

To reach the fishing spot, cross gully to "big" rock. Care must be taken for this rock gets surrounded from half tide up to half tide down. It is not prudent to stay on the rock over the high water as it gets covered, particularly on spring tides or in bad weather.

GUERNSEY	
PLACE	Soldiers Bay
PERRY MAP REF.	25-G3 (see page 98)
TYPE OF VENUE	Rocks
ASPECT FACES	East
SHELTERED FROM	Winds from south-west, through west to north.
ACCESS	Park by Vallette Bathing Pools, although long term parking in excess of 2 hours is difficult to find during business hours. Walk up steps to left of aquarium. Take cliff path and follow signs to bay - distance 500 metres.
BEST STATE OF TIDE	Half tide up to two hours down.
SPECIES	Grey mullet, plaice, pout, black bream, sole, bass, lesser-spotted dogfish, mackerel.
METHODS	Float Bottom fishing - leger.

GENERAL INFORMATION

The main fishing spot is not the bay itself but a flat-topped rocky outcrop to the south of the bay. The path down accesses both the beach and the fishing mark. When the path to the beach goes off to the left carry straight on to reach the mark.

Recent small landslides has made access a little difficult and extreme care should be taken.

Bottom at the fishing spot is all sand.

Fishing can also be done off the beach which has produced bass at both low and high water.

GUERNSEY	
PLACE	Ozanne Steps
PERRY MAP REF.	25-G5
TYPE OF VENUE	Rocks
ASPECT FACES	East
SHELTERED FROM	Winds from south-west through west to north.
ACCESS	On cliff path between St Peter Port and Fermain. Park in Becquet Road (Perry ref. 25-G5). Walk down hill and on down cliff path. Follow direction signs to St. Peter Port. Steps will be seen on your right, approx distance 500 metres.
BEST STATE OF TIDE	Low water to two hours after high tide.
SPECIES	Grey mullet, conger, ballan wrasse, black bream, red mullet.
METHODS	Float Bottom fishing - leger or paternoster.

GENERAL INFORMATION

Can be an awkward place to fish after half tide up. The lower rocks in front of the angler get covered, making it a little difficult to retrieve tackle (and hopefully fish)

Rock and weed close in and to the left. A 40-50 metre cast straight out or slightly to the right will find sand.

GUERNSEY	
PLACE	Fermain Moorings
PERRY MAP REF.	31 - G1
TYPE OF VENUE	Pier
ASPECT FACES	South
SHELTERED FROM	Winds from west through north to north-east.
ACCESS	From cliff path on north side of Fermain Bay. Park in Becquet Road (Perry Ref 25-G5), walk down hill and down cliff path. Other approach via cliff path from Fermain Bay. There is NO vehicular access permitted to the bay.
BEST STATE OF TIDE	Half tide up to two hours down.
SPECIES	Grey mullet, garfish, pollack, black bream, pout, plaice, lesser-spotted dogfish.
METHODS	Float Bottom fishing - leger.

GENERAL INFORMATION

Although it's called the 'moorings' it's currently not used as such, so mooring ropes are not a problem. Considered a good spot for grey mullet.

After dark you will get plagued with tiny pout and poor cod, but the venue does also produce some takeable specimens of various species.

Bottom, nearly all sand.

GUERNSEY	
PLACE	La Ricou, Fermain (see page 99)
PERRY MAP REF.	31-G2
TYPE OF VENUE	Rocks
ASPECT FACES	North
SHELTERED FROM	Winds from south, round to west.
ACCESS	On cliff path between Fermain and Jerbourg. A small steep path leads down through the bracken to the mark from the main cliff path. Care is needed on the climb down of the last 20 feet onto the rocks.
BEST STATE OF TIDE	Two hours up to two hours down.
SPECIES	Grey mullet, red mullet, plaice, black bream, pout, garfish.
METHODS	Float Bottom fishing - leger or paternoster.

GENERAL INFORMATION

This mark is commonly known as Lerico! An awkward place to get to! Car Parking is very difficult, nearest spot is towards the south end of Calais Road. Take the lane that runs down from the junction of Calais Road and Calais Lane. (See Perry's 31-G2). Carry on down cliff path that runs down to the left at the end of the tarmaced lane. 100 metres or so down the path there are steps down to the right. Go down the steps and follow the cliff path. The path down to the mark is on the left as the main path turns south. The entrance to the path down to the mark is a little obscure and can be a little slippery. The rock on which to fish is reached across a narrow gully. Fish from the slightly higher rock looking into the bay. Bottom is sand. Take care on spring tides - the rock covers, particularly when a swell is running. It's safe to stay on the rock on neap tides in calm weather.

If forced off the rock you can fish on the rock ledge under the side of the cliff that overlooks the bay.

GUERNSEY	
PLACE	Bec du Nez (see page 99)
PERRY MAP REF.	31 - H3
TYPE OF VENUE	Rock/Pier
ASPECT FACES	East and North
SHELTERED FROM	Winds from south-west through west to north west.
ACCESS	On cliff path between Fermain Bay and St Martin's Point. Car park across the road from Doyle Column, walk back to Bouvee Lane and go down lane, bear right down steps to cliff path, follow signs. Total distance 850 metres.
BEST STATE OF TIDE	One hour up to two hours down.
SPECIES	Ballan wrasse, garfish, red mullet, black bream, pollack, grey mullet, pout, conger, mackerel, sole
METHODS	Float Spinning, wormbait, sandeel, lure Bottom fishing - leger or paternoster.

GENERAL INFORMATION

There are three different spots to fish at this venue.

(a) Bec du Nez Harbour. Good for grey mullet and ballan wrasse. Mixed bottom sand and rock. Boat mooring ropes can make angling difficult.

(b) Rocks to the east of the harbour. Bottom rock and weed close in. Sand straight out and to the right.

(c) Rock on the south side of the Bec du Nez headland. This is separated from the rocks in (b) by narrow gully that fills, in the two hours each side of the high tide. Safe to stay on the rock on neap tides and calm weather. rock and weed close-in, sand straight out and slightly to the left. Best spot at Bec du Nez in north west to north winds.

GUERNSEY	
PLACE	Marble Bay (see page 100)
PERRY MAP REF.	31- H3
TYPE OF VENUE	Rock
ASPECT FACES	East
SHELTERED FROM	Winds from south through west to north.
ACCESS	On cliff path between Fermain Bay and St Martin's Point. Car park across the road from Doyle Column. Go down cliff path at east end of car park behind L'Auberge Restaurant and follow signs. Total distance 400 metres.
BEST STATE OF TIDE	One hour up to two hours down.
SPECIES	Ballan wrasse, grey mullet, garfish, plaice, sole, red mullet, black bream, pollack, conger.
METHODS	Float Bottom fishing - leger or paternoster.

GENERAL INFORMATION

The fishing spot is the big rock outcrop on the south side of this small bay.

Bottom is rock and weed close in, and sand straight out. Access from the cliff path out over the rocks to the fishing spot at the end is 'awash' on big spring tides. It's safe to stay on the 'main' rock if the weather is calm. There are no problems on neap tides.

The fishing spot at Les Terres Point (Cowhorn). The gully that cuts off the rock at high tide can be seen. If you look very carefully you spot an angler fishing the mark.

Soldiers Bay, the flat topped rock from where the fishing is done is to the left of the picture. The beach of Soldiers Bay can be seen in the foreground.

La Ricou, or if you prefer Lerico on the south side of Fermain Bay. The little Bec Du Nez "Harbour" can be seen in the background. Picture taken in the winter hence no moored boats

The south side of Bec Du Nez headland. The gully that cuts off the fishing spot on the outer rock can be clearly seen. Picture taken about half tide.

The fishing spot at Marble Bay

Divette, showing the rubble mound causeway bottom left. Two anglers can be seen at the fishing spot at the end of the rocks.

The "Battery" at St Martins Point taken from the top of the cliff path.

St. Martins Point, Telegraph Bay side. Picture taken when it was close to low water.

Saints Bay Harbour at low water. Taken in winter, hence lack of moored boats. Fishing normally done from the "Pier" but from the rocks to the left when the boat moorings (and boats) are down in the summer months.

Gouffre Harbour, the small fishing "Pier" can clearly be seen as well as the rocks which ar usually fished when the boats and moorings are down in the summer months.

The fishing spot at Fort Hommet is out on the end of the reef past the big rock. Access is round the far side of the rock.

The fishing spot on the west side of Port Soif as seen from the opposite headland. As can be seen it is not a place to fish when there are big swells.

Big Bill (left) and the Slipper Rock (right) at Pembroke. Picture taken at low tide. Access to the the fishing spot on Big Bill is around the right side of the rock.

The Catelain (or Cartlines) at L'Ancresse Bay. The high rock on the right is the upper (or big) Cartline, the lower rock on its left is the lower (or little) Cartline.

The fishing spot at Fort Doyle. The view from the edge of the car park looking north. Picture taken at half tide.

The Lace at Fort Doyle. The picture clearly shows the gully that seperates it from the land, from half tide up to half tide down.

GUERNSEY		
PLACE	Divette	(see page 100)
PERRY MAP REF.	31- H3	
TYPE OF VENUE	Rock	
ASPECT FACES	East	
SHELTERED FROM	Winds from south-west to north-west.	
ACCESS	On cliff path between Fermain Bay and St Martin's Point. Car park across the road from Doyle Column, go down cliff path at east end of car park behind L'Auberge Restaurant and follow signs. Total distance 400 metres.	
BEST STATE OF TIDE	One hour up to two hours down.	
SPECIES	Ballan wrasse, grey mullet, garfish, plaice, sole, red mullet, black bream, pollack, conger, mackerel.	
METHODS	Float Spinning, wormbait, sandeel, lure. Bottom fishing - leger or paternoster.	

GENERAL INFORMATION

The fishing spot on the rocks at the end of the reef is reached by transversing a man-made 'rubble mound causeway' (this spot is actually called La Divette Pier in Perry's Guide).

The bottom is rock and weed close in and out to the right. Casting for bottom fish should be to the left (or north), or straight out.

The retrieve at low water up to half tide is made a little awkward due to a rocky reef on the north-east corner of the fishing spot.

The end of the reef becomes awash on high water springs and by big swells during disturbed weather. Great care should be taken at these times. there is no problem on neaps or in settled weather.

GUERNSEY	
PLACE	Pine Forest
PERRY MAP REF.	31- H3 and H4
TYPE OF VENUE	Rock
ASPECT FACES	East
SHELTERED FROM	Winds from south-west through west to north.
ACCESS	Car park across the road from Doyle Column, go down cliff path at east end of car park behind L'Auberge Restaurant and follow signs to Divette. Instead of going down to Divette, turn right up hill between trees. Distance 450 metres.
BEST STATE OF TIDE	One hour up to two hours down.
SPECIES	Black bream, red mullet, lesser spotted dogfish, ballan wrasse, grey mullet, garfish, conger, pout.
METHODS	Float Spinning, wormbait, sandeel, lure Bottom fishing - leger or paternoster.

GENERAL INFORMATION

Fishing spot is a rocky outcrop just below the cliff path. Once you have walked up a short hill through the trees you will soon pass a seat on your right. The path down to the fishing spot is down to your left at the top of the next short rise. Take care for the path down to the rocks through the bracken can become very slippery when wet.

The bottom is rock and weed close in and to reach the sand which is straight out, it needs a cast of 50 metres plus.

Safe spot to fish, can be fished right throughout high water unless the weather is extreme.

GUERNSEY	
PLACE	St Martin's Point - Battery. (see page 101)
PERRY MAP REF.	31- H4
TYPE OF VENUE	Rock
ASPECT FACES	East
SHELTERED FROM	Winds from south-west through north-west.
ACCESS	300 metre walk down cliff path/steps. Good car park available at cliff top.
BEST STATE OF TIDE	Half tide up through to two hours down.
SPECIES	Garfish, mackerel, grey mullet, ballan wrasse, black bream, conger, scad, red mullet.
METHODS	Float Spinning with wormbaits, sandeel or lures. Bottom fishing - leger or paternoster.

GENERAL INFORMATION

Easily recognisable venue. As you go down the cliff path towards St Martin's Point take the first left turn and you will see the "battery" - it;s a saucer shaped grassed area. Bottom to the east is rock and weed, but there are sandy areas to the south and north.

If you commence fishing just after the low tide in the autumn months, black bream can be caught on the sand patch to the north.

Can be fished in strong southerly winds, if you fish tucked well in on the north side!

GUERNSEY	
PLACE	St Martin's Point (see page 101)
PERRY MAP REF.	31- H5
TYPE OF VENUE	Rock
ASPECT FACES	South
SHELTERED FROM	Winds from the north through east to south-east.
ACCESS	400 metre walk down cliff path/steps and over the bridge to the rocks at the end. Good car park available at cliff top.
BEST STATE OF TIDE	Half tide up through to two hours down.
SPECIES	Garfish, mackerel, grey mullet, ballan wrasse, conger, scad, and occasional bass and black bream.
METHODS	Float Spinning with wormbaits, sandeel or lures. Bottom fishing - paternoster.

GENERAL INFORMATION

Fish on the Telegraph Bay side of the point. Bottom is nearly all rock and weed.

Good spot to fish in easterly winds. be wary of large swells over the high water or spring tides.

Excellent spot for float fishing for garfish, grey mullet and mackerel.

GUERNSEY	
PLACE	Saints Bay Harbour (see page 102)
PERRY MAP REF.	30-C5
TYPE OF VENUE	Pier and Rock
ASPECT FACES	East
SHELTERED FROM	Winds from south-west through west to north.
ACCESS	Small car park adjacent to fishing spot.
BEST STATE OF TIDE	Two hours up to two hours down.
SPECIES	Plaice, grey mullet, garfish, black bream, red mullet, pollack, pout, ballan wrasse, sole, conger.
METHODS	Float Spinning wormbait, sandeel or lure Bottom fishing - leger or paternoster.

GENERAL INFORMATION

Rock and weed close in, a short cast will find sand. Possible to fish the "pier" or from the rocks.

There are many small boats and dinghies moored at this spot, so it follows that the mooring ropes makes fishing very difficult especially in the summer months.

These problems can be avoided by fishing from the rocks to the south of the mooring area.

GUERNSEY	
PLACE	Gouffre Harbour (see page 102)
PERRY MAP REF.	28 - D5
TYPE OF VENUE	Pier/Rock
ASPECT FACES	East
SHELTERED FROM	North through west to south-west.
ACCESS	Car park at top of cliff by Hollows Restaurant. Walk down path to Gouffre Harbour - distance 400 metres.
BEST STATE OF TIDE	Low water over high to two hours down.
SPECIES	Garfish, grey mullet, ballan wrasse, plaice, bass, black bream, sole, conger, pout.
METHODS	Float Spinning - worm bait, lures, sandeel. Bottom fishing - leger or paternoster.

GENERAL INFORMATION

There are two spots to fish at this mark.

(a) The moorings. Walk down to landing stage. Mooring ropes can make fishing a little awkward. Bottom rock and weed very close in otherwise sand.

(b) Rock outcrop to south of moorings. Better spot of the two. Climb down (and up) can be tricky so EXTREME CARE must be taken. Care will need to be taken on the high water when a swell is running. Neap tides are usually no problem. Bottom as in (a) - but all rock and weed out to the right.

GUERNSEY	
PLACE	Fort Hommet (see page 103)
PERRY MAP REF.	13-E1
TYPE OF VENUE	Rock
ASPECT FACES	North
SHELTERED FROM	Winds from south-west through south to east..
ACCESS	Car parking is available at the top of Fort Hommet headland.
BEST STATE OF TIDE	Half tide down to half tide up.
SPECIES	Plaice, pollack, bass, garfish, grey mullet, ballan wrasse.
METHODS	Float Spinning - lure, worm baits, sandeel. Bottom fishing - leger or paternoster.

GENERAL INFORMATION

Walk from car park along path on north side of headland, on path in the direction of Albecq. Distance to mark approximately 300 metres. Fishing spot is on the reef which includes a large rock. A gully must be crossed to reach the fishing area at the end of the reef. Anglers MUST get off the rock before half tide up as the fishing spot gets surrounded and covered by high tide.

The bottom is rock and weed close in, but is sand straight out, which can be reached by a 40-50 metre cast.

GUERNSEY	
PLACE	Albecq.
PERRY MAP REF.	13 - F1, G1 and H1
TYPE OF VENUE	Rock
ASPECT FACES	North
SHELTERED FROM	Winds from south-east round to south-west.
ACCESS	Parking difficult, but car park available at south end of Cobo Bay. Walk to the most distant point on rocks. 740 metres.
BEST STATE OF TIDE	Two hours up to two hours down.
SPECIES	Grey mullet, ballan wrasse, plaice, black bream, pollack, bass, sole.
METHODS	Float Spinning - worm bait, sandeel, lure. Bottom fishing - leger or paternoster.

GENERAL INFORMATION

A whole series of rocky outcrops run for 600 metres from the south end of Cobo Bay, below Le Guet to Albecq Bay. The bottom is rock and weed close in and sand within the range of a short cast.

There are many good spots that can be fished. However, some get cut off towards the high tide, so always ensure you know your line of retreat and keep an eye on the tidal position.

GUERNSEY	
PLACE	Port Soif (see page 103)
PERRY MAP REF.	8 - B1
TYPE OF VENUE	Rock
ASPECT FACES	North
SHELTERED FROM	Winds from south-west through south to east.
ACCESS	Park in car park to west of Port Soif Bay behind the 'old' Grandes Rocques Hotel.
BEST STATE OF TIDE	Half tide up to half tide down.
SPECIES	Ballan wrasse, pollack, bass, garfish, plaice, sole, lesser-spotted dogfish, conger.
METHODS	Float Spinning lures, worm baits, sandeel. Bottom fishing - leger or paternoster.

GENERAL INFORMATION

Walk north from car park onto little 'island'. You can fish off the 'island' or from the rocks that stretch out to the north.

Rock and weed close in, sand can be reached with a short cast.

The mark does get surrounded for a very short time, on the top of spring tides but it is safe to stay on the 'island'.

A place to be avoided if there is a big swell running.

GUERNSEY	
PLACE	Pembroke Bay (see page 104)
PERRY MAP REF.	6 - C1, C2 & D1
TYPE OF VENUE	Rock
ASPECT FACES	East
SHELTERED FROM	Winds from south-west to north-west.
ACCESS	Car park at Pembroke Bay Hotel or 200 metres further on at Jáonneuse. Walk across grass to fishing spots, maximum distance 400 metres.
BEST STATE OF TIDE	Two hours up to two hours down, but over the low water for Big Bill.
SPECIES	Grey mullet, plaice, black bream, garfish, mackerel, pollack, pout, bass, conger, red mullet, lesser-spotted dogfish.
METHODS	Float Spinning - worm bait, sandeel, or lures. Bottom fishing - leger or paternoster.

GENERAL INFORMATION

There are four fishing spots on the west side of Pembroke Bay. At each there is rock and weed close in but a short cast will find sand.

(a)   Big Bill. The most northerly rock, accessed by walking past east side of the disused Pembroke Fort and continuing north across the rock and boulder-strewn beach to the big rock directly ahead. you must climb around this rock on the Pembroke Bay side to get onto Big Bill, which is only accessable from half tide down to half tide up. A water filled gully cuts it off over the high water, but it is safe to stay on Big Bill over this period on neap or small spring tides and in calm, settled weather.

(b)   The Slipper. Proceed as for Big Bill but as you cross the beach in a northerly direction you will see the Slipper rock on your right. It gets surrounded for up to two hours each side of the high, but it's safe to stay on the rock.

(c+d) The Moorings and the Battery. These are two rocky outcrops on the side of the bay that are accessed straight from the grass, and do not get surrounded. The Battery fishes best on the high water.

Bass can also be caught, after dark, from Pembroke Bay beach.

GUERNSEY	
PLACE	Catelain (see page 104)
PERRY MAP REF.	7 - E1
TYPE OF VENUE	Rock
ASPECT FACES	West
SHELTERED FROM	Winds from east to south.
ACCESS	Car park at the end of Rue de la Fontenelle, Perry's Guide 7-F1. Walk over small hill to the west of the car park and you will see the Catelain down in front of you.
BEST STATE OF TIDE	Half tide down to half tide up - lower Catelain. Half tide up to half tide down - upper Catelain.
SPECIES	Grey mullet, plaice, sole, ballan wrasse, bass, garfish, pollack, red mullet, lesser-spotted dogfish.
METHODS	Float Spinning - wormbait, sandeel and lures. Bottom fishing - leger or paternoster.

GENERAL INFORMATION

This spot is also known as the 'Cartlines'. The rock consists of two levels. The lower Cartline which is fished over low water and the upper Cartline which is fished over the high. The upper Cartline is surrounded for up to 1 1/2 hours on each side of the high or the spring tides, but is safe to stay on the rock. Bottom on the lower Cartline is sand except for the area within 10 metres or so of the rock, but the upper Cartline needs a cast of 50 metres in a westerly direction into the bay to clear the rock and weed.

Note:- When red flags are flying in the area, it means the rifle range is in use and the car park is closed. The alternative in that situation is to drive over Bunker Hill and down the Longree road and park by the German concrete tower. (Tower No. 5 on Perry's Guide) You can the walk along the path alongside L'Ancresse Bay out to the Catelain (Perry's Guide 7-F3, F2 and E1). Distance 300 metres.

GUERNSEY	
PLACE	Fort Doyle (see page 105)
PERRY MAP REF.	7 - H1
TYPE OF VENUE	Rock
ASPECT FACES	North
SHELTERED FROM	Winds from south-east through south to west.
ACCESS	Very short walk over the rock from the adjacent car park.
BEST STATE OF TIDE	Two hours up to two hours down.
SPECIES	Garfish, mackerel, grey mullet, pollack, ballan wrasse, black bream, conger, lesser-spotted dogfish.
METHODS	Spinning worm bait, sandeel or lure. Float Bottom fishing - leger or paternoster.

GENERAL INFORMATION

Bottom is rock and weed close in and to the front and left of the rock. Sand out to the right, and casts should be made in the general direction of Platte Fougere lighthouse.

Popular spot which can become crowded at times. It is also possible to fish from the rocks directly below the Fort over the low water, but you will be forced off as the tide rises. However can be worth a try as it has produced big ballan wrasse close in and bream and plaice if you cast straight out.

Be wary of big swells on the main rock on high water spring tides.

GUERNSEY	
PLACE	Fort Doyle - The 'Lace' (see page 105)
PERRY MAP REF.	7 - H1
TYPE OF VENUE	Rock
ASPECT FACES	East
SHELTERED FROM	Winds from south-west through to north-west.
ACCESS	Short walk towards the east from the adjacent car park.
BEST STATE OF TIDE	Half tide down to half tide up.
SPECIES	Black bream, plaice, gurnards, red mullet, sole, garfish, mackerel, pout, bass, grey mullet, lesser-spotted dogfish.
METHODS	Spinning worm, sandeel or lure. Float Bottom fishing - leger.

GENERAL INFORMATION

Approach is across the grass in front of the fort. The 'Lace' is a seperate rock which is surrounded over the high tide and is nearly covered on the big springs.

The gully that separates the rock from the 'mainland' can only be crossed after half tide down. Anglers must leave the rock before half tide up.

The bottom is all sand, except for very close in.

GUERNSEY	
PLACE	St Sampson's Harbour
PERRY MAP REF.	11 - F3 and G3
TYPE OF VENUE	Pier
ASPECT FACES	East
SHELTERED FROM	Winds from south through to north-west.
ACCESS	End of Old Breakwater - park at fishing spot. North pier at Harbour entrance - park at fishing spot.
BEST STATE OF TIDE	Half tide up to two hours down.
SPECIES	Plaice, bass, garfish, pollack, grey mullet, flounder, red mullet, ballan wrasse.
METHODS	Bottom fishing - leger . Float. Spinning.

GENERAL INFORMATION

There are two main fishing spots. One is the end of the old breakwater, the other is the north pier at the harbour entrance, although at times access is not possible if ships are being worked. Fishing from the south pier is not permitted as it is part of the oil tanker berth. The bottom at both spots is sand. Although the venue has produced 14 Bailiwick shore records, its potential seems to have declined in recent years and it has become less popular. The area is plagued with green crabs which seem to strip the bait off the hooks within minutes. One of the few places in the Bailiwick that occasionally produces flounder. Grey mullet can be caught in the Harbour, but access is not permitted to the boat pontoons.

Access has recently been granted to fish from the rubble mound around the Longue Hougue Reclaimation site.

Anglers MUST not cross the working area of the site to gain access.

119

Alderney Shore Fishing Marks

ALDERNEY	
PLACE	Platte Saline (see page 178)
PERRY MAP REF.	37 - E1, F1, G1 and 35
TYPE OF VENUE	Beach
ASPECT FACES	North
SHELTERED FROM	Winds from south-west to south-east.
ACCESS	Parking available at top of beach.
BEST STATE OF TIDE	Low water over the high to two hours down.
SPECIES	Conger, bass, black bream, sole, plaice, tope, lesser-spotted dogfish, golden grey mullet, grey mullet.
METHODS	Bottom fishing - leger or paternoster. . Spinning with lures.

GENERAL INFORMATION

This is a steeply shelving gravel beach. The bottom in the fishing area is all sand/gravel.

Considered by many anglers to be the top fishing beach in the Bailiwick. Has accounted for five British and 11 Bailiwick shore records.

Floating seaweed can be a problem at times.

ALDERNEY	
PLACE	Doyle (see page 178)
PERRY MAP REF.	37 - G1 and 35
TYPE OF VENUE	Rock
ASPECT FACES	North
SHELTERED FROM	Winds from south-east to south-west.
ACCESS	Parking available within 100 metres of fishing spots.
BEST STATE OF TIDE	Two hours up to half tide down.
SPECIES	Red mullet, grey mullet, plaice, sole, lesser-spotted dogfish, garfish, black bream.
METHODS	Float. Bottom fishing - leger Spinning - worm baits, sandeel, lures.

GENERAL INFORMATION

This mark contains the outfall from the island's sewer so it can be a little smelly and unpleasant. The fishing spot is reached by a fairly easy short walk across the rocks.

Casting straight out or a little to the left will find sand. Fishing spot gets surrounded one hour each side of high water on spring tides. Be wary of big swells which can wash over the rock at high water. Usually there is no problems on neap tide.

ALDERNEY	
PLACE	Breakwater (see page 179)
PERRY MAP REF.	37 - H1, 38 A1 and B1
TYPE OF VENUE	Pier
ASPECT FACES	North and east
SHELTERED FROM	Winds from south-west to south-east.
ACCESS	Parking available near entrance to pier. NO VEHICLES are allowed on the Breakwater.
BEST STATE OF TIDE	Two hours up to half tide down.
SPECIES	Conger, ballan wrasse, pollack, garfish, scad, grey mullet, pout, black bream, ray, tope.
METHODS	Float. Spinning - lures, worm bait, sandeel. Bottom fishing - paternoster or leger.

GENERAL INFORMATION

Considered to be the 'mecca' of shore fishing venues in the Bailiwick. Consistently produces a string of specimen fish, covering many different species. Has produced 15 Bailiwick records. Can be fished almost along its entire length on both sides. Bottom is rock and weed from the back of the breakwater and a mixture of sand, rock and weed on the inner, harbour side. Excellent results can be obtained by spinning off the end and from the Queen's Steps near the end. Fishing off the high back wall with float gear can produce superb catches of mullet, but a drop net is required to bring your catch up the wall. However, can be an EXTREMELY DANGEROUS mark in adverse weather, particularly when a swell is running; huge waves are flung 100ft into the air and almost engulf the entire structure. Always seek the advice of the locals, preferably the Harbour Office if there is ANY doubt about the conditions.

ALDERNEY	
PLACE	Commercial Quay
PERRY MAP REF.	38 - A1
TYPE OF VENUE	Pier
ASPECT FACES	North and east
SHELTERED FROM	Winds from south-west to south-east
ACCESS	Parking available near the pier but access for fishing can be restricted when shipping operations are in progress.
BEST STATE OF TIDE	One hour up over the high to half tide down.
SPECIES	Bass, ballan wrasse, grey mullet, scad, garfish, coalfish, plaice.
METHODS	Float. Spinning, lures, worm bait, sandeel. Bottom fishing - paternoster or leger.

GENERAL INFORMATION

Can be fished from either side of the pier. Bottom is a mixture of sand, rock and weed.

Anglers must be aware that this is a working port and they must be prepared to move their gear due to shipping movements.

ALDERNEY	
PLACE	Roselle Point (see page 179)
PERRY MAP REF.	38 - C2
TYPE OF VENUE	Rock
ASPECT FACES	north and west
SHELTERED FROM	Winds from east to south.
ACCESS	Parking available just above the mark, near the entrance to Fort Albert.
BEST STATE OF TIDE	Two hours up to two hours down.
SPECIES	Plaice, sole, black bream, ballan wrasse, grey mullet, garfish, pollack, mackerel, conger, ray.
METHODS	Float. Bottom fishing - leger or paternoster. Spinning - worm baits, sandeel, lures.

GENERAL INFORMATION

This mark is situated below the west side of Fort Albert on the east side of Braye Bay. It is also known as "The Lights" due to the remains of the German constructed concrete buildings that housed navigation lights.

Access is down to the site by means of a fairly steep path, and a short walk on the rocks.

Bottom is predominately sand which can be reached by a modest cast. Rock and weed very close in and out to the right.

ALDERNEY	
PLACE	Arch and Corblets Bay
PERRY MAP REF.	39 - E2, F2
TYPE OF VENUE	Beach
ASPECT FACES	East
SHELTERED FROM	Winds from south-east through to north-west
ACCESS	Parking available at top of bay(s)
BEST STATE OF TIDE	Half tide up to half tide down.
SPECIES	Bass.
METHODS	Bottom fishing - leger .

GENERAL INFORMATION
Good spots for night fishing for bass.

ALDERNEY	
PLACE	Cats Bay (see page 180)
PERRY MAP REF.	39 - G3
TYPE OF VENUE	Rock
ASPECT FACES	North
SHELTERED FROM	Winds from south-east through south to west.
ACCESS	Parking available right by the fishing spot.
BEST STATE OF TIDE	Half tide up to two hours down.
SPECIES	Grey mullet, garfish, black bream, bass, plaice, sole, pollack.
METHODS	Float. Spinning worm bait, lures, sandeel. Bottom fishing - leger.

GENERAL INFORMATION
This is the bay to the north-west of the lighthouse. Parking is by the lighthouse wall, and fishing is done from the rocks, which run along the bay adjacent to the lighthouse.
Bottom is all sand.

ALDERNEY	
PLACE	Lighthouse (see page 181)
PERRY MAP REF.	39 - G3
TYPE OF VENUE	Rock
ASPECT FACES	East
SHELTERED FROM	Winds from south to north-west.
ACCESS	Parking available by the lighthouse.
BEST STATE OF TIDE	Two hours up to half tide down.
SPECIES	Plaice, grey mullet, bass, sole, garfish, ballan wrasse, black bream.
METHODS	Float. Spinning - worm bait, lures, sandeels. Bottom fishing - paternoster or leger.

GENERAL INFORMATION

This mark is the bay to the east of the lighthouse, which is bounded by Fort Quesnard on its south side. It is also known as Godfrey's Bay.

Fishing is done either from the rocks at the west end of the bay "in front" of the lighthouse, or from the rock alongside Fort Quesnard.

Area is predominately sand, right up to the rocks.

ALDERNEY	
PLACE	The Slides (south of Fort Quesnard)
PERRY MAP REF.	39 - G4
TYPE OF VENUE	Rock
ASPECT FACES	East
SHELTERED FROM	Winds from south-west to north-west.
ACCESS	Is across the grass to the rocks from the adjacent cart track. As parking is limited it's recommended you park near the lighthouse.
BEST STATE OF TIDE	Two hours down to half tide up.
SPECIES	Grey mullet, ballan wrasse, garfish, pollack, mackerel, conger.
METHODS	Float. Spinning - worm bait, lures, sandeels. Bottom fishing - paternoster.

GENERAL INFORMATION

As the name suggests the rocks are partly made up of formations of smooth rock with a 45° slope. It follows that the anglers must fish from areas of flat rock. It can be dangerous if there is a swell running, for the waves tend to wash right up the sloping rocks - it follows that great care is needed.

Bottom is all rock and weed.

ALDERNEY	
PLACE	Les Bouffresses (see page 182)
PERRY MAP REF.	39 - F4
TYPE OF VENUE	Rock
ASPECT FACES	South
SHELTERED FROM	Winds from west through to north
ACCESS	Parking available at the venue.
BEST STATE OF TIDE	Four hours down to two hours up..
SPECIES	Plaice, sole, bass, black bream, ray.
METHODS	Bottom fishing - leger or paternoster.

GENERAL INFORMATION

This mark is also known as the 'Targets'. Fishing is done from a number of rock outcrops. Bottom is all sand, right to the edge of the rocks.

Be aware of gullies behind your fishing spot, which can fill up and cut you off as the tide rises. Always be aware of the tidal situation and your path of retreat.

ALDERNEY	
PLACE	Raz Island (see page 182)
PERRY MAP REF.	39 - E5
TYPE OF VENUE	Rock
ASPECT FACES	South
SHELTERED FROM	Winds from north-west round to north-east.
ACCESS	Across a causeway out to Raz Island Note:- There is parking for vehicles at both the island and Alderney ends of the causeway.
BEST STATE OF TIDE	Half tide down to half tide up.
SPECIES	Grey mullet, ballan wrasse, garfish, pollack, black bream, conger, ray, plaice, lesser-spotted dogfish.
METHODS	Float. Bottom fishing - paternoster or leger. Spinning - worm baits, sandeel, lures.

GENERAL INFORMATION

It must be noted that Raz becomes surrounded two hours each side of high water. It is safe for anglers to stay on Raz over this period. DO NOT attempt to cross the causeway once it has become awash.

Bottom at the venue is predominately rock and weed. However, there is sand if you cast across the mouth of Longy Bay.

ALDERNEY	
PLACE	Longy Bay
PERRY MAP REF.	38 - D4 and 5 and 39 - E4
TYPE OF VENUE	Rock
ASPECT FACES	East
SHELTERED FROM	Winds from south-west to north.
ACCESS	Parking available along the track on the west side of the bay.
BEST STATE OF TIDE	Half tide up to two hours down.
SPECIES	Black bream, sole, plaice, red mullet, ballan wrasse, lesser-spotted dogfish, bass, mackerel.
METHODS	Float. Bottom fishing - leger or paternoster.

GENERAL INFORMATION

The majority of the fishing is done from the rocks on the west side of the bay. There is a particularly good spot for grey mullet at the south end of the rocks at the mouth of the bay, called the Frying Pan.

Access down to the rocks is by steel ladder. DO NOT attempt to go through the private property at the Frying Pan end.

Bottom is rock and weed close in, but a cast of 40-50 metres will find sand.

ALDERNEY	
PLACE	Cachaliere Pier (see page 183)
PERRY MAP REF.	37 - G5
TYPE OF VENUE	Pier
ASPECT FACES	South
SHELTERED FROM	Winds from north-west to north-east.
ACCESS	The pier is at the base of the cliffs on the island's south coast. It's approached down a steep path.
BEST STATE OF TIDE	Half tide up to two hours down.
SPECIES	Grey mullet, black bream, garfish, ballan wrasse, conger.
METHODS	Float. Bottom fishing - paternoster. Spinning - lure, worm bait, sandeel.

GENERAL INFORMATION

This pier is commonly known as Chicago! The path down to the pier is steep and can be slippery. It follows that EXTREME CAUTION is needed. It is strongly recommended that this mark is fished in the company of one of the local anglers who knows the approach across the fields and the way down the cliff.

A superb spot for grey mullet, particularly in the late summer, autumn and early winter. A drop net is required to bring up your catch. Note:- the approach to the cliff path is across private property. Always ensure all gates are shut and no damage is done to fences.

Sark Shore Fishing Marks

SARK	
PLACE	Maseline Harbour (see page 183)
PERRY MAP REF.	Page 40
TYPE OF VENUE	Pier
ASPECT FACES	North-east
SHELTERED FROM	Winds from south-east through south to north-west.
ACCESS	Sark's commercial harbour, so there is easy and continuous access.
BEST STATE OF TIDE	One hour up through to half tide down.
SPECIES	Pout, pollack, black bream, red mullet, conger, scad, garfish, lesser-spotted dogfish, mackerel, grey mullet, ballan wrasse.
METHODS	Float. Spinning - worm bait, lures, sandeels. Bottom fishing - leger or paternoster.

GENERAL INFORMATION

The pier gets very busy at times, particularly during the summer months, so anglers must be prepared for interruptions due to shipping operations. Nevertheless, considered by some to be the easiest and best shore fishing spot in the island, especially as regards the number of different species. Bottom is rock and weed close in, otherwise sand. Casting should be done straight off the end of the pier or a little to the right or even over the back wall. Shipping activities permitting, grey mullet are usually found by the steps at the shore end of the pier.

NOTE:- Another angling spot can be found if you go through the road tunnel and continue towards the bottom of the Harbour Hill. There are some steps leading down to the sea, a spot that produces catches of grey mullet, garfish, pollack, black bream and a few ballan wrasse.

SARK	
PLACE	Creux Harbour
PERRY MAP REF.	Page 40
TYPE OF VENUE	Pier
ASPECT FACES	East
SHELTERED FROM	Winds from south-west to north.
ACCESS	Easy, just walk through the road tunnel onto the pier.
BEST STATE OF TIDE	Half tide up to half tide down.
SPECIES	Black bream, ballan wrasse, garfish, pollack, conger, bass.
METHODS	Float. Spinning - worm bait, lures, sandeels. Bottom fishing - paternoster.

GENERAL INFORMATION

This is Sark's 'old' harbour, now mainly used for pleasure craft although commercial shipping does use it very occasionally. Fishing is done over the back wall. Bottom is mixed rock and weed.

The best spot for bass is to cast across the harbour entrance towards the south-east on the low tide. It follows that great care must be exercised as regards boats moving in/out of the harbour.

(The British, Channel Island and Bailiwick black bream shore-caught record was caught at this mark, a 6-8-6 specimen landed by Roseanne Guille in October 2001)

SARK	
PLACE	Derrible Bay
PERRY MAP REF.	Page 40
TYPE OF VENUE	Beach and rocks
ASPECT FACES	South
SHELTERED FROM	Winds from the west round to the north-east.
ACCESS	A steady walk down a long flight of steps.
BEST STATE OF TIDE	One hour before low water through high to two hours down.
SPECIES	Pollack, ballan wrasse, garfish, grey mullet, black bream, bass.
METHODS	Float. Bottom fishing - leger or paternoster.

GENERAL INFORMATION

Bottom nearly all sand. High tide is usually fished from the flat rocks on the east (or left side) of the bay. Otherwise fish from the beach and follow the water down and up!

SARK	
PLACE	Dixcart Bay
PERRY MAP REF.	Page 40
TYPE OF VENUE	Beach and rocks
ASPECT FACES	South
SHELTERED FROM	Winds from the west round to the north-east.
ACCESS	Well defined path right down to the bay, with steps down to the beach.
BEST STATE OF TIDE	One hour before low, right up to high tide.
SPECIES	Bass, plaice, ballan wrasse, pollack, black bream.
METHODS	Float. Bottom fishing - leger or paternoster.

GENERAL INFORMATION

It is possible to fish off the beach or from the rocks each side of the bay.

As the beach and rocks cover the angler merely retreats up the beach, back towards the access path.

Bottom is nearly all sand.

SARK	
PLACE	Havre Gosselin (see page 184)
PERRY MAP REF.	Page 40
TYPE OF VENUE	Rock
ASPECT FACES	West
SHELTERED FROM	Winds from south through east to north.
ACCESS	Follow the road from the old Beau Regard Hotel Site, and past the Pilcher Monument. Take the well defined cliff path down to the landing stage.
BEST STATE OF TIDE	Two hours up to two hours down
SPECIES	Ballan wrasse, grey mullet, conger, pollack, black bream, sole, garfish.
METHODS	Float. Spinning - worm bait, lure, sandeel. Bottom fishing - leger or paternoster.

GENERAL INFORMATION

Fishing is usually done from the rock at the steps that "looks out" towards the boat moorings. Bottom is rock and weed close in, but sand out towards the moorings. Fishing from the steps of the landing stage is not usually very prolific.

A second spot, which is very good for ballan wrasse, is accessed by going over the wall and crossing the gullies over to the outlying rocks. Bottom is rock and weed. This spot is fished from half tide down to half tide up. CARE must be taken regarding the tide. As it rises this fishing spot gets cut-off so always ensure that you are aware of the tidal situation.

SARK	
PLACE	L'Eperquerie (see page 184)
PERRY MAP REF.	Page 41
TYPE OF VENUE	Rock
ASPECT FACES	East
SHELTERED FROM	Winds from south through to north-west.
ACCESS	Well defined cliff paths take you right down to the spot which is situated almost at the north tip of the island.
BEST STATE OF TIDE	Half tide up to half tide down.
SPECIES	Ballan wrasse, sole and plaice, garfish, pollack.
METHODS	Float. Spinning - worm bait, lure, sandeel. Bottom fishing - leger or paternoster.

GENERAL INFORMATION

In the past, this spot was a recognised landing point. It can be observed from a vantage point above the mark where there are seats and a cannon on display. The path down to this spot is a little south of the vantage point.

Bottom is rock and weed.

SARK	
PLACE	Banquette Landing
PERRY MAP REF.	Page 41
TYPE OF VENUE	Rock
ASPECT FACES	East
SHELTERED FROM	Winds from south through to north-west.
ACCESS	Steady walk down the cliff path and a small clamber over a flat rock.
BEST STATE OF TIDE	Half tide up to half tide down.
SPECIES	Pollack, garfish, ballan wrasse, grey mullet.
METHODS	Float. Bottom fishing - paternoster.

GENERAL INFORMATION

Bottom mostly rock and weed. Float fishing is the favoured method at this spot.

Herm Shore Fishing Marks

HERM	
PLACE	Harbour
PERRY MAP REF.	Page 34
TYPE OF VENUE	Pier
ASPECT FACES	West
SHELTERED FROM	Winds from north-east to south.
ACCESS	This is the high water landing point for passenger (and cargo) boats and pleasure craft.
BEST STATE OF TIDE	Four hours up to two hours down.
SPECIES	Grey mullet, pollack, ballan wrasse, bass.
METHODS	Float. Spinning - worm bait, lure, sandeel. Bottom fishing - paternoster.

GENERAL INFORMATION

Mixed bottom of sand and stones.

Comfortable place to fish, but it is a VERY busy harbour, particularly in the summer months to the point where consistent fishing is almost impossible.

Worth a try, in the more quiet days in late autumn or early winter.

Ray Records

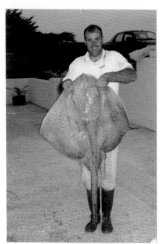

Alderney angler Paul Williams with the 36-2-7 Bailiwick boat-caught record blonde ray caught in the Alderney Swinge in June 2005

A truly remarkable shore catch, Richard Torode with a 59-0-0 record sting ray caught at Vermerette in October 2009

The 10-14-11 Bailiwick and British marbled electric ray boat record landed by visiting angler Gary Crane off the east coast of Sark in October 2010.

Wayne Calladine with the Bailiwick 18-4-0 boat record thorn back ray caught off Sark in June 2009

138

Freshwater Catches

The Bailiwick's biggest recorded fresh water fish. Captor Jim Rosbrook holds the 38-3-0 carp caught in La Landes Quarry in September 2006.

Paul Berryman with the 5-14-0 fresh water record tench.

Greg Whitehead with the 6-1-6 record fresh water eel caught in La Lande Quarry

Christopher Byng with his 1-1-4 record rudd caught at Les Rouvets lake.

Tim Cotterill with the 5-11-10 record chub.

Paul Priaulx with a 16-5-8 grass carp caught at the Grande Mare pond.

Richard McCarthy a much respected and popular member of the Guernsey Freshwater Angling Society who tragically died at a young age. The GFAS' newly constructed water will be known as the Richard McCarthy Memorial Lake

The new coarse fishing water, Corbletts Quarry in Alderney

One of the rarest and most bizarre fish ever landed in the Bailiwick. It was caught in
a gill net set by Stuart Exall and Casey Brehaut near Lihou Island in July 2010.
Casey holds the 1-7-11 specimen that was finally identified as a Cornish black fish. A
species normally found in very deep water off the continental shelf in depths in
excess of 200 meters.

Successful Women Anglers

Davina De La Haye with her 8-8-6 boat section winning bass in the 2009 GBASS festival.

Dawn Marley with her 7-6-6 shore section winning bass in the 2009 GBASS festival.

Keen Sark angler Liz Dewe with a fine grey mullet

One of the most colourful fish in local waters, Olivia Williams with her 1-12-12 cuckoo wrasse caught in 2009

Jersey angler Steve Mullins with the 50-14-13 Bailiwick and Channel Island record shore-caught tope. Steve caught it while fishing in the 2004 Alderney Angling Festival. Prizes from the festival and other competitions gave him total winnings of over £12,000.

The Bailiwick's Lieutenant Governer enjoyed competitive angling success. Sir Fabian Malbon (right) accepting his two trophies from GSAC president Mike Weysom in February 2007.

Colin Tranter with the 8-15-6 record shore caught gilt head bream.

Specimen Fish Hunt

Every year shore catches in the WCSAC's Specimen Fish Hunt confirm the wonderful angling the Bailiwick has to offer as these pictures from the 2007 competition clearly illustrate.

Dave Saunders (left) 10-12-11 bull huss, Peter Taylor 5-2-7 grey mullet and Billy Forman 10-0-5 bull fuss

Marc Eppelein (left) 6-7-1 ballan wrasse and Shane Bentley 1-15-12 golden grey mullet

Paul McLaren 2-2-2 sole, 6-6-7 grey mullet & 9-5-15 bull huss

Another fine bass. Brian Montgomery's GBASS shore record fish of 16-7-3 caught in 2010.

Mick Le Sauvage with his 1-11-4 boat caught record megrim caught at Godine in April 2011.

Alderney angler Richard Smith on his kayak in Longy bay with the Bailiwick boat record grey mullet of 8-7-6.

145

HERM	
PLACE	Rosaire
PERRY MAP REF.	Page 34
TYPE OF VENUE	Rock and Pier
ASPECT FACES	West
SHELTERED FROM	Winds from the north-east to south..
ACCESS	This is the low water landing stage for passenger boats.
BEST STATE OF TIDE	Half tide down to half tide up.
SPECIES	Ballan wrasse, grey mullet, black bream, conger, garfish.
METHODS	Float. Bottom - leger or paternoster.

GENERAL INFORMATION

Fishing is done from the rocks that stretch away south from the landing stage. It is also possible to fish on the landing stage, in particular for grey mullet but you are continuously disturbed by the boats.

Bottom is rock and weed for 30-40 metres out, then sand. Fishing into the rough ground usually produces good catches of ballan wrasse.

Difficult to fish over the high water due to the very strong tide, which runs north to south.

HERM	
PLACE	Putrainez (see page 185)
PERRY MAP REF.	Page 34
TYPE OF VENUE	Rock
ASPECT FACES	East and South
SHELTERED FROM	Winds from south-west round to north.
ACCESS	A short climb down from the cliff path and a few steps across the stony beach.
BEST STATE OF TIDE	Two hours up to half tide down.
SPECIES	Ballan wrasse, pollack, garfish, mackerel, grey mullet, plaice, sole, conger, lesser-spotted dogfish, black bream, pout, bass.
METHODS	Float. Spinning - worm bait, lure, sandeel. Bottom fishing - leger or paternoster.

GENERAL INFORMATION

Putrainez is a small grass-topped island off Herm's east coast, south of Belvoir. The short climb down from the cliff path can be a little tricky and care must be taken. It gets surrounded up to 2 1/2 hours each side of the high water on spring tides, less on neap tides, but it is safe to stay on the islet during this period.

The bottom is rock and weed close in and to the north and east. Sand can be found by casting to the south.

Arguably the best fishing spot in Herm, which consistently produces good catches in the autumn and early winter months. Hugh catches of garfish have been reported with conger, dogfish, black bream, and sole giving well after dark. Grey mullet are taken at this spot on a regular basis.

HERM	
PLACE	South coast cliffs
PERRY MAP REF.	Page 34
TYPE OF VENUE	Rock
ASPECT FACES	South
SHELTERED FROM	Winds from the north-west through north to north-east.
ACCESS	Take the southerly cliff path that starts up the steps just in from of the Rosaire Landing. Walk down cliff to fishing spot.
BEST STATE OF TIDE	Half tide down to half tide up.
SPECIES	Ballan wrasse, pollack, garfish, grey mullet, black, bream, conger.
METHODS	Float. Spinning - worm bait, lure, sandeel. Bottom fishing - leger or paternoster.

GENERAL INFORMATION

EXTREME CAUTION MUST BE TAKEN when going down (or coming up) the steep slope to the fishing spot. The surface is slippery and crumbly in parts.

The effort needed to access this particular spot is usually worth it, for it has produced excellent catches.

The bottom is rock and weed close in and out to the left. Sand can be found by casting towards Jethou, or out to the west into the channel that runs up to the Rosaire Landing.

The venue can be fished over the high water, but there is a very strong tide run that makes angling difficult.

Anglers are requested to avoid this spot from February 14 to July 14 due to nesting sea birds.

HERM	
PLACE	Belvoir (North)
PERRY MAP REF.	Page 34
TYPE OF VENUE	Rock
ASPECT FACES	East
SHELTERED FROM	Winds from south, through west to north-west.
ACCESS	The mark is the rock ledge that starts on the north side of Belvoir Bay. It can be accessed from the beach at low water or by a short climb down from the cliff path above the ledge.
BEST STATE OF TIDE	Two hours up to two hours down.
SPECIES	Ballan wrasse, grey mullet, garfish, black bream, pollack, plaice, sole, bass and occasional ray.
METHODS	Float. Spinning - worm bait, lure, sandeel. Bottom fishing - leger or paternoster.

GENERAL INFORMATION

The rock ledge extends from Belvoir to a point overlooking the Shell beach. The bottom along its length is rock and weed very close in and then sand.

Care should be taken when climbing down from the cliff path, for the path through the bracken and the rocks themselves, are very slippery when wet.

Fish can be found at almost any point, casting out from the ledge, but the favourite spots are the two extremities, casting out into Belvoir Bay and out to the left of the big rock in front of you, which is called Mouliere. Obviously grey mullet and garfish can be tempted close in by the use of shirvy.

HERM	
PLACE	Belvoir (South)
PERRY MAP REF.	Page 34
TYPE OF VENUE	Rock
ASPECT FACES	East
SHELTERED FROM	Winds from south through west to north-west.
ACCESS	Short climb down from cliff path to rock ledge.
BEST STATE OF TIDE	Two hours up to half tide down.
SPECIES	Grey mullet, garfish, plaice, black bream, sole, ray.
METHODS	Float. Bottom fishing - leger or paternoster.

GENERAL INFORMATION

The bottom is sand. The best approach is to follow the cliff path south from Belvoir Bay.

The rock ledge will soon be seen below you a few hundred metres from the bay.

HERM		
PLACE	"Camp-Site"	(see page 185)
PERRY MAP REF.	Page 34	
TYPE OF VENUE	Rock	
ASPECT FACES	East	
SHELTERED FROM	Winds from south-west round to north.	
ACCESS	Short walk down a medium slope through bracken from the cliff path.	
BEST STATE OF TIDE	One hour up through high to half tide down.	
SPECIES	Grey mullet, garfish, mackerel, pollack, black bream, plaice, sole, lesser-spotted dogfish, ballan wrasse, red mullet, conger, ray.	
METHODS	Float. Spinning - worm bait, lure, sandeel. Bottom fishing - leger or paternoster.	

GENERAL INFORMATION

This is an outcrop of rock across the bay to the south of the islet of Putrainez. It is opposite the outlying rock called Selle (or Saddle) rock.

It has been nicknamed "Camp Site" because most anglers go through the campsite on the top of the island on the way to it!

It is a large area of flat rock making it a comfortable place to fish. the bottom is sand to the north and east of the mark. there is rock and weed close in and this gets more pronounced towards the southern end of the mark.

HERM	
PLACE	Shell Beach
PERRY MAP REF.	Page 34
TYPE OF VENUE	Beach/Rock
ASPECT FACES	North and east
SHELTERED FROM	Winds from south through west to north-west.
ACCESS	Walk across common to beach.
BEST STATE OF TIDE	Half tide down to half tide up.
SPECIES	Ballan wrasse, black bream, lesser-spotted dogfish, bull huss, plaice, grey mullet, golden grey mullet, bass.
METHODS	Float. Spinning - lures, worm baits, sandeels Bottom fishing - leger or paternoster.

GENERAL INFORMATION

Fish from the Shell Beach - bottom all sand - northern end of beach best.

Most favoured is on the reef at the north-east corner (called La Pointe du Gentilhomme in Perry's guide). Reef gets covered on rising tide. Fishing over the high tide is virtually impossible due to the very strong tide race.

Boat Angling

Boat anglers have an even greater variety and number of marks to fish than the shore anglers.

The varied environment, the huge tidal range and the strong currents produce an almost endless number of places where fish can be found.

The commercial fisherman and the more experienced boat anglers will have the knowledge of dozens of marks which gives them an incredible choice, whatever the state of tide, or weather conditions.

Some of the spots will be common and known to many boatmen, while others are highly prized, almost secret marks, that may have been passed down from father to son, through the generations.

All the marks used to be pinpointed by visual means, the boat skipper using landmarks which he would line-up to ensure he was on the right spot.

Obviously each mark would require more than one line of coordinates. Two bearings were usually used, the mark being where the imaginary lines crossed.

Many of these co-ordinates were never written down but existed purely in the memory of the boat skipper.

When they were recorded they often did not make much sense to anyone else!

The problem is clearly illustrated by two examples taken from an old record of "whiting" (pollack) marks.

1. "A chimney with the corner. Delancey house open with castle"

2. "Rabbit Warren house with the north chimney of Watermans house. Grange with coal store."

This may well have been quite clear to the boat skipper concerned, but very confusing to anyone else. As years passed landmarks were altered or disappeared. Who would know now which is the Rabbit Warren house? — or which is Waterman's house? or where the coal store is (or was)? As changes occurred different co-ordinates had to be used.

Nevertheless it was a simple system that worked well, as good catches landed over the years will confirm.

In recent years new technology started to make the need for such records and knowledge superfluous.

The introduction of the Decca Navigation System and more recently the Global Positioning System (GPS) has enabled boat skippers to find and record their fishing spots with incredible accuracy at the touch of a button. The availability of chart plotters was another huge leap forward, for they have the added advantage of a visual rolling display of the chart showing the boats' actual position. In addition the colour echo sounders/fish finders have given the anglers further advantages in his attempt to locate the fish.

All this, coupled with faster, more reliable boats has opened up a whole new range of marks.

Good examples are the exploitation of the wrecks and distant sandbanks and reefs, many that are well out of sight of land, where the use of 'visual' marks would have been impossible. The new technology also meant that for the first time marks could be fished in times of poor visibility when landmarks could not be seen.

However, the ability to pinpoint fishing marks only solves half the problem.

Fish do not feed at a particular spot throughout the 12 hour cycle of the rise and fall of the tide.

When I was still at school many happy days of my holidays were spent out with the late Otto Enevoldsen, a professional fisherman who mainly worked crabpots along Guernsey's south coast or in the Big Russel between Herm and Sark.

Before the tide run had eased sufficiently for the crabpot bobbers (marker buoys) to surface, he would go for a few pollack (or whiting, as they used to be called) using handlines with artificial rubber eels for bait.

This, for me, was the best part of the trip, so I would get quite frustrated when Otto would say "pack up your line my son, we're moving."

I couldn't understand this for a while, as we were still catching the odd fish, so why move?

I soon realised that Otto knew that the fish would stop feeding at that particular mark and consequently move the boat onto the next spot where he knew the fish would bite at a slightly different state of tide.

My disappointment and frustration would instantly disappear, when we immediately started catching at the new spot!

All this means that the boat skipper, whether professional or angler has a terrific amount to learn and retain if he is to be successful.

Besides the navigational skills and knowledge he must have to safely negotiate the numerous rocks and reefs at all the varying states of tide, he needs to be able to understand and use the latest technology and be aware of the pattern of the sea and its inhabitants.

For the sports newcomers there is no short cut. Although navigation and boat handling can be learned at Further Education evening classes, the majority of the necessary knowledge that needs to be acquired can only be gained by experience.

Going out with an established skipper over a period of time is probably the best way to start, until you feel you have gained enough knowledge and confidence to start out on your own.

Visitors to the islands who become aware of the strong tides and the enormous numbers of reefs and rocks will not be surprised to learn that there are no 'self-drive' hire boats available.

The only way they can get afloat is either with a friend, or to go out on one of the locally based licensed charter boats.

Compared with many United Kingdom angling centres the Bailiwick is very poorly served by charter boats. This is not a slur on the charter skippers who do an excellent job, it refers solely to the small number of charter boats available.

Many angling resorts in the UK can boast of 10 to 15 boats, but here in the Bailiwick there are usually just two or three.

A visit to any of the local tackle dealers will give you the up-to-date information on charter boat availability.

As in the case of shore angling fishing spots it is absolutely impossible to include detailed information on the hundreds of boat marks.

However there is one publication which lists details of the strike marks for 140 rocks or reefs around the coasts of Guernsey, Herm and Jethou, as well as the three wrecks which lie in the approaches to St. Peter Port Harbour.

For each of the 143 marks it gives comprehensive details of at least two co-ordinates to enable you to locate the mark and the amount the reef dries, or the depth of water that covers the rock at low water.

As a bonus, it includes details on local lights and fog signals, clearing and leading marks, beacons, safe anchorages and tidal streams. The title of this excellent source of information is the "General Pilots Pilotage Examination for Class One Licence, Islands of Guernsey, Herm and Jethou".

It can be obtained from the St Peter Port Harbourmasters Office, at a reasonable cost..

Obviously the list of 143 marks does not include their fishing potential or the right state of tide to fish each spot.

Nevertheless it will at least lead you to a large number of marks, many of which have given good sport in the past.

In spite of the availability of this information, further details are now provided on a small number of boat marks selected from the hundreds that exist in Bailiwick waters.

The GPS numbers, strike marks, tidal information, details of the reefs, and the distances and directions quoted on the following pages *must only be considered as a general guide and must not* be used for navigational purposes.

Kayaks

The early 2000's were to see a new type of angling activity introduced into the Bailiwick for fishing from kayaks became extremely popular. They gave the angler opportunities to fish in gullies, over reefs and other restricted areas that were not easily accessible to normal boats.

It was a completely new concept which grew rapidly in popularity. The early pioneers included Paul Clark and Jamie Falla but in a very short time they were joined by dozens of anglers who realised the kayaks potential and were keen to give it a try.

Many of the kayaks became quite sophisticated, being fitted out with electronic equipment including fish finders and chart plotters.

By 2009 it had become so popular there was enough support to hold the first kayak open competition.

It didnt take long for kayaks to prove their worth for Alderney angler Richard Smith became the first to break a Bailiwick boat record from a kayak. On the 21st of December 2008 he caught an 8-7-6 thick-lipped grey mullet in Longy bay. (see page 145)

Guernsey Boat Fishing Marks

GUERNSEY	
MARK	Great Bank
GPS (Lat./Long.)	49 25 367 02 30 870 (Southern end)
TYPE OF MARK.	Sandbank
BEST STATE OF TIDE	Three Hours before high water to two hours down.
SPECIES	Brill, turbot, bass, mackerel, whiting, lesser-spotted dogfish, scad, herring, pilchard, garfish, red gurnard, John Dory, plaice, sole, pollack.
METHODS	Float Spinning — lure, sandeel, worm baits Bottom fishing — leger or paternoster, Feathering.

GENERAL INFORMATION

This sandbank off Guernsey's east coast is the most popular boat mark in the Bailiwick. In the summer months it's not unusual for over 50 boats to be fishing on the Bank at the same time! It consistently produces good catches and has accounted for one British and 37 Bailiwick boat records. In part, its popularity is due to its close proximity to St Peter Port Harbour. The Bank runs roughly parallel to the island's east coast from St Martin's Point right up past the harbour. However most of the fishing is done at the southern end where the bank rises up from 45 metres to 15 metres or less! This area is 2 nautical miles south of the harbour and 1/2 nautical mile east of St Martin's Point.

In the early summer, feathering produces excellent catches of mackerel, with herring, pilchard and scad as an added bonus!

There are other spots on the Bank that produce good catches with each angler having his own favourites. Bass sometimes make an appearance in some numbers on the east side of the Bank. One combination of strike marks for this spot being the Martello tower in Fermain just open of the north 'cliff' of Fermain Bay and the Salvation Army building in Clifton in line with Victoria Tower, or the houses on Cambridge Park just open Terres Point.

More plaice would be caught if a baited spoon with worm baits were used from the drifting boat. A UK angler who was temporarily resident in the island had great success, but it's not a method that's 'caught on' so far with local anglers.

GUERNSEY	
MARK	The "Cement" Wreck
GPS (Lat./Long.)	49 26 404 02 29 786
TYPE OF MARK.	Wreck
BEST STATE OF TIDE	Neap - 2 hours after low or high for one hour. Spring after low or high water for two hours.
SPECIES	Conger, pout, pollack, mackerel, scad, lesser-spotted dogfish, red gurnard, black bream.
METHODS	Bottom fishing — leger or paternoster

GENERAL INFORMATION

This wreck is situated approximately 1.4 miles south-east of St Peter Port Harbour in the Little Russel.

Visual strike marks are the St Peter Port Breakwater light in line with the big cranes on the container berth and Barbe 'pole' on the extreme lower edge of the southern side of Jethou.

GUERNSEY	
MARK	Grunes and Fourquies, off Jerbourg
GPS (LatjLong.)	-
TYPE OF MARK.	Reef
BEST STATE OF TIDE	Four hours up to one hour down.
SPECIES	Pollack, bass, mackerel, garfish.
METHODS	Float
	Spinning — lure, sandeel, worm baits

GENERAL INFORMATION

These two marks are in close proximity to each other just off the south coast between St Martin's Point and the Peastacks.

The strike marks for the Grunes are Saint's Bay Martello tower open west of the Peastacks and St Martin's Point lighthouse on the north-west hill of Herm, and for the Fourquies, Longue Pierre pole to the north end of the beach on Herm's west coast and the black rock in the cliff in line with conical shaped rock on foreshore.

Spinning is the favoured method here. Fish can be found over the whole area and not just right on the marks.

GUERNSEY	
MARK	'Rousse', off Point de la Moye (Gouffre)
GPS (Lat./Long.)	49 24 408 02 35 428
TYPE OF MARK.	Reef
BEST STATE OF TIDE	Two hours before high, up to high water.
SPECIES	Pollack, bass, mackerel, pout.
METHODS	Spinning - lures, sandeels and worm baits. Bottom fishing - leger

GENERAL INFORMATION

This reef is situated appoximately 1/2 mile off La Moye Point and 2 1/2 miles from St. Martin's Point.

Visual strike marks are red bungalow over Petit Port peeping over Icart Point, White house on Icart just showing. High rock on La Moye Point in line with a "diamond shaped" field which is green or yellow depending on the season!

GUERNSEY	
MARK	Boue des Kaines
GPS (Lat./Long.)	49 24 680 02 38 060
TYPE OF MARK.	Reef
BEST STATE OF TIDE	Two hours before high to one hour after.
SPECIES	Pollack, bass, mackerel.
METHODS	Spinning - lures, sandeels and worm baits.

GENERAL INFORMATION

This boue/reef is situated approximately 3/4 mile off Guernsey's south coast and three miles south-east off Hanois Lighthouse.

Visual strike marks are, Hanois Lighthouse with east side of Herpin rock, Creux Mahie Pump House just peeping Torteval Church.

GUERNSEY	
MARK	Hoffets
GPS (Lat./Long.)	49 31 200 02 34 417
TYPE OF MARK.	Mixed reef and sand
BEST STATE OF TIDE	Half tide down to half tide up.
SPECIES	Pollack, bass, mackerel, turbot, brill.
METHODS	Spinning - lures, sandeels and worm baits. Bottom fishing - leger

GENERAL INFORMATION

This mark is situated approximately 1 1/2 miles north-west of Rousse Pier in Grande Havre.

It is a rock mark with sand as you drift away from the rock. It dries half a metre on low water.

Visual strike marks are, Grandes Brayes close north of Rocque au Nord. Castel Church in line with Black Rock.

GUERNSEY	
MARK	'Capt Niko' Wreck
GPS (Lat./Long.)	49 32 769 02 35 354
TYPE OF MARK.	Wreck
BEST STATE OF TIDE	2 1/2 hours after high water to four hours down.
SPECIES	Black bream, bass, pout, pollack, conger, cod, ling.
METHODS	Bottom fishing - leger or paternoster.

GENERAL INFORMATION

This wreck lies approximately three miles north of Port Grat on Guernsey's north coast.

GUERNSEY	
MARK	Brayes
GPS (Lat./Long.)	-
TYPE OF MARK.	Reef
BEST STATE OF TIDE	One hour before high to half tide down.
SPECIES	Predominately pollack.
METHODS	Spinning - sandeel or lure

GENERAL INFORMATION

This is one of the many marks around the Brayes, north of Guernsey.

The visual marks are Castel Church in line Vale Church and the north beach on Herm in line with the Platte Fougere Lighthouse.

GUERNSEY	
MARK	Petites Canupes
GPS (Lat./Long.)	49 30 309 02 28 985
TYPE OF MARK.	Reef/Sand
BEST STATE OF TIDE	Two hours before high to half tide down.
SPECIES	Pollack, bass, black bream, mackerel, garfish, red gurnard. Occasional brill and turbot.
METHODS	Spinning - sandeels, worm bait or lures. Bottom fishing - leger.

GENERAL INFORMATION

The Petites Canupes rock is marked with a yellow/black south cardinal beacon and is situated approximately 0.6 miles south of the Platte Fougere Lighthouse.

The normal practice at this mark is to start the drift just north of the rock. The bottom is rock and weed at the start and gets progressively sandy as you drift north. If you wish you can drift all the way up to the Lighthouse, with a chance of fish over the complete drift. Do not let yourself get carried to the west as there are a number of reefs that dry as much as 5.5 metres on the low water.

GUERNSEY	
MARK	Brehon Tower
GPS (Lat./Long.)	49 28 35 02 29 20
TYPE OF MARK.	Mixed rock/sand
BEST STATE OF TIDE	South of Tower half tide down to half tide up. North of Tower high water to half tide down.
SPECIES	Pollack, bass, mackerel, ballan wrasse, black bream.
METHODS	Spinning - sandeels, worm bait or lures.

GENERAL INFORMATION

The strike marks for the best spot on the north side of the Tower is: the Tower just on lower edge of St Martins Point and Corbettes Beacon between the two 'humps' on Herm.

The best fishing on the south side, is to drift away from the lee side of Brehonnet Rock on the ebb. A fairly long drift will take you over a sandy area, which produces at times.

Alderney Boat Fishing Marks

ALDERNEY	
MARK	Casquets (See page 180)
GPS (Lat./Long.)	49 43 35 02 22 55
TYPE OF MARK.	Mostly rocky reef, but a few sandy areas.
BEST STATE OF TIDE	Two hours down to two hours up.
SPECIES	Pollack, bass, ballan wrasse, mackerel
METHODS	Spinning - sandeels or lures. Bottom fishing - leger.

GENERAL INFORMATION

This infamous lighthouse and reef is situated some 20 miles north of Guernsey and six miles west of Alderney. Angling boats from Guernsey usually go up on the flood tide and return on the ebb so it follows that most fishing is done over the low water. It is an extremely dangerous place to fish if there is anything more than a moderate breeze. The very strong tides interacting with any wind causes the build up of huge overfalls.

It is an excellent mark for bass and pollack. The best catches of pollack are generally made early in the season, in late April or during May. Although fish can be taken almost anywhere in the area, the best spots are West rock, Black rock, off the steps on the south side of the reef, close in to the north-east corner of the main reef, and the area near the Fourquie rock which lies a few hundred metres to the east of the main reef. As the name suggests West rock is the most westerly of the Casquets group and is usually fished on the last of the flood tide. Black rock is the large separate rock just west of the main Casquets reef and is fished on the flood tide.

ALDERNEY	
MARK	Alderney South Banks
GPS (Lat./Long.)	49 42 538 02 09 422 North end
	49 40 424 02 12 486 South end
TYPE OF MARK.	Sand banks
BEST STATE OF TIDE	All states of tide.
SPECIES	Turbot, brill, pollack, cod, bass, red gurnard, mackerel, tope.
METHODS	Spinning - sandeels or lures.
	Bottom fishing - leger.

GENERAL INFORMATION

This is an extremely long sandbank that runs parallel to Alderney's south coast. It is one to one and a half miles off Alderney and is at least four miles long.

It follows that long drifts along the bank are possible.

Fish can be found anywhere along its length, but anglers who fish the bank on a regular basis have discovered "hot-spots" for both bass and pollack.

Although it is possible to fish it on any state of tide, the main run of a big spring tide, either on the ebb or flood, can prove to be a little difficult due to the speed of the drift.

Sark Boat Fishing Marks

SARK	
MARK	Banc de la Schole
GPS (Lat./Long.)	49 35 003 02 13 325
TYPE OF MARK.	Sand bank
BEST STATE OF TIDE	Half tide down to half tide up.
SPECIES	Turbot, brill, bass, mackerel, red gurnard, lesser-spotted dogfish. Occasional ray.
METHODS	Bottom fishing - leger.

GENERAL INFORMATION

This is a four mile long bank, situated roughly midway between Sark and Alderney, some 14 miles from St Peter Port Harbour.

It is quite a dramatic bank for on the ebb tide the bank is marked by a line of short white capped overfalls. It follows that it can become extremely rough if there is even a moderate westerly wind.

The edge of the bank is very shallow and the bottom can clearly be seen on low water of a big spring tide.

Every angler will have his own favourite spot on the bank, but fish can be found anywhere along its length.

SARK	
MARK	Banc au Nord
GPS (Lat./Long.)	49 27 722 02 19 247
TYPE OF MARK.	Sand bank
BEST STATE OF TIDE	Two hours before high water to two hours down.
SPECIES	Brill, turbot, bass, mackerel, lesser-spotted, dogfish, pollack, red gurnard. Occasional ray.
METHODS	Bottom fishing - leger. Feathering

GENERAL INFORMATION

This is a sandbank eight miles from St Peter Port and nearly two miles east of the Nez of Sark.

Visual strike marks are St Martin's Point peeping just over the Nez, Conchee Rock showing east of the Burons.

SARK	
MARK	Conchee
GPS (Lat./Long.)	49 25 360 02 30 589
TYPE OF MARK.	Sand bank/reef.
BEST STATE OF TIDE	Half tide up to half tide down.
SPECIES	Turbot, brill, bass, mackerel, pollack.
METHODS	Spinning with lures or sandeels. Bottom fishing - leger.

GENERAL INFORMATION

This sandbank is only a quarter of a mile outside Sark's Creux Harbour. It is usually fished on the flood, although the ebb can also produce fish.

Normally boats will start their drift from just north of the Conchee rock and end the drift as the boat is swept past the east side of Les Burons, a total distance of approximately half a mile.

It should be noted that there is rough ground for a short distance north of the Conchee rock and on the east side of the Burons. If follows that care should be taken at the beginning and end of the drift, otherwise lost tackle will be a result.

SARK	
MARK	Godine
GPS (Lat./Long.)	49 22 435 02 24 790
TYPE OF MARK.	Sand bank
BEST STATE OF TIDE	Half tide down to two hours up.
SPECIES	Turbot, brill, bass, pollack, whiting, mackerel, cod, red gurnard.
METHODS	Feathering Bottom fishing - leger.

GENERAL INFORMATION

This sandbank is nearly seven miles from St Peter Port and just over two miles south-west of Sark.

Visual strike marks are the Nez of Sark, just showing on the east side of the Gouliot Passage.

Pierre du Cour in line with the point of Derrible Bay (which is opposite the Conchee Rock).

And in good visability the 'chimney' of the Burons in line with the bottom of Derrible Point

165

SARK	
MARK	Brecqhou
GPS (Lat./Long.)	49 26 750 02 23 470
TYPE OF MARK.	Mixed ground
BEST STATE OF TIDE	On the flood - one hour before high tide to one hour down. On the ebb (neap tide) start two hours after low.
SPECIES	Pollack, bass, mackerel, ballan wrasse, turbot, brill, red gurnard.
METHODS	Spinning, lures, sandeel, wormbait. Bottom fishing - leger.

GENERAL INFORMATION

This area is also known as "Roman", and is situated to the west and north of Brecquou.

The area close to Brecqou is rock and weed and sand when you drift north. The sand "starts" when Little Sark can be seen through the Gouliot Passage.

Many anglers have a long drift here, starting on the rock and going onto the sand.

One mark in the rough ground can be located by the following strike marks: Pilcher Monument on Sark peeping over Brecqhou. Small rock just clear east of La Neste rock (as the tide falls put Pilcher Monument on the cleft in Brecqhou.)

SARK	
MARK	Gouliot Passage
GPS (Lat./Long.)	-
TYPE OF MARK.	Rough ground
BEST STATE OF TIDE	Half tide down to half tide up.
SPECIES	Pollack, scad, mackerel, bass, ballan wrasse, garfish, grey mullet.
METHODS	Spinning, lures, sandeel, wormbait.

GENERAL INFORMATION

The Gouliot passage lies between Brecqhou and Sark. On the ebb tide which flows north to south, good fishing can be enjoyed on the south side of the passage by spinning on the edge of the tide stream.

The fish here tend to be modest in size but give good sport and a lot of fun in the comparatively shallow water.

It is sheltered from winds from any easterly direction.

Although they are not so prolific in this spot as they used to be, grey mullet can be sometimes found (and caught!) out of the tide run, by the rocks on the south-east corner of Brecqhou.

Herm Boat Fishing Marks

HERM	
MARK	Platte Boue
GPS (Lat./Long.)	49 31 232 02 25 179
TYPE OF MARK.	Reef.
BEST STATE OF TIDE	Two hours down to low water.
SPECIES	Pollack, mackerel, bass, ballan wrasse.
METHODS	Spinning, lure, sandeel, worm.

GENERAL INFORMATION

This boue (or reef) is approximately 3/4 mile north of Grande Amfroque and 2 1/2 miles NNE of Herm.

One set of visual strike marks are the two beacons on Grande Amfroque in line and Brehon Tower east of Tautenay Beacon.

The boue dries 1.8 metres on low water.

HERM	
MARK	Amfrocque
GPS (Lat./Long.)	-
TYPE OF MARK.	Mixed - rough ground and sandbank.
BEST STATE OF TIDE	Half tide down to two hours up.
SPECIES	Pollack, bass, mackerel, garfish, ballan wrasse, black bream, red gurnard, turbot, brill.
METHODS	Spinning, lures, sandeels, wormbaits. Bottom fishing - leger.

GENERAL INFORMATION

There are many marks that can be fished in the Amfrocque area. However, the most popular three are:

(a) The "top corner". This is the area just to the east of Cul de L'Autel. Care must be taken when approaching the marks as there are a number of boues/reefs that uncover with the falling tide. The normal method is to carefully go up to the reefs and drift away on the ebb tide. Spinning produces pollack, mackerel and the occasional bass, black bream and ballan wrasse.

(b) Amfroque Bank. Long drifts can be completed over this sandbank on the ebb, starting 1/4 mile south of Grande Amfroque and continuing for nearly a mile. Bottom is sand except for a few small rough patches. When the Platte Fougere closes to the north of Tautenay Beacon, terminate the drift as the bottom suddenly gets very rocky.

For flatties keep Goubiniere just open of Selle (or Saddle) rock.

(c) The tide runs on the full ebb just to the west of Grande Amfroque. Trolling or spinning with Rapala type lures can produce bass.

HERM	
MARK	Noire Pute
GPS (Lat./Long.)	49 28 348 02 24 933
TYPE OF MARK.	Reef
BEST STATE OF TIDE	Half tide up to two hours down.
SPECIES	Pollack, bass, mackerel, black bream.
METHODS	Spinning, lures, sandeels, wormbaits.

GENERAL INFORMATION

Noire Pute is the large rock out in the 'middle' of the Big Russel, approximately one mile east of Herm. It never covers, not even on a big spring tide.

The majority of the fishing at this spot is done on the flood tide. The best results are obtained by spinning, as the boat is allowed to drift from just north of the rock. The drift is usually terminated when a flat bottom is reached, after all the reefs have been passed over. Spinning in the main tide run slightly to the east can produce bass. Care must be taken north of Noire Pute as there are reefs which become exposed at low water, one drying 1.6 metres.

Jethou Boat Fishing Marks

JETHOU	
MARK	Les Barbees
GPS (Lat./Long.)	49 26 90 02 28 60
TYPE OF MARK.	Mixed rock/sand
BEST STATE OF TIDE	Half tide up to two hours down.
SPECIES	Garfish, pollack, mackerel, bass, ballan wrasse.
METHODS	Spinning - lures, worm baits, sandeels.

GENERAL INFORMATION

This mark is situated nearly three quarters of a mile south-west of Jethou and is one of the many rocks in the general area known as the "Ferrieres". It never covers and is marked by a yellow pole beacon topped by a barrel. Fishing is done on the flood on the north side of the rock. There is a clear approach into the mark from the direction of St Peter Port Harbour.

It may not be the most prolific mark but produces very well at times, so it's always worth a "stop-off" on the way to more distant marks.

JETHOU	
MARK	Fourquies
GPS (Lat./Long.)	49 27 212 02 26 581
TYPE OF MARK.	Mixed bottom, sand and rock.
BEST STATE OF TIDE	Half tide down to half tide up.
SPECIES	Pollack, bass, mackerel, red gurnard. Occasional brill and turbot.
METHODS	Spinning, sandeels and lures Bottom fishing - leger

GENERAL INFORMATION

This reef lies approximately three quarters of a mile east of Jethou and is a very popular mark.

The Fourquies rock dries up to 2.3 metres and is marked with a North Cardinal Buoy. Anglers must remember that this buoy is sited some 100 metres north of the rock. It follows that when drifting down over the mark on the ebb-tide, the drift must not start by the buoy as this will take you over the rock! All drifts should begin at least 200 metres south of the buoy. There is rough ground just south of the rock at the beginning of the drift, but the bottom gets less rocky and more sandy the further south you go!

JETHOU	
MARK	Goubiniere
GPS (Lat./Long.)	49 27 068 02 26 581
TYPE OF MARK.	Reef/Sand
BEST STATE	Half tide down to half tide up - south of rock.
OF TIDE	Half tide up to half tide down - north of rock.
SPECIES	Pollack, bass, mackerel, black bream.
METHODS	Spinning, lures, sandeels, wormbaits.

GENERAL INFORMATION

This is a big rock that never covers and is situated half mile south of Jethou.

Basically it can be fished on the north side on the flood and the south side on the ebb.

The more favoured side is the south, which has rock and weed at the start of the drift and sand as the drift progresses. There have been instances of turbot, brill and ray being taken, once the boat has drifted well down from the rock.

Catches at this mark seem to have declined in recent years, but is always worth a try.

Care should be taken to avoid Les Anons rock, a reef situated less than a quarter of a mile southwest of Goubiniere which dries up to 3.3 metres on the low water.

Chapter 6 — Sea Angling Clubs/Organisations

The Bailiwick's first sea angling club was the Guernsey Sea Anglers. The club's early records have disappeared in the mists of time, but available club documentation, including the updated General Rules Booklet that was issued in 1964, states that the club was founded in 1938.

As a consequence the club proudly celebrated its 50th Anniversary in 1988. Events held to mark the auspicious occasion included a four-day open angling festival and a dinner attended by the Lieut. Governor Sir Alexander Boswell and Lady Boswell.

It now seems that the club got it all wrong, for it's older than the post-war records indicate!

Recent research has confirmed that a meeting was held at the offices of the Guernsey Evening Press on 31 July, 1937, where it was unanimously decided to inaugurate the Guernsey Amateur Sea Anglers Club.

The first elected chairman was W T Pealling, but it was decided to leave the post of President vacant until a later date. One of the first decisions made by the committee of the fledgling club was to organise the Bailiwick's first open angling competition for the evening of Tuesday 24 August, 1937. It seems that the word "Amateur" was dropped from the club's title almost immediately and it was under the shortened name of the Guernsey Sea Anglers Club that the inaugural competition went ahead. It was a great success. It took place on the New Jetty, at St Peter Port Harbour and over 100 senior and junior anglers took part. Sadly the fishing didn't match the occasion. At the end of the three-hour event, the senior winner was L. Freeman with a weight of 1-9-8. The winning junior was Roy du Moulpied with 1-2-4. The report of the match confirms that Roy landed the heaviest fish, a 1-1-8 specimen, so his other fish must have weighed just three quarters of an ounce! Either the new club didn't have any size limits, or it was a roselet (atherine smelt)!

The winning senior's prize was a guinea (£1.05) and 100 cigarettes, while the top junior was presented with a wrist watch plus a fishing rod and a five shillings (25p) fishing tackle voucher for catching the heaviest individual fish.

By the time the new club held its first Annual General Meeting in January 1938, Gervase F. Peek had been confirmed as the club's first president and the club had obtained the patronage of both the Lieut. Governor and the Bailiff of Guernsey!

In addition a number of club competitions had already been held.

The German Occupation put a stop to the club's activities from 1940 to 1945 but soon after the Liberation by the Allied Forces, fishing recommenced.

By the early 1950's the club had introduced most of the things that angling club members take for granted today.

They had a championship programme of boat and shore competitions there were size limits, albeit a lot lower than the present standards, an overall record list, 14 trophies covering both competition and specimen fish awards and even a series of bass competitions.

It was inevitable that being the first club they were to be responsible for the introduction of a number of interesting innovations which would greatly influence the future of Bailiwick angling.

Junior Section (see page 63)

The club was the first to have a completely seperate junior section, which was formed in the early 1950's and is still going strong over 55 years later!

The youngsters have their own programme of boat and shore competitions, and fish an annual match against the seniors.

They have a wide range of trophies covering not just the competitions, but also for the best fish of the year, the best flatfish, and for the most species landed.

On each competition they are looked after, helped and given instruction by the junior section secretary and other senior members. Safety is paramount and all juniors must wear a life jacket when taking part in club activities.

Although some of the other Bailiwick clubs do accept junior members, the GSAC remain the only club to have a seperate section with a full programme of events for the youngsters.

Competition Points System

This was a new, unique concept which was to make a fundamental change, not only to the club's competitions at the time, but to have a profound effect, right up to the present day.

From the outset the GSAC competitions were run on a 'heaviest weight' basis, an accepted method which was, and still is, used by the vast majority of both sea and freshwater clubs throughout the United Kingdom and in many other countries.

Many angling venues have a restricted number of similar species and in these cases, competitive anglers have to settle for what's available. In these situations the heaviest total weight principle is quite satisfactory.

However, the Bailiwick is blessed with an enormous variety of fish and the GSAC committee had to be persuaded to accept that the 'heaviest weight' system only encouraged members to ignore many species in order to target the heavy fish such as ballan wrasse, almost to the total exclusion of everything else.

Peter Witterick a member of the GSAC committee designed and suggested the use of a unique points system, which would be a different approach, that would encourage anglers to fish for other species during competitions

Four points per pound, or alternatively one quarter of a point per ounce would be awarded irrespective of the type of fish caught. In addition, bonus points would be awarded for each fish of each species.

The higher value bonus points would be given to the rarer species or those deemed more of a challenge to catch. There was of course much debate on the value of the points to be given to the various species.

GSAC members embark on a non-competitive angling trip on 17 July 1958

A more modern angling trip - GSAC members boarding 2 boats in May 1997

174

However, it was recognised that it was a flexible system which would allow the 'species points' to be amended in light of use, particularly if fish availability and patterns changed.

It was decided to adopt the system on a trial basis. By 1957 the species points allocation was as follows;

Sole	10 points
Red mullet	9 points
Dab, flounder, garfish	8 points
Mackerel, plaice, black bream, grey mullet, John Dory, gurnard	7 points
Whiting, common eel, bass	6 points
Coalfish, turbot, brill, scad	5 points
Ling, cod, dogfish, pollack	4 points
Pout, roselet (atherine smelt)	3 points
Skate/ray, wrasse, red bream	2 points
Conger	1 point .

The list looks quite quaint today with what appears to be glaring anomalies. Garfish 8 points, roselet 3 points and bass the same value as common eel must look strange, but it must be remembered that it was considered right for the type of angling and fish patterns prevailing over 50 years ago.

Suffice to say only three species, conger, pout and whiting remain at the same values in the club today.

The points system became a permanent feature of the club's competition rules and although the points values have been refined and amended a number of times over the years, it is still in use today.

For one year in 1974, the club members did decide to revert to a weight-only basis for a trial period. However, there was so much criticism and adverse reaction, there was an immediate switch back to points for the following year!

Since those early days many newly formed clubs have adopted the points system.

Naturally they have varied the species points values to suit their own needs, but the principle remains.

It was the GSAC which introduced the first open competition in the Bailiwick. There was, of course, that 1937 event, but the first open match in the modern angling calendar that was to become a regular feature was the annual Fur and Feather competition, so called because it's held just before Christmas with prizes of turkeys, chickens and other meats as well as other festive fare including wines, spirits, chocolates and Xmas pudding!

The first one was held on 27 November 1966 when 173 anglers took part. It was to prove quite an eventful occasion, but maybe not quite in the way that everyone expected.

The competition was run using the club's points system and was won by the GSAC President of the day, Ernie Baker, who landed three pollack and 60 roselet for a weight of 6-13-0 and 99 1/4 points.

John Newton came second with seven plaice for 7-15-0, including a

175

3-10-0 fish, for 80 3/4 points.

The result caused a lot of comment. After all, there is no doubt that seven plaice is a far better catch than three pollack and 60 roselet!

It was obvious what had happened. Plaice rarely get caught in club matches and a catch of seven was quite unusual even in those days, consequently this anomaly in the points system had never cropped up before.

As a result the club had a fresh look at its species points allocation and introduced no fewer than 17 changes for the following season, a simple task due to the flexibility of the system.

It was also agreed that although the points system was excellent for club matches, it was not suitable for large one-off open competitions, and as a consequence all future opens would be on a "weight only" basis.

Just one small postscript on that 1966 Fur and Feather. In that year roselet were worth one point, now it's a quarter of a point; plaice were seven, now they are worth 20!

The same result today under the present points allocation would give John victory with 171 3/4 points to Ernie's 50 1/4!

Bailiwick Record Committee

In 1966 the GSAC proposed another far-reaching innovation. They started the moves necessary that resulted in the formation of the Bailiwick of Guernsey Record (Rod-Caught) Fish Committee which is described in some detail in chapter nine.

Inter-Insular Competitions

Back in 1951 the club had been responsible for yet another new first, an inter-insular competition, with the Jersey Sea Fishing Club providing the opposition. The GSAC came out on top in the team match, but JSFC member Dick Smith had the distinction of winning the first individual contest between the club champions of each

The well dressed GSAC Inter Insular teams in 1958! Back row left to right, Joe Merrien, Ernie Baker, Jim Ikeringill, John Petit, John Carre, P. Wingrave, Front row left to right, P. Jackson, S. Turville, J.J. Falla, P. Witterick, P. Marette

176

island. As the inter-insular developed it became a four-match contest with trophies at stake for both the senior and junior team events and the individual matches between the club's senior champions and top women anglers. In the 1990's the JSFC junior section closed down, which ment the junior team and individual matches came to a sad end. In 2001 the inter-insular competition celebrated it's 50th anniversary.

The GSAC won the match fished in Guernsey waters, which meant that over those 50 years the local team held a lead in the senior team competition by 36 wins to 14!

The GSAC v JSFC inter-insular in 1959, all aboard the "Lady June". Over 20 anglers on one boat would not be tolerated in later years!

Sadly it was to prove to be the last such event for the JSFC went into rapid decline, and soon went out of existence.

Other newer clubs have also held inter-insular matches but interest in all such events seemed to fade away to the point where competitive sea angling between the islands almost ceased completely.

Although there had been some interest and discussion about starting an annual inter island match between selected teams of the top anglers of Guernsey and Jersey, in effect an angling "Muratti", it has never come to fruition.

The only such fixture left is an annual get together of Jersey and Alderney anglers, up in the northern isle in the early Spring.

In the early 1960's the GSAC went through a very difficult period. Apathy was rife and the club membership fell to a critcally low level. Under the leadership of Ernie Baker, the newly elected club president, the club's problems were quickly resolved

A more modern club outing. Anglers on Roy Taylor's Belle de Serk in the mid 1990's.

177

Platte Saline Bay Alderney.

The Doyle with Platte Saline Beach beyond.

178

Alderney Breakwater

Roselle Point showing The Lights and the Alderney Breakwater in the background.

The rocks that provide good fishing at Cats Bay, which is adjacent to Alderney Lighthouse.

The infamous Casquets reef/lighthouse south elevation.

Alderney Lighthouse

A good fishing spot. The rocks along the north side of Fort Quesnard in Alderney.

The rocky fishing spots at Les Bouffresses (or The Targets) showing their relative position to the east of Raz Island.

Raz Island.

Cachaliere Pier (or Chicago) on Alderney's south coast

Maseline Harbour Pier in Sark

Havre Gosselin in Sark showing the steps and adjacent rocks from where to fish.

The fishing spot L'Eperquerie Sark

Putrainez off Herm's east coast, whch clearly shows that it gets surrounded over the high water.

The "Camp-Site" shore mark in Herm. Note, the outlying rock called the Saddle and the anglers down at the mark.

185

and its future was assured. During the years since, the club have continued their comprehensive competitive programme which has been amended from time to cater for changing trends. The top club anglers during the 48 year period up to 2010 were Ernie Baker, who won the club's senior championship seven times, and Peter Frise, who won on 23 occasions in a 28 year period a remarkable record of consistent competitive angling! (see page 58)

VIP Member!

In 2006 the GSAC were delighted to welcome the Lieutenant-Govenor Sir Fabian Malbon as a club member. In spite of his busy programme of commitments he found time to enter many of the club competitions. He enjoyed success in his first season, winning two trophies. One was for a top place finish in a competition, the other for the heaviest bass of the year an 8-10-1 fish.

(see page 143)

New Clubs

The Guernsey Sea Anglers club was to remain as the only sea angling club in the Bailiwick for 25 years. In 1962 this situation was to change. The Gas AC was formed, the first local club attached to a company. In addition the first specialist club was founded, ironically due to problems within the GSAC itself. There was a growing unrest among a number of club members who were becoming increasingly disenchanted with the club's policy of fishing its boat competitions on inshore marks where the main quarry was invariably small pollack and wrasse.

It was known that there were bigger and more exciting species further afield. It was not the wrecks that were the attraction in those days but the presence of shark!

Discussions with the professional fisherman had confirmed that blue and porbeagle sharks often attacked the fisherman's mackerel lines and were taken in nets and on longlines.

The club anglers were determined to have the opportunity to try for the sharks and it was suggested to the club committee that deep-sea trips should be organised.

The request was firmly rejected, and as a consequence, a number of members decided that the only option was to form another club.

On 26 November 1962 a group of anglers including GSAC members Ernie Baker, Peter Witterick, John Petit and Jim Ikeringill met at the Dorset Arms.

It was decided to form the 30 Fathom Club. The name was suggested by Peter Witterick and was the average water depth of the offshore areas where the club intended to fish for the shark.

The club's first officers were, president Ernie Baker, secretary, Peter Witterick and treasurer/trip organiser Jim Ikeringill.

The club was to prove extremely successful in meeting its aims and with the help and co-operation of local trawler skippers, porbeagle and blue shark were soon being caught on a regular basis, the majority from the area south of Guernsey known as the "exchange".

An early success in the 30 Fathom Club John Martel (Left) and Jim Ikeringill with their catch of the day.

John Petit, one of the Bailiwick's most successful shark anglers in the 1960's

These were the only species of shark landed by the club members. Mako and thresher shark are known to be in this area of the English Channel but none were ever hooked by the club members.

All did not go smoothly. The members were taken by surprise by the sheer power of the sharks and some of the anglers were to find out the hard way of the inadequacy of their tackle, as lines, rods and even reels proved not to be up to the task.

Members' budgets were strained as heavier tackle was obtained, but as a result the members' success rate rapidly improved.

John Petit was probably the most consistent of the club members boating both porbeagle and blue sharks topped by a 120-0-0 blue shark which held the Bailiwick record from August 1973. This record was to stand for 29 years until it was beaten by a 132-13-3 specimen caught by Paul Priaulx west of Guernsey in August 2002.

The heaviest porbeagle to be caught in Bailiwick waters in those early days fell to the rod of club member Peter Rouxel. His 220-0-0 specimen caught in August 1972 was to stand as the record for 35 years. It was finally beaten by a 295-8-6 fish caught by Jamie Allen near the Hanois in August 2007. (see page 222)

The capture of two porbeagles by Peter Witterick stand out as quite remarkable highlights of the club's early years.

The shark baits, usually a whole mackerel, were presented on float tackle, which were allowed to be towed quite a few yards away from the drifting trawler.

This gave the members the opportunity, while waiting for a shark take, to fish for bottom feeding species, and a second, lighter rod was bought into use.

The catches were excellent, for in those days big red and black bream were plentiful and there was always a chance of gurnard, dogfish, pout, ling and many other species.

On this particular day Peter had discovered a fault in the butt locking system

of his shark rod. He did however have his second rod, which at best could only be described as a light to medium spinning rod. Nothing daunted Peter decided to use it for shark! He subsequently hooked a 90-0-0 porbeagle, which he boated after a prolonged, exciting fight. It was a superb angling feat on such light gear.

Peter Witterick with a catch of porbeagle in the early days of the 30 Fathom Club.

On the second occasion Peter had a shark run, struck and immediately felt the weight and power of an enormous fish. Although on this trip he was using his standard sharking gear he could make little impression on the apparently monster fish. Angler and fishing gear was to take a terrible hammering for nearly three long hours before the shark was even seen.

Finally the reason for the terrific battle became evident, Peter had foul hooked a 175-0-0 porbeagle in the pectoral fin! Anglers who have had the same experience with a much more modest fish will know the difficulty that such a hook position causes.

Peter finally managed to boat his catch after literally playing the enormous shark side-on which was an incredible achievement, so much so that the German rod manufacturer awarded him a rod of his choice in recognition of his great feat of angling!

The club became more adventurous and organised annual week-end trips to the Minquiers reef, south of Jersey, which was known to be a shark hot-spot!

The effort paid off, for in 1969 club member Des Bougourd caught a 430-0-0 porbeagle, which was to become the World, British, Channel Island and Jersey record, but more on that outstanding catch in a later chapter.

One lasting memory of the first years of the club was the costs involved.

Anglers who charter commercial angling boats today will be flabbergasted to learn of the cost of the deep sea trips in the mid 1960's. The cost of the boat trip was £10. That was not the cost to each angler, but the total

Peter Rouxel (left) and boat skipper Frank le Page, with Peter's 220-0-0 Bailiwick record porbeagle shark caught in August 1972

189

charter cost of boat, skipper and crew for the day!

The club also organised their first annual dinner, the chosen menu costing £1 per head.

In the 1970's the interest in sharking waned and finally disappeared altogether. As new members joined the club the emphasis steadily switched to bank fishing for turbot, brill and bass.

There is no doubt that sharks are still present in our waters. They will give great sport to any angler who is prepared to give the time and effort to pursue these exciting species.

In recent years a small number of trips by anglers in private boats have had some success as indicated by that shark records boated by Paul Priaulx and Jamie Allen.

'Watershed' in Local Angling Club History

The formation of the Gas AC and the 30 Fathom Club in 1962 was to prove a watershed in local angling history. For 25 years there had been just that one sea angling club, over the next 35 years new clubs would be founded with almost monotonous regularity.

They would fall into five different categories: clubs such as the 30 Fathom that were formed to pursue "deep sea" angling, clubs that would target one species, clubs attached to a company, general clubs similar to the Guernsey Sea Anglers Club and clubs that would specialise in specimen fish. The 30 Fathom club was to stay in existence for 29 years, although it's name was later changed to the 30 Fathom Specimen Hunters Club. As the years progressed new navigational aids that became available meant that almost pin-point accuracy in positioning could be achieved.

This opened up the deep water wrecks to the local angling clubs. This type of trip was added to the club's annual programme and the members soon experienced good catches of ling, pollack, cod and conger.

It's not surprising that other clubs with the same aims and interests were formed. In 1980 the Drifters AC came on the scene. Although their origins were anglers who worked at Brennans furniture shop, their membership was open to all island anglers.

They were followed by the Royals AC in 1990 and the Castaways AC in July 1991.

The success of any angling club is dependent on the enthusiasm of its members, coupled with the leadership and good management of its elected officers, but the new clubs were soon to realise that there was one other necessary ingredient for success — size!

In the early days the 30 Fathom Club had soon discovered that a membership of at least 30 members would be necessary to ensure that the club would be able to regularly fill the 12 places on chartered commercial angling boats that had been booked for their deep sea trips.

It was obvious that on the proposed date for any trip some members would be unavailable due to holidays, illness or family or work commitments.

The situation was to get worse as the years progressed. Anglers started to cut back on their charter boat trips. This was due to considerable rises in boat fees and the fact that more and more anglers were purchasing their own boats.

Consequently the new clubs were soon to have problems. They all had comparatively small memberships, some below 20, and they experienced difficulties in finding enough members to fulfil their charter boat bookings. Even the long established 30 Fathom Specimen Hunters' Club had the same problems as their membership had started to decline. It was inevitable that something had to be done. In late 1991 an agreement was reached with the Royals AC to merge into a single new club, which would be known as the Royal Fathomers AC.

The amalgamation forced the members of the 30 Fathom Specimen Hunters Club to abandon one of their main principles that had stood since the club's formation in 1962.

All the other Bailiwick angling clubs have a comprehensive range of awards to the point where many anglers feel that there are just too many. Cups and shields seem to be awarded, almost at the drop of a hat, for every conceivable competition or specimen fish.

It's actually got to a situation where some clubs have more trophies than members!

The 30 Fathom Specimen Hunters Club were unique, they didn't have any! The club's main object had been to pioneer and exploit the local deep-sea fishing potential and they always had a strictly non-competitive policy.

However, as the new Royal Fathomers AC had inherited trophies from the Royals AC, members that came from the 30 Fathom Specimen Hunters Club had no option but to accept the situation and found themselves with the chance of becoming a trophy winner for the first time!

Support for this type of club continued to decline which was to cause the demise of the Castaways AC in the autumn of 1997 and the Drifters AC in November 1999. This left the Royal Fathomers AC as the only remaining club that exclusively used commercial angling charter boats for their planned deep sea trips.

Even they were to find it difficult to get the level of support from its members that was essential if it was to continue. In spite of much hard work by club secretary Eddie Osborne to keep the club going it finally succumbed to the inevitable and closed down in January 2008.

This ended 46 years of club organised charter boat trips to the more distant "deep sea" marks.

Company Clubs

In the 1960's no fewer than four company angling clubs were founded. The Gas AC in 1962 were followed by the Telephone AC early in 1966, Tektronix AC later in 1966 and the Electrics AC on 11 October 1968.

Although they were, in practice, the angling sections of the company's sports and social clubs, they acted like independent angling clubs and set out to give their members all the opportunities and facilities as those enjoyed by the members of the long established GSAC.

They adopted the GSAC designed points system, started club record lists, introduced programmes of shore and boat competitions, obtained trophies and where there were equivalent companies in Jersey, set up annual inter-insular competitions.

They were joined by the Post Office Angling Club in 1972 and the Uncatchables AC, which was based at St Martin's Garage, in January 1992.

The clubs set up inter-club competitions and for many years, the Electrics, Gas and Telephone fished a series of two-leg, six-a-side boat matches against each other.

Unlike general island-wide clubs, the fortunes of the company- based clubs seemed to ebb and flow depending on the staff working in the company at any one time, the fluctuating interest within the organisation and the calibre and dedication of the anglers who took on the administration responsibilities. Sadly, none were to have a very long term future.

Tektronix were a large electronics manufacturing company and their club ceased to function in the 1980's just prior to the company closing their activities in Guernsey and moving to a new location elsewhere.

The Post Office AC disbanded in 1995 due to a decline in interest to a level that the club was no longer viable.

The Uncatchables AC from St Martin's Garage lasted just two years, closing down in 1994.

By December 1998 only the Telephone AC, Gas AC and Electrics AC were left. Even these three clubs that had been in existance for over 30 years were seeing a steady decline in both interest and levels of membership.

It was not just a temporary downturn in support and all three finally closed down during 2000 or 2001.

Although they had not been in existence since they decided to disband on 4 December 2000 the TAC did manage to scrape a team together and fish an inter-insular match in Jersey in June 2002, following an invitation from their colleagues at Jersey Telecom. Even a win in that last inter-island match failed to rekindle any enthusiasm or support for a reformation of the club.

As a consequence the era of company based clubs that had lasted for 40 years from 1962 - 2002 finally came to a sad end.

There were certainly a number of other company-based clubs. As the interest in angling grew, groups of work colleagues in a number of organisations considered forming their own club.

Many of the prospective clubs were to remain as only ideas that were never to get off the ground. Others did get formed but only lasted a very short time, usually due to the administrative inexperience of the organisers, but sometimes because there just weren't enough members to ensure their long-term viability.

Specialist Clubs

The mid-1970's saw a new trend as some anglers became more discerning and began to target a selected species. It wasn't to be long before a specialist club would be formed by anglers with a shared common interest.

Chippy Corbet (right) first president of the Guernsey Bass Anglers Sportfishing Society, his successor Bill Solway (left) and Dave Le Feuvre the holder of the post in 1998.

Bass Clubs

At a meeting of bass enthusiasts, held at the Couture Inn on 17 February 1975 the Guernsey Bass Anglers Sportfishing Society came into existence.

Under the leadership of its first President, Chippy Corbet, and later Bill Solway, it was an incredible success and quickly became the biggest and most affluent club in the Bailiwick. Due to the hard work by the club's officers and the enthusiasm of the local bass anglers its membership climbed to over 140! A further measure of its popularity was the fact that at one annual dinner and presentation evening at the Carlton Hotel, over 300 members and friends attended.

Although the Society awarded trophies for both boat and shore- caught fish, the main emphasis was very much on shore fishing.

The quality of the fish consistently caught by the members and entered in the Society's competitions was truly remarkable. Up to the end of 2006 the Society had awarded 72 gold bars to members who had caught bass of 10-0-0 or over more than 60 silver bars for fish between 9-0-0 and 10-0-0 and more than 80 bronze bars for fish between 8-0-0 and 9-0-0. Over the same period the best fish caught by a member was the 15-9-7 specimen caught by Brian Robson at Cobo in June 1982. This fish became the Bailiwick shore-caught record that stood until November 1996 when it was beaten by a 16-8-4 fish from Alderney.

Althought the Society has ended the presentation of the bars the high standard of the members catches were to continue in subsequent years. As illustrated by club president Brian Montgomery's catch in 2010 when he established a new club shore record with a 16-7-3 specimen. (see page 145)

John Hanley has been the Society's most successful member. He has landed 12 shore-caught bass over 10-0-0, topped by a 14-10-2 specimen. His haul included the Society's heaviest bass from Herm, a 12-12-0 fish and he won a whole string of awards, including the club championship on nine occasions.

Jean Mauger had the top fish by a woman member, a 12-0-6 fish, Patrick Hanley's 10-0-4 bass was the heaviest by a junior, while Tom Brock had the top boat caught fish a 12-12-7 specimen landed in 2009.

In 1981 the Society introduced the first Open Bass Festival which is covered in detail in a later chapter, but suffice to say at this point, it was to prove to be another outstanding success for the Society.

In the 1990's the Society's fortunes surprisingly started to wane and the membership steadily declined.

Over the same period, bass catches, which had been below average for some years, took a dramatic upturn. Bass had been considered almost an elusive species, with dedicated shore anglers usually fishing in the dead of night, catching just an occasional specimen!

Suddenly they seemed to be everywhere, particularly on boat marks and quite huge catches became almost the norm!

Obviously more anglers than ever before started to specialise in this popular sporting fish and yet this considerable surge of interest did not result in any increase in GBASS membership.

It eventually became apparent that there was dissent and even animosity among the different factions of the bass angling community.

It came to the point when it was obvious that any reconciliation would be impossible and as a result a second bass club was formed, the Bailiwick Bass Club coming into being in February 1998 under the presidency of Mark Fletcher. The new club set out to give its members, at least the same facilities as the longer established GBASS, even to the point where the new club introduced their own Open Bass Festival.

At the time the formation of a second club was considered an unnecessary backward step by many enthusiasts and indeed Bailiwick anglers generally.

However in spite of the doubts and concerns expressed of having two competing bass clubs in a small island, few problems have arisen and the two organisations have sucessfully co-existed each maintaining a satisfactory level of membership.

The animosity between the two groups has been overcome to the point where they have even run inter-club competitions.

The Bailiwick Bass Club's comparitively short history has been a successful one. There has been keen competition in the club's championships, where Mark Fletcher and Terry Dodd have been the club's most successful members, Mark winning the shore championship on five occasions and Terry four times in the boat championship.

The members caught 32 double figure bass in the club's first thirteen years, topped by the club's shore record, a 14-8-4 specimen caught by Mark Amies in 2002 and the boat record, a 12-11-11 fish caught by Terry Dodd in the same year.

Dawn Marley has had the top fish by a female club member, a fish of 7-6-6, Joe Collenette the best by a junior 9-5-0, while Colin Patch's 6-3-5 fish is the clubs best from Herm.

In spite of the much improved relations between the two club's there is no possiblility of an amalgamation into one club still considered by some anglers to be a logical final outcome. Anglers will therefore have the choice of two similar clubs and two similar Bass Festivals for the forseeable future.

Mark Fletcher, first President of the Bailiwick Bass Club, pictured with a large ballan wrasse.

Guernsey Mullet Club

The local mullet enthusiasts followed their bassing colleagues and formed their own club in April 1984, their first President being Ron Harris. The Guernsey Mullet Club differed from the bass clubs for they targeted not one, but three species. These were the thick- lipped grey mullet, the thin-lipped grey mullet and the golden grey mullet.

For the first four years the club championship was decided on the top aggregate weight of mullet caught by the member during the club year.

The club placed a great emphasis on conservation, with members being encouraged to return their fish once they had been

Ron Harris, first president of the Guernsey Mullet Club, seen here with a turbot!

weighed. This was a very successful policy and 95% of the catches were returned alive. Exceptions were the odd fish kept for eating, or outstanding specimens that had to be formally weighed and identified for record or competition purposes.

The club realised the overall weight principle for deciding the club championship was not compatible with their conservation philosophy and consequently as from 1988 it was decided that the championship would be based on the member's top 10 fish. This lasted for nine years, until in 1997 it was amended to the member's best 10 mullet out of their top fish of each month!

In 1986 the club introduced the Open Mullet Competition which is discussed in Chapter 8.

It's true to say that the club has attracted many of the best mullet anglers in the island who are very adept in catching this shy and unpredictable species.

As a result many outstanding catches have been made by the members. In 1996 Martyn Torode won the championship with 10 mullet for a combined weight of 66-11-9, an average weight of 6-10-12. This really was a superb achievement. It was a result way above the wildest dreams of the vast majority of anglers, who would be very satisfied if they managed to catch even one mullet over 6-0-0!

Martyn Torode recorded the highest number of mullet caught by a club member in a year, 78 for a total weight of 299-4-11. Over the period 1984 to 2010 members landed a massive total of 6082 mullet for an overall weight of 21975-15-10.

The most sucessful club member over the club's 27 year history has been Mike Weysom for he won the club championship on ten occasions, his total catches over the years amounting to 881 fish for 2892-7-9. Martyn Torode and Mark Gillson were his nearest rivals with four championship wins each.

The club records, as at April 2011 were:

Thick-lipped grey mullet	Martyn Torode	11-8-12
Thin-lipped grey mullet	Mike Weysom	3-5-2
Golden grey mullet	Andy Le Lerre	2-8-10

New General Clubs

The new company-based, and specialist clubs were joined by at least five new general island-wide clubs that were open for membership to all island anglers.

These new clubs would experience varying degrees of success, but by the end of 1994 only one would remain in existence.

By far the most successful was the Jamaica Inn Angling Club. It was formed in 1969, the first chairman being mine host at the Inn, R. W. (Nobby) Clark, with the first committee members being Larry Burtenshaw, Alf Solway and John Palmeri. Trophies were acquired and the new club soon embarked on their first competitions.

For a couple of years the club was to be quite informal and fairly low key. In 1971 there was a considerable upsurge in interest and the club was placed on a more formal footing. The new President was Roy Barrasin with the secretary's post being filled by Mick Le Sauvage. He was to remain in the post for 18 years.

There is no doubt that largely through his hard work and influence the club became one of the most ambitious and innovative in the Bailiwick. Initially the club followed a similar pattern adopted by other previously formed organisations.

It was decided to run the competitions on the GSAC designed points system, a full programme of boat and shore matches, including some on Herm were introduced and a club record list was inaugurated.

However, it wasn't long before the club brought in many new ideas and innovations. They were to be the first Bailiwick club to organise regular competitions with a club from the United Kingdom. In common with other local clubs the JIAC had started annual matches against Jersey opposition, their

John Hanley (left) receives an award from Nobby Clarke, Chairman of the JIAC, in the early days of the club.

opponents being the St. Catherine's Angling Association. The series of competitions proved to be comparatively short-lived and as a result, in the early 1980's they began annual competitions with the South Devon Sea Angling Club. This started a friendly relationship that was to last for many years. Overseas excursions didn't stop there, for they also introduced matches against the Alderney Sea Angling Club!

The club were the first to invite the Bailiff of Guernsey to an annual angling club dinner, Sir Charles and Lady Frossard being their honoured guests at the 1985 function.

Further innovations followed. A small boat championship, a unique concept in local angling, was included as part of their overall programme and they became the first club to fish shore matches on Jethou.

The JIAC were the first Bailiwick club to affiliate to the British Conger Club and also the South West Federation of Sea Anglers. This gave their members the opportunity to qualify for awards from both organisations and as a result many medals and certificates for specimen fish have been won by local anglers.

The club's trophy list grew steadily until they had the most comprehensive range of angling awards of any Bailiwick club. These were not just for competitions but also for the captors of the best specimen fish in a number of different species. The growth in awards was matched by the enthusiasm of the members as they sought good catches or fish that would give them success and a share of the spoils.

Shaun Long with his vast collection of awards at the JIACs 1986 Annual Dinner.

The pinnacle of success was surely that achieved by Shaun Long in the 1985/6 season. He won no fewer than 13 trophies including the club's overall shore, boat and Herm championships. Without doubt this was one of the best achievements in Bailiwick club history.

In 1993 the club shook the angling community by deciding to change both their name and headquarters. After being based at the Jamaica Inn for 24 years they decided to move out to the Wayside Tavern at Grandes Rocques.

The JIAC was disbanded and on 19 January 1993 a new club which would be called the West Coast Sea Angling Club was formed by basically the same members. Its first president was Chris Massey.

The new club adopted the same policies and traditions of the JIAC including its program of events and competitions.

Like the JIAC the WCSAC continued to run both their shore and boat competitions on the GSAC designed points system, but attitudes of the club members soon began to change. Although the points systems would continue to be used for some competitions members increasingly favoured the idea of specimen fish contests.

As a result the club introduced a new imaginative concept. In 1993 they launched the Winter League, a shore competition that would run from January to March and October to December each year.

Members could fish where and when they wished, the object being to catch the greatest number of different species. The weight of the anglers best fish of each species would be expressed as a percentage of the Bailiwick Record (Rod-caught) fish. The winner of the League would be the angler with the highest aggregate percentage.

A pairs league was run in parallel, based on the same format. It was an immediate outstanding success, it really caught the imagination of the members and it became a fiercely competitive competition.

Up to 2010 Mark Thomson was top competitor, winning the league on four occasions. Each year more species were caught, until in 2010, winner Billy Foreman managed to find 16!

The incredible success of the new event, encouraged the club to abandon their small boat and charter competitions and start a summer league, which would run from April to September. The boat based event was run on the same principles and was a similar success story. Dan Slimm won the first two leagues which were held in 2005 and 2006, boating 17 and 18 species respectively.

In 2008 Tim Froome was the winner and Andy Le Lerre the runner up both landing 20 species. George Jennings tops the list of winners with success in 2007, 2009 and 2010.

There is no doubt that the new style competitons have been instrumental in a big rise in the club's membership, to the point where it had the highest number of senior members of any sea angling club in the Bailiwick.

They have ensured that local anglers have a real viable alternative to the only other similar club, the GSAC. The four remaining general clubs were all formed with great enthusiasm, but all were set to fail within a comparatively short length of time, the longest lasting 13 years, the shortest just three!

The Dreamers AC was the most successful. It was formed in 1982 by a number of friends who regularly fished with one of the charter angling skippers. It quickly became established with a full programme of boat and Herm shore competitions. However, declining interest from the members, coupled with the fact that their regular skipper left the island, forced it to disband in 1994.

The Mare Multipliers were formed in 1978 by the staff and friends of Mare de Carteret School. They were to last 10 years, the club closing down in 1987. The Foresters Arms, no doubt conscious of the success of the angling club at the Jamaica Inn just down the road, decided to form their own club in 1980, but this was to last just seven years until 1986. The Kingfishers AC was formed by employees and friends at the States Electricity Board. It was to have the shortest history of the new general clubs, lasting just three years from 1991 to 1993.

The GSAC and WCSAC (ex JIAC) were to be the Bailiwick's only general clubs for a nine year period from 1994.

However, in March 2003 they were joined by the Sark Angling Club, which had been formed by a group of local enthusiasts.

The club's first president was Glyn Williams who steered the fledgling organisation through it's formative years.

It got off to a flying start, with its first competition being held in April 2003.

It had a membership of over 40, a full programme of shore competitions, an annual dinner and presentation night and a fine array of trophies.

Specimen Fish Clubs

In the 1980's and early 1990's there was a general growing awareness of the dangers to fish stocks due to their possible over-exploitation by both commercial and sport fishermen. The question of fish conservation and the need to safeguard the stocks started to become a real political and environmental issue. In many ways the Bailiwick's angling community had already been taking action in this regard. All the clubs had fish size limits, many of which had been increased over the years, and as a result many club limits have become considerably higher than those prescribed by law. Some clubs, the Guernsey Mullet Club being the best example,introduced a catch and return policy, while many others switched the emphasis of some of their competitions to specimen fish inpreference to the heaviest catch principle.

Anglers who had strong views on the conservation issue and considered that competition fishing for heaviest bags resulted in the unnecessary killing of fish, soon banded together to form new general clubs that would concentrate purely on the pursuit of specimen fish. Two such clubs would be formed in Guernsey, but in reality, they were beaten to the punch by the Alderney Sea Angling club.

It came into existence in 1974 under the chairmanship of James Roberts. The specimen fish principle was the club's policy from the beginning, even though there is some evidence to suggest that for a very short time a few "heaviest bags" competitions were held. It is primarily a shore fishing club, although there were a small number of awards for boat-caught fish.

The club has had a rather chequered history, its members enjoying success with the incredible fishing to be had in the Bailiwick's northern isle and a whole string of specimen fish, including many Bailiwick and British records, have been a result.

The club also held competitions against anglers from Jersey, as well as a Guernsey club, as we have already noted. However, in spite of those great catches and initial enthusiasm, support for the club over the years as been spasmodic at best and it finally expired in 2010.

The first specimen club to be formed in Guernsey was the Guernsey Shore Anglers Premier Pursuers. It came into being in September 1985, its first President and main instigator being Alan Drillot. Bearing in mind that it was a shore fishing club, its high size limits confirmed its intention to only target the top fish. To be eligible for club competitions, ballan wrasse had to be 5-0-0, bass 5-0-0, grey mullet 4-0-0, conger 20-0-0 and cod 5-0-0. Limits for other species are equally demanding.

In it's early years GSAPP was extremely successful. It had a fine array of superb trophies, an enthusiastic membership and well attended annual dinners. Sadly in the mid 1990's the membership started to decline to the point where it was no longer a viable or worthwhile club, and it finally folded in January 2007, after being in existence for 22 years.

In September 1991, a second specimen club was formed. A group of anglers who were already members of a club that judged its competitions on the "heaviest bag" principle decided that they could no longer support such a policy and agreed to form their own club As a result the Sarnia Specimen Club was born under the presidency of Mark Giles.

Unlike GSAPP the newer club accepted competition entries from boat-caught as well as shore-caught fish. They encourage their members to catch and return fish wherever possible.

The club members were to achieve outstanding successes. In 1993 two of its members caught British Record fish. In March Jason Le Noury had a shore-caught ballan wrasse of 8-10-13 and in June, Marc Eppelein boated a 4-1-12 sole.

The club duly honoured the two record breakers at its annual dinner with special awards to mark their achievements. There were also successes in the South West Federation of Sea Anglers. For three years in succession they finished third in the Federation's club specimen fish medal table, beating many larger and longer established clubs from the south west of England in the process.

List of Clubs

Anglers have mixed views on clubs; either you're a club type angler or you're not!

Some anglers feel clubs are too restrictive, they have no time or interest in competitions of any sort and certainly have no wish to get involved in angling administration. They consider that it's all quite unnecessary and just want to quietly pursue and enjoy their fishing with the minimum of outside interference.

Others really enjoy the excitement of competitive angling, the friendships that club life can bring, and the chance to swap stories with their colleagues, as well as picking up tips and suggestions, which can help to improve their own chances of angling success.

It can be quite difficult for an angling beginner to learn all that is necessary to be successful in the sport. In the late 1970's and early 1980's the States College of Further Education ran an eight week evening class course entitled 'Sea Angling for Beginners'.

Currently the sports newcomers do not have access to such a course, so it follows that there is a definite advantage for them to join a club. They will be able to learn an awful lot just by talking to, and observing, the more experienced anglers. Once they are established and more conversant with the intricacies of the sport, they can then make a reasoned decision whether they wish to belong to a club or not.

A list of all the clubs that existed in the Bailiwick in June 2011 follows, each described with a few relevant details that will help a prospective club member to choose the club they feel will be best for them.

Once you've made your choice any one of the tackle dealers should be able to advise you on whom to contact.

1.   **General Clubs**

Name	**Guernsey Sea Anglers Club.**
Formed	1937

Open to   All anglers, including women.
Junior anglers as from their ninth
birthday.

Size of   40 seniors, 20 juniors.
Membership

Type of fishing   Boat competitions for both seniors
and juniors. Shore competitions,
including day and night matches on
Herm, for both seniors and juniors.
Awards given for competitions for
heaviest bags of fish, based on a
points system, and for specimen fish.

Other events   Annual dinner/presentation night.
Annual Open Fur and Feather
Competition.

Name   **West Coast Sea Angling Club.**
Formed   1993

Open to   All anglers, including women, over the
age of 16.

Size of   80
Membership

Type of Fishing   Boat competitions. Shore competitions
including day and night matches on Herm.
Awards given for competitions for heaviest
bags of fish, based on a points system
and for specimen fish.

Other events   Annual dinner and presentation
Annual Open Specimen Fish Hunt.

Name	**Sark Angling Club.**
Formed	2003
Open to	All anglers, seniors, juniors, women
Size of Membership	20
Type of fishing	Shore competition, including day and night matches. Awards given for heaviest bags of fish based on a point system, and for specimen fish.
Other events	Annual dinner and presentation night.

2.   Clubs that target selected species

Name	**Guernsey Bass Anglers Sportfishing Society.**
Formed	1975
Open to	All anglers, including women and juniors
Size of Membership	70
Type of fishing	Boat and shore competitions for bass. Awards given for specimen fish.
Other events	Annual dinner and presentation night. Annual open bass festival.
Name	**Bailiwick Bass Club**
Formed	1998
Open to	All anglers, including women and juniors.
Size of Membership	45
Type of fishing	Boat and shore competitions for bass. Awards given for best specimens.

| Other events | Two annual open bass festivals. |
| | Annual dinner and presentation night. |

| Name | **Guernsey Mullet Club** |
| Formed | 1984 |

| Open to | All anglers, including women. No junior under 14. |

| Size of Membership | 45 |

| Type of fishing | Shore only, for thick-lipped, thin-lipped and golden grey mullet. |
| | Awards given for specimen fish. |

| Other events | Annual open mullet competition. |

3. **General Clubs that specialize in specimen fish**

| Name | **Sarnia Specimen Club.** |
| Formed | 1991 |

| Open to | All anglers, including women and juniors. |

| Size of Membership | 20 |

| Type of fishing | Boat and shore for specimen fish. |

| Other events | Annual dinner and presentation night. |

Club Scene

The Bailiwick club scene differs from many other angling centres due to the sheer number of existing clubs.

The majority of the well-known angling venues in the United Kingdom usually cover much bigger catchment areas, and consequently have many more anglers than there are in the Bailiwick and yet they usually have just two or three major clubs.

In comparison the Bailiwick is almost awash with sea angling clubs. In March 2011 there were seven and at one time there were as many as 17!

Initially this would appear to be an ideal situation. It gives anglers a wide choice to join a club that suits their style of fishing and seems to confirm that local angling is in a healthy, thriving position.

Unfortunately, this is not necessarily the case. So many clubs for such a relatively small total number of available anglers, has meant that some of the newer, smaller clubs have struggled to survive. As we have already noted some find they cannot attract enough members to make the club administratively viable and this has forced a number to fold up in recent years.

In addition, all clubs, both large and small, tend to be very insular in their views and attitudes. As a result, angling administrative efforts in the Bailiwick has become very fragmented. Each club "does its own thing" which has meant that there is very little collective will to come together for the good of the sport as a whole.

One aspect that clearly illustrates the problem is the complete lack of facilities that anglers elsewhere take for granted.

In the majority of United Kingdom angling centres, clubs have quite palatial premises, with meeting rooms, bars, games rooms, locker rooms and even restaurants or cafeterias. Where the club premises are situated right on the sea-front which is often the case, there are usually many other facilities provided that help the angler to enjoy his sport. These can include boat launching, retrieval and storage, designated areas where competitions are organised (including registration and the weighing in of catches) and even places set aside where fish can be gutted, cleaned and filleted.

Although angling is one of the Bailiwick's biggest participant sports, the local angler can enjoy none of these things.

The size of the local angling fraternity may not justify the grandeur of the comprehensive club premises found elsewhere, but the local angling community surely deserves a modest angling headquarters.

Many feel that the main reason that this has not been achieved is due to the ease with which the Bailiwick angler can enjoy his sport.

Some United Kingdom anglers have to travel dozens, or even hundreds of miles to get to their chosen angling venue. They therefore need the facilities when they arrive and again before they depart on the long journey home.

In the Bailiwick anglers can get to their shore fishing spot, or boat embarkation point in minutes and argue that there is no need for all the things that are necessary elsewhere.

Visiting anglers, national angling administrators and journalists from the national angling press are absolutely astounded that in such a thriving angling community there is nowhere for anglers to get together socially and that the registration and weighing-in of both open and club competitions are forced to take place in car parks or other convenient spots!

Central Angling Administrative Organisations

There has been efforts to try and bring Bailiwick anglers together in an attempt to improve the situation, but to date all have failed.

In the late 1970's an ad-hoc investigation committee was formed to consider all aspects on the possible formation of a central administrative body. As a result the Guernsey Federation of Sea Anglers was formed in March 1981 under the presidency of Harold Bewey.

The much-loved and respected Harold Bewey. One of the Bailiwick's finest angling administrators who was the first President of the Guernsey Federation of Sea Anglers. Seen here with a fine plaice.

For a while it enjoyed success and support. Its membership, through both its affiliated clubs and personal members rose to nearly 300 at one stage.

In 1986 it even organised an International Boat Angling Festival, but this proved to be a major disappointment for it only attracted six visiting anglers!

By 1988 support for the Federation was failing rapidly. Apathy and increasing disinterest from the angling community sounded the death knell for the organisation and by the middle of 1989 it ceased to exist.

In spite of the failure of the Federation a hard core of anglers remained convinced that a central angling organisation was essential. A number of issues were arising that could adversely affect angling in the Bailiwick.

Changes in fishing laws were being considered, restrictions on access for anglers at some parts of the harbours were being experienced for the first time, and there were discussions being held on the possible creation of marine conservation areas. Angling needed a central body that would be able to meet these challenges by putting forward the anglers' point of view.

As a consequence the Guernsey Association of Angling Clubs was formed in July 1990. Although the majority of Bailiwick clubs joined the new association, it was to suffer the same fate as the old Federation.

In spite of sterling work by committee members, support from local anglers was abysmal. Eventually a number of clubs didn't bother to renew their membership and in 1996 it just seemed to slip into oblivion!

In 1997 the States Sea Fisheries Committee proposed the introduction of a new Fishing Ordinance.

They were aware that sections of the Ordinance, particularly those covering the laws on the use of trots and nets in inshore waters would be of great interest to the angling fraternity.

The committee were keen to involve the anglers in discussion on the matter, but soon realised they didn't know who to contact.

They made a strong plea to the angling community to form a central body that could act as a liaison point, not just on this occasion but to be available to discuss all matters that would be relevant to angling in the future.

As a result the Sea Anglers Representative Committee was formed. Its size was kept deliberately small, just five members, and its mandate was solely to provide the basic function as requested by the Sea Fisheries Committee.

There was no intention of SARC taking over the aims and objects of the defunct Guernsey Federation of Sea Anglers or Guernsey Association of Angling Clubs. Initially it was to prove a success. A good rapport with the Sea Fisheries Committee was quickly established. The discussions that were held not only had a direct bearing on the final wording of the new Ordinance, but the SFC became aware, at first hand, of the anglers' problems and concerns for the future. SARC was absolutely delighted when the SFC invited anglers to put forward a candidate to fill a vacancy on the committee, and recommended his election at a States meeting.

This was just what the angling community had always wanted. Official States recognition, not only of the sport itself, but also its value to the economy of the island. It would enable anglers to make their views known at the highest level and be part of the policy making process.

Sadly, it was all to come to naught! At the May 1998 States meeting the commercial fishermen, who were strongly against angling representation, put forward a candidate even though they already had one representative on the Committee. They received strong support from a senior States member, who made an impassioned speech in favour of the fishermen. This resulted in overwhelming support for the fishermen's candidate, who was elected by a huge margin.

A second effort was made to get a seat in the SFC at a later date, but this was also unsuccessful.

In spite of the disappointment on the failure of the anglers' representative to get elected, there is no doubt that the setting up of SARC was a great step forward.

Regular meetings between the SFC and SARC were to continue for a while, but inevitably SARC was to experience the same fate as the Guernsey Federation of Sea Anglers and the Guernsey Association of Angling Clubs.

A joint approach to the relevant authorities by SARC and the SFC concerning the provision of these elusive angling facilities had got no-where, and there seemed to be little enthusiasm for further discussion on other matters.

The last joint meeting of SARC and SFC was held in December 2003, with the combined group being formally wound up in March 2004.

207

Chapter 7 - Freshwater

The Bailiwick has very few indigenous freshwater fish. This is hardly surprising for an area that has no rivers, lakes or large natural ponds.

Historical text dating from 1840 confirms that the only indigenous species were the stickleback and the migratory common eel, both of which existed in ditches and douits (streams).

It appears that the first fish to be imported into the Bailiwick, were carp, which were brought into the area by members of early religious orders who kept and bred the fish for food.

The thriving granite trade in the late 1800's and the early part of the 1900's was to be responsible for enormous changes to the local aquatic environment.

As the trade declined the large number of quarries that had been excavated fell into disuse. They were abandoned and allowed to fill with water. Some were ultimately filled in, but many still remain.

As Guernsey's population grew the increasing need for a guaranteed supply of water became a major requirement.

The States Water Board, which came into being in 1920, purchased a number of quarries, chiefly in the north of Guernsey and installed a separate mains system to supply untreated water to the up-and-coming horticultural industry, which was taking over from granite as the island's main source of income and prosperity. Although this went a long way to satisfy the industry's needs, it was realised that the increasing demand from domestic consumers would also need to be addressed, and in October 1936 the States approved the construction of St. Saviour's Reservoir.

Building began in 1938 but World War II and the occupation of the islands by the German forces caused its construction to be halted. After the war the work recommenced and the dam was finally completed in 1947, thus creating the largest area of freshwater in the Bailiwick.

It wasn't to be long before these new water-filled areas would see the introduction of fish.

Not all tomato growers obtained their water from the States supply. Some had access to private quarries and pumped water from them directly on to their properties.

Apparently some of these growers introduced fish into the quarries as a crude indicator of the water's purity. If the fish died then the water was considered too toxic to irrigate the precious grape and tomato crops.

Other fish were imported to stock ornamental garden ponds or aquariums, while some fish undoubtedly arrived in egg form attached to the imported aquatic plants.

It was inevitable that unwanted fish were soon finding their way into the quarries. They were put in by owners who had lost interest in keeping fish or found they had too many due to their fish breeding and multiplying!

As a result of all this unplanned and rather haphazard stocking, the previously barren areas of water soon became home to a surprising number of different species of fish.

Over the same period the quarries themselves were undergoing a quite startling natural transformation.

The stark stone quarry faces and adjacent work areas which had reverberated to the noise, dust and bustle of industry soon became covered with trees and bushes as nature started to repair the ravages left by man's activities.

The quarries were completely changed from ugly, unattractive areas into quiet and quite beautiful parts of the landscape, a haven not just for the newly introduced fish, but also to birdlife and a multitude of different wild flowers and plants. (see page 218)

It's not surprising that local anglers soon began to consider the potential of all these new freshwater facilities.

Guernsey Trout Society

In 1933 the Guernsey Trout Society was formed, almost certainly the first ever angling club in the Bailiwick.

The society was soon to give more impetus to the introduction of fish, albeit in a more controlled manner.

They began to stock some of the quarries with trout and this activity continued right up to the German occupation in 1940.

Following the completion of St. Saviour's Reservoir in 1947 the Society sought and obtained permission to introduce trout and stocking began in March of that year.

Fishing was allowed to begin in September 1948 and has continued with just one small break until the present day.

The interruption was in 1973 when a toxic algae caused widespread mortality amongst the trout. Thankfully this problem was to be short-lived.

The intention had always been to keep the reservoir as a trout only water. In spite of the considerable costs and difficulty of obtaining and transporting fish from the United Kingdom this policy has been supported by regular and frequent stocking of both brown and rainbow trout.

One can therefore understand the concern of the Society's members when in 1983 carp were seen in the reservoir. The presence of the carp has always remained a complete mystery for it has never been established how they got into the water, although in all probability it was someone who decided to get rid of unwanted fish and thought that the reservoir was as good a place as any!

Worse was to follow, for in 1984 rudd appeared. These multiplied at an alarming rate and are now present in vast numbers. It is believed that the original rudd escaped from an ornamental pond into a stream that feeds the reservoir.

There have been a few attempts to catch and transfer the coarse fish to other waters in the island, but due to the enormous numbers present, these efforts have had very little impact, and the unwanted species continue to be a problem.

There is absolutely no doubt that the Guernsey Trout Society has been an incredible success story.

For over 75 years they have quietly, efficiently and without fuss achieved their aims, and enjoyed their sport.

The Society are a private club, who have to pay an annual lease to be able to use the reservoir.

As it is their only water it has been necessary for the club to have strict policies to ensure that the well being of the water and its associated environment is maintained.

It is a "fly fishing only" water. Spinning and float fishing are not allowed. In addition members have a limit on the number of fish they can take from the reservoir on each fishing session and over a calendar year.

They have a strict membership limit and only members of the club are permitted to fish in the reservoir.

Although there is always a queue of anglers wishing to join, with usually a four or five year wait, the Society do not allow this to influence their necessary policy to restrict the size of the club.

Coarse Fishing

The start of organised coarse fishing was to take a bit longer!

A very few anglers who had access to private waters had enjoyed a small amount of occasional fishing for some years, but it was not until 1973 that the first real moves were made to discover the overall freshwater angling potential.

It was Martin Nickolls and Peter Sherbourne who decided to undertake an in-depth research, which amazingly was to take over three years to complete. They studied large scale maps of Guernsey, made a comprehensive list of the surprisingly large number of freshwater areas and went on to complete the difficult task of confirming the ownership of each site.

Then followed the tricky problem of obtaining permission to have access to each site. It would be necessary to do some fishing in all the waters in order to assess their potential.

It was to take much discussion, correspondence and negotiation before this hurdle was overcome.

A few private owners steadfastly refused to grant permission but finally clearance was given by the States Water Board who owned most of the sites, and also from the majority of private owners.

Over the next two years Martin and Peter methodically visited and fished all the waters, where access had been approved.

It wasn't an easy task. If the two anglers didn't have any bites did it mean the water was devoid of fish? Were they using the wrong bait? Was it the wrong time of the year? — or were the fish there, but off the feed?

After much effort and deliberation, it became fairly clear that a few sites were barren, but the majority did contain fish, to varying degrees!

Carp, eels, rudd, tench, trout and goldfish were the main species caught.

Finally a small group of enthusiasts got together and formed the Guernsey Freshwater Angling Society. Over the next few years some effort was made to catch and move fish from one water to another in an attempt to spread the fish out more evenly and provide a more balanced stock in each water.

Sadly, all the considerable effort expended to date, was to come to nought. Interest seemed to wane, Martin Nickolls one of the early prime movers in the project left the island and problems of access to some waters was causing difficulties.

Consequently by the early 1980's it seemed possible that coarse fishing in the island could once more sink back into obscurity!

A meeting of the GFAS held on 31 May 1983 seemed to confirm the worst.

The society's membership was down to five and no annual subscription fees had been received from the members for three years.

It seemed that the only member who was prepared to see the society continue was Martyn Foxen, who now found himself virtually as the sole survivor!

However it was to be due to his persistence that coarse fishing was to have a future in the island.

He refused to give up and soon teamed up with David Copperwaite, a freshwater angling enthusiast who had recently become an island resident.

An advertisement was placed in the personal column of the Guernsey Press in the summer of 1983 asking anyone interested in freshwater fishing to get in contact.

It was to prove the major turning point in the Society's history. Within weeks the membership was up to 15 and just continued growing.

The new committee enthusiastically tackled the existing problems, drawing up new rules and policies which would ensure that the Society would have a firm foundation on which to base its future.

What size membership that the club should support was an early decision that had to be made.

Unlike their sea-angling colleagues, the Society's waters covered a finite area and, therefore, could not support an infinite number of anglers.

Two main factors influenced the decision on the ultimate size of the Society.

One was the environment surrounding the water at the various quarry sites. Steep sides in parts of the quarries and the luxuriant undergrowth meant that the number of available fishing spots, or swims, at each venue was restricted. In addition there were the more mundane problems, such as access and parking.

The other main factor was the limitations imposed by the States Water Board who own the majority of the waters. They imposed a limit on the total number of anglers that would be given permission to have access on to their properties.

It's therefore no surprise they have had to copy their Guernsey Trout Society colleagues and adopt a firm policy concerning the size of their membership in spite of the fact that there is sometimes a waiting list of anglers wishing to join.

The membership is organised into two sections. Anglers joining for the first time become associate members, who are only allowed to fish in the Society's privately owned waters. As vacancies occur associate members move up to become full members who have full access to all 11 waters currently used by the Society.

At the present time the size of the membership is restricted to 90 full members and 45 associate members.

The undoubted success of the club since that turning point in 1983 has not been achieved without considerable work and effort.

Many hours have been spent by members clearing undergrowth to give access to fishing swims, removing rubbish from the quarry surrounds and from the water, removing fallen trees and even providing fishing pontoons where access to the water would have been impossible to provide in any other way.

There have been problems with drastically falling water levels in times of drought, due to natural evaporation, water extraction by the States Water Board which is, of course, absolutely essential in order to maintain the island's water supplies and use of the water by private owners to irrigate their gardens and commercial crops.

Conversely, access paths and fishing platforms have often been submerged after periods of heavy rainfall!

In the 1990's the Society took a positive step to safeguard their future by deciding to purchase their own waters, a big decision and a major financial commitment for such a small organisation. As a result they became the owners of La Lande Quarry and part owners of Le Lorier Quarry. In 2006 they made a decision to add to their waters by embarking on a major development to create a brand new fishing lake in the Marais area. Work started on this ambitious project in 2007.

It was completed in 2010, and officially opened for fishing on June 5th 2011. It will be known as Richard McCarthy Memorial Lake in rememberance of a much respected member who tragically died at a young age.

As we have already learnt there were fish in many of the waters long before the GFAS was formed. Nevertheless the two Societies have had regular restocking programmes covering many different species.

Consequently it's largely due to their efforts that there are now at least 13 different species in local freshwater sites: carp, grass carp, chub,rudd, roach, tench, eels, brown trout, rainbow trout, catfish, bream, perch and crucian carp. (see page 139)

Shags and cormorants have been unwelcome guests. They have become almost permanent residents on some waters, helping themselves to an easy food supply by taking the fish, many of which had been introduced by the Societies at considerable trouble and expense!

Over the years the GFAS have built up a full programme of competitions for its members, and each year do battle with the Jersey Freshwater Angling Association members, not only in the inter-island team match but also in the Channel Islands Individual Freshwater Championship. This annual competiton is now the only inter-island fishing events that is still held.

One major highlight of the society's history must be the incredible success enjoyed in 1992. David Copperwaite, Mike Weysom and Martyn Foxen were part of the Channel Island team that entered the World Freshwater Angling Championships for the first time.

It was fished on the River Erne at Enniskillen in Northern Ireland and to everyone's astonishment, not least the team itself, they finished third of the 39 countries taking part and won the bronze medal, pushing the reigning champions England back into fourth place!

Make no mistake this was an absolutely incredible result. The Channel Island anglers were up against the world's best, who regularly fish the lucrative coarse fishing match circuit in the United Kingdom or on the Continent — anglers who are household names in their own countries, many being heavily sponsored by the world's top tackle manufacturers.

The Channel Island team, bronze medal winners in the 1992 World Freshwater Angling Championships (left to right) Bill Twigger (Jersey), Martyn Foxen (Guernsey), Eddie Scoltock (Jersey), Mike Weysom (Guernsey), David Copperwaite (Guernsey), Phil Noel (Jersey), Peter Chesney (Jersey), and Graham Carver (Jersey)

It was akin to a Channel Islands football team entering and getting to the semi-finals of the World Cup, losing the semi-final but going on to beat England in the third/fourth place play-off!

The comparatively recent availability of local freshwater angling has created quite a challenge for local sea anglers.

Those who have been fortunate enough in obtaining membership of either of the two freshwater societies, have almost experienced a culture shock.

They found they had to put aside their 12 or 20lb class rods, their large fixed spool or multiplying reels, the 20lb BS lines, 5/0 hooks, six ounce grip leads, the heavy floats and the large baits and deal with small reels, line as light as one lb BS, tiny shot, small stick floats, hooks down to size 14 or less and baits that comprise of maybe just one maggot or an artificial fly.

They found they had an incredible lot to learn about choosing the right float for the prevailing conditions or the right fly to tempt the wily trout.

They realised more accurate casting was required. Casting a heavy weight and large bait a considerable distance out into the open sea was one thing, but placing a light float into the precise spot between overhanging bushes, or casting a fly to just the exact spot where the trout are rising was to prove much more difficult.

The sea anglers who had fished for mullet had the easiest transition for mullet fishing had become steadily more refined over the years with anglers using very light tackle for that shy species.

Suffice to say the sea anglers acquitted themselves very well and soon became quite proficient.

Some even switched to fishing with freshwater poles, which for the uninitiated, literally means angling without a reel, the pole being extended in sections to enable the bait to be placed over the spot where the fish are feeding. The poles are made of extremely light but strong materials and are often capable of being extended to well over 40 feet!

A number of sea anglers adapted so well to all aspects of freshwater angling that they soon began to enjoy considerable success. Bailiwick freshwater records fell to their rods, they began to figure in the GFAS annual list of prizewinners and a few even managed to beat the more experienced coarse fishermen who had previously fished in the United Kingdom, to win the GFAS championship!

Although there are fewer than 250 freshwater anglers in the Bailiwick, the local tackle dealers rose to the challenge and now stock a wide range of freshwater tackle and accessories which had not previously been available locally, at least not in such a range or quantity.

Fly rods, reels, lines and flies to cater for the trout fisherman's needs, while fishing poles, coarse fishing rods, keepnets, low breaking strain lines, small barbless hooks, a vast range of freshwater floats and shot are just part of a comprehensive selection of gear now held for the coarse fisherman.

Coarse fishing bait has also become available, including carp boilies, ground baits, worms and regular imports of live maggots.

Bearing in mind all the effort and enthusiasm that has been made to create all the freshwater facilities, it was extremely sad that comparitively few anglers had the opportunity to participate.

It was clear why this situation existed. Due to the comparatively small amount of water available and the associated restrictions it meant that the societies had no option other than to limit the number of anglers that could be accommodated and naturally put their members first.

There is, however an increasing opportunity for non-society members, local or visitor to sample the local coarse fishing potential!

The Guernsey Freshwater Angling Society do allow a minimal number of outsiders to fish their waters, but the non-member is restricted to privately owned waters and must be accompanied by a full member of the Society at all times. The society do not issue day tickets to individual anglers visitors or locals.

The breakthrough for day ticket accessability came with the creation of two new coarse fisheries.

In 1996 a private fishing syndicate led by Chris Hubbard, developed a new half acre fishery called Willow Lake on a virgin site situated in the Marais area of the Vale. Members of the syndicate can enjoy the well stocked waters which contain bream, tench, chub, carp, koi carp and orfe. They do issue day tickets, which can be obtained from Mick's Fishing Supplies, the tackle shop at Aladdins Cave at Les Canus.

In 2006 new owners decided to develop Les Rouvets Lake as a coarse fishing venue. The large lake used to be part of the Tropical Gardens tourist attractions in the 1970's, but since it closed down it has been inaccessable to the public.

Nature took over and the lake and it's surroundings almost disappeared. Extensive clearance of the tangled mass of brambles and undergrowth has been undertaken, both around the lake itself and the access paths. Work has also proceeded in providing swims for anglers at various points around the lake.

Species known to be in the lake are carp, rudd, roach, eels and bream. There are plans to add other species including tench. Full membership to fish the lake is available, but day ticket holders are particularly welcome, and can get their day passes from either the owners Richard and Cindy Lawson or from Mick;s Fishing Supplies. (see page 218)

In Alderney there used to be a privately owned quarry that contained a few trout and coarse fish. Fishing could be done with the owners permission but all that became irrelevant as the quarry was almost completely drained during a period of drought conditions!

It seemed that was the end of coarse fishing in the northern isle, but in November 2010 Jon Gates established a new coarse fishing facility at Corblets Quarry (see page 141)

Initially it was stocked with carp but there are plans to introduce tench at a later date. Anglers who have fished the new water have been surprised to land a number of brown trout, no doubt survivors of those drought conditions. Annual membership of the fishing facility is available as well as day tickets. Both can be obtained from either Alderney Angling and Sports in Victoria Street or Jon Gates.

Chapter 8 — Competitions

When it comes to competitions, Bailiwick anglers are spoilt for choice. A comprehensive range of competitions are organised by the angling clubs for their members, but in addition there are numerous annual open events that can be entered by residents and visitors alike.

As we have already seen the first open competition was the 1937 event run by the fledgling Guernsey Sea Anglers Club, which was also responsible for the introduction of the first open competition of the modern era in 1966.

Since then the number of annual open matches has grown enormously. Sponsorship obtained from local companies not only gave angling clubs the necessary financial assistance to help in the introduction of open matches but also ensured that the organisers could offer a worthwhile range of prizes and awards.

From humble beginnings when the prizes were worth just a few pounds, the value of the awards has escalated to almost unimaginable heights. A holiday in Florida, gold plated reels, cash prizes of £3,000, a hi-fi, a microwave oven, tackle vouchers worth hundreds of pounds and rods and reels are just a few of the items won by anglers in recent years. In 1998 a new high was reached with individual prizes of £10,000 on offer!

The majority of clubs took up insurance to cover the pay-out of such huge amounts.

However, when these prizes were starting to be won with some regularity, the premiums charged by the insurance companies became prohibitive, and as a consequence the big cash awards have dropped considerably to a more sensible level.

Tackle dealers have naturally been the main source of sponsorship for club-organised events but they have also held open competitions of their own, for they saw this as an additional opportunity to advertise and promote their businesses.

However, problems were to arise. There is no doubt that the best shore fishing in the Bailiwick is in the period from mid-August through to the end of the year. As nearly all the opens are shore competitions, they tend to be compressed each year into a comparatively short period in the autumn months. Naturally club shore matches follow a similar pattern.

The result is a fixture pile-up to the point where it has become difficult for club and open organisers to find a clear date with a suitable tide to fit in their proposed events.

With such a congested programme, with some competitions even clashing with others on the same date, anglers had to become selective, and as a result support for the competitions started to decline.

The number of annual opens reached a peak in the late 1980's but due to the fall in support from the anglers, it was inevitable that some would be discontinued.

Fur and Feather

The Fur and Feather that was started by the Guernsey Sea Anglers Club in 1966 has proved to be the most resilient of all the open events. Each year in the 45 years up to 2010, it has been held on a Sunday in late November or early December depending on the best suitable tide. The only year it was not held was 2007 when severe gales on the planned and rescheduled dates caused it to be cancelled. It was intended very much to be a fun competition to be held just before Christmas and it certainly achieved that aim. It set out to attract all anglers, including women and juniors, the casual angler as well as the most dedicated. Consequently the match has always been kept to a modest length, four hours in the early days, seven hours in more recent times. The prizes have been awarded across a whole range of different concepts in an attempt to cater for all anglers' tastes. The heaviest bags, the best fish, the top fish of each species, the most different species, the greatest number of roselet, special prizes for the women and juniors and team competitions have all been included at some time or other in the event's history. The prizes themselves have remained practically unchanged: Christmas fare, turkeys, chickens, meat vouchers, wines, spirits, chocolates and biscuits with fishing tackle vouchers being added in more recent years.

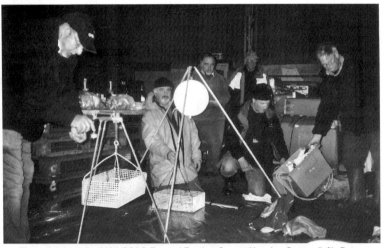

The weigh-in at the 2006 GSAC Fur and Feather Competition Joe Gomez (left), Peter Frise, Mike Weysom, Len Hall, John Davey and Dave Tostevin

The only major alteration came in 1991. In the previous year the club had given a questionnaire to all competitors, seeking their views on how the event could be improved. Except for the inaugural year when the competition was run on the club's points system the main prizes had always been awarded for the heaviest bags of the day. However it became clear from the replies that anglers wanted to see more emphasis placed on specimen fish. As a consequence the

A typical quarry scene where nature has covered the ravages of industry.

Part of Les Rouvets Lake. A water open to day ticket coarse anglers.

Peter Guille with the Bailiwick shore-caught record trigger fish. The 3-10-12 fish was caught at the Hog's Back in Sark in 2004.

Rosanne Guille with the 6-8-6 Bailiwick, Channel Island and British shore-caught record black bream which she landed at Sark's Creux Harbour in October 2001

Justin Robert with the 30-4-0 Bailiwick and Channel Island boat-caught record turbot caught at Banc au Nord in April 2005.

Paul Carre with his 65-14-10 Bailiwick and Channel Island shore-caught record conger caught at Bec du Nez while fishing in the 2000 Specimen Fish Hunt.

Shane Huxster with the Bailiwick and Channel Island shore-caught 3-1-0 record three bearded rockling caught on St Peter Port breakwater in August 2007

Jon Cataroche with his 11-0-5 John Dory caught on the Great Bank in May 2001. It is the Bailiwick and Channel Island boat-caught record.

Jason Le Noury with his 8-10-13 Bailiwick shore-caught ballan wrasse record. It also held the Channel Island and British records until beaten by a Jersey fish.

The 1-12-9 Bailiwick, Channel Island and British shore-caught cuckoo wrasse record landed by Mark Hooper in Herm in October 1999.

Shark Catches

The heaviest fish taken on rod and line ever to be landed in the Bailiwick. Des Bougourd with his 430-0-0 porbeagle shark. It was caught in Jersey waters in 1969 and gained the Jersey, Channel Island, British and World Records! Note the Domestos bottle float!

Surely the smallest shark ever caught in the Bailiwick. Blake Jackson with the 9-8-0 thresher caught off Alderney in 2007. The fish was returned alive.
(Picture by Chris Tett)

Proof - as if it were needed - that there are sharks in Bailiwick waters. A shark attack left visiting angler David Woolcombe with only half of his pollack!

Jamie Allen with the 295-8-6 Bailiwick record porbeagle shark caught in August 2007

The Bailiwick blue shark record. Captor Paul Priaulx (right) and Richard Le Ray hold up the 132-13-3 specimen that was caught in August 2002.

Raymond Fallaize with his 6-9-7 British, Channel Island and Bailiwick boat-caught record Couch's sea bream.

Simon Rowe with the Bailiwick and Channel Island shore-caught record bass. He landed the 18-6-5 fish at Pembroke while fishing in the 1999 Specimen Fish Hunt.

Sam Robins with a rare fish, the 1-12-12 shore record twaite shad caught while fishing in the 2008 Specimen Fish Hunt

Paris Broe Bougourd with the Bailiwick and Channel Island boat-caught record cuckoo wrasse. The 2-1-11 fish was caught at Anfre in January 2007.

Visiting angler Brett Adams with the Bailiwick and Channel Islands boat-caught bass. The 18-6-12 fish was caught in September 2005 in the Alderney Race from the English charter boat, Peace and Plenty from Weymouth.
(Apologies for picture quality)

Olly Bailey with his 5-9-1 Bailiwick and Channel Islands shore-caught record tub gurnard caught at the Chouet in June 2005.

Frederik Van Zyl with the 3-8-13 record boat caught pout caught in June 2008.

Almost a rare fish in local waters, John Holdaway with a 5-4-5 record shore-caught salmon caught at the Longue Hougue in February 2007.

Jonathan Beck with the 16-5-0 bull huss. This Bailiwick boat-caught record was caught east of Sark in June 2006.

Simon Newton with the 3-4-7 Bailiwick, Channel Island and British record shore caught Couch's sea bream caught at Bel Grave Bay in July 2008.

Lee Le Poidevin with the 8-0-2 Bailiwick and Channel Island record boat caught tub gurnard caught at Godine in July 2010

Charter boat skipper Richard Seager with his 14-3-0 boat record starry smooth hound caught east of Sark in October 2008.

club changed the format and decided to give equal top awards to both the captors of the heaviest bags and the best fishes of the day. The event has attracted steady support, with an average entry of 148 anglers, with the best attendance 235 in 1977.

Many anglers have done consistently well over the years, taking home armfuls of Christmas fare, but the most successful has been Stuart Tostevin.

Over the years 2000 to 2006 he never had to buy his Christmas dinner for he won the top heaviest bag award five times and the top fish prize twice!

The top year for catches was 1988, the year that enormous shoals of coalfish appeared in St. Peter Port Harbour as well as a number of other shore marks along Guernsey's east coast. It was no surprise that they would figure highly in both open and club competition results.

Nigel du Jardin landed 42 coalfish for 40-5-0 to win the competition, his catch being a record for the event at the time. The overall catch in the 1988 competition was also the best ever, 514 fish for a total weight of 678-15-0.

In 2004 Andy Carre created a new individual record for the competition when he caught one garfish, nine ballan wrasse, two grey mullet and one black bream for a total weight of 43-15-0. Ironically, Stuart Tostevin who came second, also broke the old record weighing in 13 ballan wrasse for 42-14-0.

In comparison the lowest weight to win the competition was the 6-13-0 landed by Ernie Baker in the inaugural event in 1966, when it was decided on the GSAC points system. The lowest when it was decided on the heaviest bag principle was the 7-11-0 brought back to the weigh-in by junior angler P. Barratt in 1972, the only occasion that a junior has won the top award.

Winners at the 2005 Fur and Feather, Daryl Butcher (left) and Stuart Tostevin, the most successful angler in the history of the competition

One of the outstanding fish in the events history was the 2-11-11 garfish caught by John Rothwell in 2002. Not only was it the Bailiwick shore record but it was landed at the most unlikely mark, the end of the Crown Pier! As from 2004 interest in the event steadily declined. In the years 2004-2006 and 2008-2010 the average entry slumped to 70. In fact in 2010 it reached an all time low with just 53 anglers taking part. As a result of the downturn the GSAC committee concidered the options for the future of the event and finally decided to discontinue the heaviest bag section.

The GSAC introduced three other open competitions, but none have stayed the course. They all became victims of the decline in anglers' support for open events in the early 1990's.

Open Roselet

The Open Roselet (atherine smelt) event was the least attractive of all the opens as far as prizes were concerned, for, it was run purely to raise money for Royal National Lifeboat Institution funds. It was a fairly low key event, lasting just three hours on an evening during the winter months. It was unique, for anglers who won the modest cash prizes were expected to give them back to help swell the donation to the RNLI!

The forerunner to the event was an annual inter-club roselet competition started by the GSAC in 1968. A number of clubs including the Telephone AC, Tektronix AC, Electrics AC and the Jamaica Inn AC took part. As the number of anglers representing each club differed, the result was calculated on a fish per rod basis. The competition ran for nine years, from 1968 to 1976. The GSAC won on four occasions the JIAC three and the Telephone AC and Tektronix AC one each. The top club score was 54.8 fish per rod achieved by the JIAC in 1972. Individual prizes were also awarded, the top anglers being John Hanley from the JIAC and Tiny Rogers from the GSAC with three wins each.

In 1977 it was decided to make it a straightforward individual event. The inaugural competition attracted 27 anglers who landed a total of 1,068 roselet.

Anglers at the GSAC Open Roselet Competition in 1980.

Dave Brouard had the honour of winning the first such competition, catching 163.

There was no competition in 1978, as it was decided to switch the timing of the event from November to January. In those days the first months of the year were considered the time for roselet. An old saying that went back many years was, "the colder the weather, the better for roselet." Consequently the next competition in the series was in January 1979. The move wasn't to prove a longterm success. The roselet seemed to change their habits. The shoals now peaked before Christmas and disappeared almost completely in the New Year. In 1984 it was decided to switch back to November It meant that there would be two competitions in 1984, the last January contest and the one that would initiate the new series of November events. The results of the two matches were to completely justify the club's decision.

In the January match Joe Gomez created a record by catching the lowest number of roselet ever to win the competition. In spite of using catbait(white ragworm) which is the best bait for this species, he could only manage to find eight! The total catch also created a record, just 28 being caught by the 16 entrants. In the November event, Richard Seager won with 163, with the total catch from 34 anglers amounting to 1,344! Ironically, Joe Gomez also holds the record for the best catch in the competition. In the 1992 event three records were established that were to remain unbeaten, Joe caught 231, 39 anglers took part and the total catch was 1,726.

The top anglers in the history of the event were Peter Frise and Joe Gomez with four wins each.

In 1996 only 12 anglers entered the competition, the lowest ever It was confirmation of what the club had realised for some time, support for the event was on a steady decline, in addition the competition was experiencing another more fundamental problem, it was becoming almost impossible to sell the roselet. The donation to the RNLI was made up of the anglers' entry fees, donations (usually returned winnings!) and proceeds from the sale of the catch. The fishmongers who had always helped out by selling the roselet, were finding it increasingly difficult to find customers who wished to buy the little silver fish.

The club committee agreed that the competition was no longer a viable proposition and with reluctance it was decided to drop it from the club calendar from 1997.

Since that time there has been a dramatic decline in fishing for roselet, generally.

Why this has happened is open to conjecture. The improvement in the shore fishing in the late autumn and winter months for other larger species, coupled with the closure of many of the best roselet spots, including the New Jetty and the White Rock area may well be to blame.

It is possible that the new generation of anglers cannot be bothered with such small fish, but whatever the reason interest in his species has almost completely disappeared.

Olympic Open

In 1974 the Guernsey Sea Anglers Club introduced a new competition called the Olympic Open. It was so called, as the main prize would be the Olympic Trophy. This had been donated to the club by its President, Ernie Baker, who, as one of the local tackle dealers was agent for the Olympic Tackle Company of Japan.

The new competition was to have a chequered history! It would be a six-hour roving shore event, similar to the Fur and Feather competition, but held earlier in the year. Prizes would be modest; in addition to the trophy there would be tackle vouchers, the top value of which was never going to exceed £40.

It appeared in the beginning that the club couldn't decide which part of the year to schedule the event. For the first two years it was held in the autumn, then it switched to May for one year. In 1977 and 1978 it was held in Herm in May, but finally settled as a Guernsey shore match in August.

In 1980 the competition was to experience a most unique and unpleasant situation.

An angler returned to the weigh-in with a catch weighing 28-

Alan Godfrey, winner of the Open Olympic Competition in 1979.

11-0. It consisted of nine garfish, one red mullet, eight mackerel, two bass and one grey mullet. The catch would have given him the top award for heaviest bag, plus four of the six subsidiary prizes.

The weighing-in team were suspicious of the catch. The mackerel split easily when being handled, allowing putrid innards to spill out and the bass had "white" eyes which suggested that the bass had been frozen and had not thawed out completely.

The GSAC committee came to the conclusion that the fish were stale and had not been caught during the match. On being informed of the committee's views, the angler became very indignant and withdrew his fish from the competition.

Previously there had been very little evidence of cheating in Bailiwick open competitions. There had been the odd bit of speculation and at times, some suspicions, but there had never been a situation where it had become necessary to institute formal proceedings against an angler.

229

This was very different. Although the club didn't take any immediate action other than to disqualify the angler concerned, it was to cause unpleasant repercussions throughout the local angling community. Prior to this open, the angler had been making entries in many other competitions, at club, island and even national level. Subsequently the organisers of all the other events thoroughly investigated his entries and involvement in their competitions. Almost without exception the anglers' entries in all the various contests were declared null and void, and he was expelled from all the clubs concerned. Even the Police became involved due to the possibility of fraud, but no formal charges were ever made.

Thankfully, this unfortunate episode was to prove to be an isolated case and no similar problems have occurred since.

The competition never became very popular. Although the number of entrants reached a maximum of 130 in the 1979 event, on average it only attracted 85 anglers, half that achieved by the Fur and Feather.

The first winner of the event was Ron Harris. His winning catch in the inaugural competition was 10 grey mullet for a total weight of 33-12-13. He repeated his success in the following year, with five grey mullet for 15-6-0. The best catch in the history of the competition was the 14 ballan wrasse for 39-0-0 caught by Michael de la Haye to win the 1987 event. The heaviest single fish was the 10-9-0 bull huss (greater spotted dogfish) which gave Chippy Corbet victory in the 1977 match

Chippy Corbet in 1977 with the 10-9-0 bull huss, that gave him victory in the GSAC Open Olympic.

that was held in Herm. By the end of the 1980's attendances at the Open were dropping steadily and when they reached a low of 46 in the 1991 match, the club decided to call it a day!

Open Conger

In 1986 there was a suggestion from club members that an Open. Conger competition should be held. The committee agreed and the first one took place in the following year. It was always scheduled to be held in November over a 14-hour period from the Saturday evening through to the Sunday morning. Prizes were fishing tackle vouchers and items of fishing gear, including rods and reels.

There were awards for both heaviest bags and the best fish. Initially it was a great success. The first event was won by Richard Seager who landed eight conger for 72-10-0. He was to be the only angler to record two wins in the competition, being successful again in 1990 when he landed five for 81-0-0. The best catch in the history of the competition was the six conger for 108-4-0 landed by Anthony le Pelley in 1991. Peter Frise caught the heaviest single fish, a 46-12-0 specimen in 1989. The competition came to an end in 1995. Not only was the anglers' support dwindling but conger catches fell alarmingly. The 1991 event saw 43 conger brought to the scales.

This went down to 14 in 1992, nine in 1993, eight in 1994 and finally six in 1995. Over the period 1990 to 1995 attendances slumped from the high of 78 down to just 35.

In 2003 Shaun Hindmarch and Rob Kerry decided to resurrect the competition, and managed to obtain sponsorship from Boatworks +.

It was won by Paul Frampton with a 34-14-0 fish, eight conger were caught for a total weight of 159-11-0.

Support for the event was disappointing for only 33 anglers entered.

This was lower than the worst supported competition in the nine years of the GSAC organized event.

Although there was some speculation that it would once again become an annual competition, it has not seen the light of day since!

Bass Festival

The Open Bass Festival, the event that would become the most popular competition in the Bailiwick's angling calendar, was introduced by the Guernsey Bass Anglers' Sportfishing Society in 1981. The event had a number of innovations. It was the first local open competition that would not be completed in a 24-hour period. It ran over the entire week-end from 7.00 p.m. on the Friday evening through to 7.00 p.m. on the Monday. This proved to be a most successful format which has been used, ever since. It was the first to offer cash prizes.

From the beginning the Society had been fortunate to obtain sponsorship. This enabled them to offer the most attractive prizes that had ever been presented to the winners of a local angling event. The top prize of £100 in the inaugural event was to grow to £300 in latter years. The Society were to be the pioneers of the really big prizes. In 1983 they included a prize of £1,000 for any angler who beat the current Bailiwick shore-caught bass record in the Festival. Within a few years the value of this special prize was to rise to £3,000.

Up to 2010 it has never been won! However the idea was copied by other opens in latter years and a number of anglers in those competitions did succeed in winning this major prize, but more of that later!

The new Bass Festival began life as a strictly shore event and at the start there was little indication of its future outstanding achievements.

The inaugural event in 1981 attracted 137 anglers which was considered to be a great success. They entered 14 fish over the 72- hour Festival. The honour of being the first winner fell to a visiting angler Bruce Yorke from Lewes, who caught an 11-5-6 bass.

Amazingly his winning fish was caught on a defrozen sandeel at Fermain on a bright calm and sunny afternoon and not from the more usual bass marks that were generally fished after dusk. The first local angler to win the event was Nigel du Jardin who was successful in the following year with a 9-8-7 fish.

The shore only Festival was to run for seven years, during which it attracted an average attendance of 173. The most fish in one year was 16 in 1986, when it was won by Adrian Bailey with a 13-7-6 specimen, the heaviest bass to win the competition up to that time. In 1987 catches slumped. Although 204 anglers entered only four fish were caught. The winner was Mick Price with a 6-8-12 fish, the smallest ever to win the main prize of £300, which meant the bass was worth £2.86 per ounce!

Possibly due in part to the poor results in 1987 the Society decided to introduce a boat section for the first time. This would be run in parallel with the shore competition over the same week-end. The Festival was immediately transformed! Attendances rocketed! No fewer than 333 anglers entered in 1988. This rose to a new high of 397 in 1991 and to a staggering 464 in 1992. This was easily a record, not just for the Festival itself but for all the open angling competitions held in the Bailiwick. The record still stood at the end of 2010.

Australian visitor Paul Berry with the 11-3-5 boat section winning bass in the 2005 GBASS Open

The first winners of the combined event were John Shuker, who had the honour of being the first-ever winner of the boat section with a 11-9-3 bass, and Charlie Le Garff who won the shore section with a 10-0-2 specimen. This enormous success would be sustained. For a number of years bass catches had been generally below par, but the 1990's would see a quite fantastic improvement in bass catches generally. This was reflected in the Festival results,

232

both as regards quantity and quality. Many fish over 10-0-0 would be caught in the competition with the top shore fish being Tim Froome's 14-0-2 bass in 1994. The best boat-caught bass was Denis McKane's 16-4-3 fish in 2007, the heaviest ever caught in any local bass festival. (see page 62) Louise Le Prevost became the first female angler to win the top prize in a local bass festival for she won the shore section with an 8-12-4 fish in 1993.

Carl Foulds with his 10-2-8 shore section winning bass in the 2004 GBASS Open.

Quite early on in the Festival's history the Society had introduced optional pools, something that was unique in local angling at the time. For the uninitiated this was basically the opportunity for the angler to bet on himself (or herself) to get top aggregate weight in the event, for although the Festival was a specimen fish contest with the prizes going to the captors of the best individual fish, the pools were usually awarded for the heaviest individual total weight taken during the Festival. The entry fee for each pool (boat or shore) was only £1 but as the payout could be well over £100, it's no surprise that anglers in the pool made certain to bring all their catches back to the weigh-in.

This situation coupled with the increase in bass catches generally, meant that Festival catches rose dramatically each year. In 1988, the first year with separate boat and shore sections, 50 bass were presented at the Festival's control centre. By 1992 this had risen to 184 which weighed a grand total of 1,031-2-2.

This began to be an embarrassment to GBASS. As a sportfishing organisation the Society realised that they could not continue to condone a situation where commercial size catches were being brought back to the weigh-in. Consequently as from the 1993 Festival the money pools were based on the top fish only. As a result the number of fish brought in for weighing in the following years fell quite dramatically.

Up to 2010 only one angler had won a top honour on three occasions. Mark Fletcher won the shore section in 1992 with an 8-11-5 fish, in 1997 with a 6-10-9 specimen, and finally had one of 9-5-5 to win in 2005. In 1995 the Society split the boat and shore sections over two separate dates, the shore competition being held in June and the boat competition in August. It wasn't a success, for only 162 anglers entered the shore section and 153 the boat section. In the following year it reverted to its original combined format, but surprisingly the number of entries only reached 247. This was disappointing bearing in mind the attendances achieved a few years before, but it was still higher than other opens were achieving at the time.

As we have seen in an earlier chapter, a second bass club was formed early in 1998 and as a result the Bailiwick had the rather unique situation of having two Bass Festivals in one year!

The first held in the year was the Bailiwick Bass Challenge which was held in July. This was organised by the new Bailiwick Bass Club which introduced a level of prizes that had never been experienced in the Bailiwick before.

The captors of the heaviest bass over the Bailiwick boat-caught or shore-caught records would each receive £10,000! The top prizes for the heaviest shore and boat-caught bass were £500.

Father and son have success in the GBASS 2009 festival.
Callum Mclaren (left) Junior winner with his 7-5-14 bass and Father Paul
with the 8-14-13 shore section winning fish.

The older Guernsey Bass Anglers Sportfishing Society scheduled their Open Festival for early August with the same level of prizes as in previous years. The top fish over the Bailiwick boat-caught record would receive £2,000, with £3,000 for the best fish over the Bailiwick shore-caught record. The top boat-caught bass would get £200 and the best shore-caught bass £300.

There was some speculation whether two Open Bass Competitions held within a month of each other would be a viable proposition. The attitudes of the Guernsey anglers would be the deciding factor.

Would they favour the event with the bigger prizes? — would they remain loyal to the older organisation and its competition? — or would they enter both?

In the end circumstances prevailed which meant that no conclusions could really be drawn!

234

The Bailiwick Bass Club event coincided with a period of awful weather with strong winds and outbreaks of rain that lasted the length of the weekend-long competition.

Boats could not get out beyond the shelter of the bays, and as a result there is no doubt that many anglers just didn't bother to enter.

The event attracted 170 anglers, but due to the conditions bass were hard to find. Only three boat-caught fish were landed, John Le Noury having the honour of catching the heaviest fish in the new competition, a 7-4-13 fish that gave him victory in the boat section. There were 11 shore-caught fish, the shore section winner being Matthew Reynolds with a 6-15-11 specimen. Needless to say many prizes including the two £10,000 awards were not won.

In comparison the Guernsey Bass Anglers' Sportfishing Society's Open Festival was blessed with perfect weather, sun, no wind, good visibility and calm seas, so it's probably not surprising that expectations were high that good catches including many double figure fish would be recorded.

It didn't happen! Only six shore-caught fish were caught, the shore section winner being Paul Clark with a 6-2-10 specimen; while the boat section saw just 20 bass, with Max Dorfner topping the catches with a 9-6-3 fish.

For the second time in the year no bass over 10-0-0 were caught and the top prizes went unclaimed.

Up to 2010 the top fish caught in the Bailiwick Bass Club Open were the 13-11-7 boat-caught specimen by Roger Berry in 2003 and the 9-8-6 shore-caught fish by John de la Mare in 1999. In 2007 a female angler beat all of her male colleagues to become the first woman to win the BBC bass festival, Caroline Froome with an 11-10-1 boat-caught specimen. (see page 62)

In 2010 there was an unusual result in the BBC open. For the first time in any local bass festival both shore and boat sections were won by junior anglers. Callum McLaren won the top shore prize with an 8-1-8 fish while Brandon La Touche took the boat award with a 9-1-1 specimen. (see page 65)

At the beginning there was real concern whether two bass festivals each year would be a viable proposition.

There was even some conjecture whether an amalgamation into one bigger annual festival would be a better option. Such a move in the future would seem very unlikely, for Guernsey anglers have continued to give sufficient support to both events.

It is just as well they did for in 2010 a third open festival was added to the competitive angling program. The BBC introduced a spring open. The weekend long shore event is held in memory of Jason Piriou, a much loved and respected member who died suddenly while shore fishing for bass. All proceeds of the event go to a charity chosen by the family. The inaugural event held in February 2010 got off to a slow start. Although 56 anglers entered no fish were caught. It was rearranged for late April when 66 took part. 4 bass were caught, the event being won by Kevin Handley who had fish of 9-1-4 and 4-14-4. In future years the open will be held in May.

The halcyon days of the late 1980's and early 1990's when 300 to 450 anglers took part in the GBASS open are gone.

Entries for both of the summer festivals are now in the 150 to 250 range which is more than enough for both events to continue.

The two bass organisations even run an inter-club competition in conjuction with the two events.

Winners in the 2005 Quayside Marine & Leisure Bailiwck Bass Challenge - Paul Benstead with the 8-8-5 shore section winning fish and Julie Crittell with the 7-3-6 specimen which won the women's prize.

Mullet Open

In 1986 the Guernsey Mullet Club followed the lead taken by the Guernsey Bass Anglers Sportfishing Society and organised their own open competition. It would be run as a six-hour roving shore event, usually in the October of each year, although in more recent times it was held in January or February. It would be open to all anglers, including women, juniors and visitors.

The Open managed to obtain sponsorship right from the beginning and the prizes on offer were fishing tackle, including rods and reels for the top awards and fishing tackle vouchers for the subsidiary prizes. Mullet are extremely exciting and satisfying to catch and invariably produce a spirited fight on the light tackle that must be used to catch this shy species. As a result some anglers have become mullet fanatics, pursuing this one species to the exclusion of everything else. However, many other anglers feel that there is almost a mystique surrounding the species. The mullet's finicky nature means that different techniques, more suitable for freshwater angling are needed to become a successful mullet angler.

As a consequence mulleting is considered by some to be a rather specialist form of sea angling and therefore they do not appear to have the same overall attraction to anglers as bass and other species.

Probably, as a result, the Mullet Open has not achieved the same level of support as the Bass Festival, or indeed the majority of the other open events.

Nevertheless, it has received steady and enthusiastic support from the mullet anglers, with a top attendance of 67 being reached in 1998 and an average attendance of 44 over the first 26 years of its history. From 1986 to 1990 it was run on the heaviest bag concept. However Bailiwick anglers were progressively becoming more in favour of competitions based on the best specimen fish as opposed to heaviest bags. In view of this trend the Guernsey Mullet Club decided to run the open on a heaviest fish basis as from 1991.

The first competition in 1986 attracted 34 anglers who brought 12 mullet back to the scales.The heaviest bag recorded in the period 1986 to 1990 was a weight of 15-7-0 achieved by Robert Foss in 1990. His catch was seven mullet, the biggest weighing 4-10-0.

Mike Weysom has been, by far, the most successful angler in the event's history, winning the competition on five occasions.

He had the honour of being the first winner in the event's inaugural competition in 1986 with a bag of four mullet weighing 5-14-8.

Ironically his next success was in 1991, the first year of the new format, when his winning fish was a 4-4-0 specimen.

In 2002 he won with the heaviest fish recorded in the Open up to that time, one of 6-3-3.

Incredibly his fourth win in 2006, was with a fish of 3-8-11, the smallest ever to win the heaviest specimen prize.

Mark Thomson (left) winner of the 2004 rearranged Mullet Open with his 4-12-8 fish with second place Charmaine Slimm 3-12-0

In 2008 the club celebrated it 25th anniversery. To honour the occasion the open was extended to run over two weekends in February and April with the event culminating in a presentation evening. It was won by Tim Cotterill with the heaviest mullet a 6-4-7 fish. The new format of the two weekends was to be retained for future years. In 2009 Mike Weysom recorded his fifth victory in the open competition with a 5-8-11 specimen.

The only other anglers to win the event more than once was Bill Dowinton who was successful in 1988 and 1993, and Andy Le Lerre in 2010 and 2011.

The 2004 Open proved to be a most bizarre event, for it established a most unwanted record. There was a good turn out of 60 anglers, but not one fish was caught, the first and only time this has ever happened in a Bailiwick Open Festival. It was refished a fortnight later, when eight mullet were caught, the winner being Mark Thomson with a 4-12-8 fish.

Alderney Angling Festival
Another new open event that first saw the light of day in 1986 was the Alderney Angling Festival.

This was, and still is, the longest competition in the Bailiwick's angling calendar, running for a complete week from Saturday to Saturday. It has been by far, the most successful open event in attracting visiting anglers to the Bailiwick. Every year the attendance is boosted by many anglers from both the United Kingdom and Jersey, who are obviously keen to sample the magnificent fishing offered by the Bailiwick's northern isle.

The fishing potential in Alderney is confirmed by the fact that in 2010 it held four British shore records and 14 Baiiwick shore records which represents nearly 30% of the Bailiwick record list. Surely an incredible achievement for an island that measures only 3 1/2 miles long by 1 1/2 miles wide!

The Festival is a shore specimen fish competition open to all anglers, including women and juniors, with prizes being awarded for the top five specimens in a number of categories including black bream, conger, bass, plaice/sole, ballan wrasse, grey mullet and all other species.

Sponsorship has meant that attractive cash prizes have been on offer since the start of the Festival. The total has climbed to over £6,000 in recent years, including a £3,000 prize for any angler breaking a British Record during the competition.

Other opens offer a similar prize but in 1991 the Festival had the distinction to become the first to pay it out! In view of Alderney's reputation for producing so many specimen fish it's an achievement that had been anticipated for some time and the only surprise was that it had taken six years to happen.

It was Jonathan Reeves who hit the jackpot, his winning fish being a 3-0-4 golden grey mullet. With a number of subsidiary prizes his total winnings came to £3,350 making his fish worth £69.43 per ounce! It was ironic that Jonathan had held the British Record for golden grey mullet on a previous occasion with a 2-12- 12 fish, but this had subsequently been beaten. His catch in the Festival meant that besides winning the cash prize he also regained his national record status.

It is common practice for open competition organisers to cover the possibility of such a big win by taking out insurance cover. Naturally the insurance company will not pay out until the record claim has been formally approved by the British Record (Rod- Caught) Fish Committee. As they only meet twice a year and had met just prior to the Festival, Jonathan had to be patient and wait six months to collect his winnings!

In 1986 the first event had been held in August and attracted 68 anglers. However, as from the following year it was rescheduled to an October date, where it has remained ever since. Interest in the new Festival grew rapidly and reached a high of 207 in 1990, which later settled down to an average attendance of 133.

The Festival has always attracted the keen specimen hunting anglers which has produced a friendly, yet highly competitive event. Probably as a result it has not been possible for one or two anglers to dominate the competition. Some anglers have been very successful and have won numerous prizes, sometimes spread over a number of years, but the real story of the Festival is not so much the participants but the stream of superb specimens that have been caught.

If we look at the records of the first 25 years of the event up to 2010 it will become apparent just how good the results have been.

No fewer than 35 ballan wrasse over 7-0-0 were caught, including three over 8-0-0. The top wrasse was the 8-5-10 fish caught by Jersey angler Tim Morley in 1997. Women anglers also enjoy success in the Festival for in 1996 Lucy Earl-Davies had the second best wrasse, her 8-2-8 fish giving her the award for the best fish in the competition in that year.

Conger was another successful species with 24 over 40-0-0 being landed, the top specimen being a 57-0-0 fish caught by UK angler Alan Kershaw in 1993.

There was a terrific upsurge in black bream catches throughout the Bailiwick in the second half of the 1990's and the Festival results reflect this trend with 55 over 3-8-0 being caught. They were topped by a 5-1-2 specimen caught by Guernsey angler Jason Le Noury in 2005.

Alderney is noted for its grey mullet so it's no surprise that 43 over 5-0-0 have been landed, the best a 7-1-14 fish by UK angler Shane Roach in 1996. (What a great name for an angler!).

The Festival has produced a steady stream of double-figure bass with 19 over 10-0-0 being caught. The best was a 16-3-12 fish caught by Mick Maurice in 2002.

Four pollack over 10-0-0 have been caught, heaviest 12-7-8 by UK angler Steve Harder in 1998.

Ten sole over 4-0-0 were caught, best one 4-14-2, 12 plaice over 4-0-0, best 5-11-0 and 14 bull huss (greater-spotted dogfish) over 10-0-0, the heaviest weighing 12-13-6.

There were red mullet up to 3-0-4, undulate ray up to 14-2-2 as well as many excellent specimens in many other species including cuckoo wrasse, garfish, pout, small-eyed ray and Couch's sea bream.

239

A number of national and Bailiwick record fish were caught. There was the 3-0-4 golden grey mullet of Jonathan Reeves which obviously attained national and Bailiwick record status, but there was also the Bailiwick record trigger fish of 3-4-4 caught by Jersey angler Serge Keenan in 1994 and the Bailiwick record marbled electric ray of 12-5-14 caught by UK angler David Rose in 1995.

It must be borne in mind that these statistics were taken from the records of the top five fish in each category over the years. The comprehensive overall list of specimens is probably even higher than those quoted!

On top of all that success there was the momentus year of 2004. There was some incredibly exciting shore fishing when over 30 tope were caught. The majority were in the 30-0-0 to 40-0-0 range, the catches being topped by the Channel Island and Bailiwick record fish of 50-14-13 landed by Jersey angler Steve Mullins.

There were high hopes that the outstanding sport given by the tope run, would become an annual occurance, but it seems to have been a one-off for it hadn't happened prior to 2004, or in any year since.

There can be little doubt why the Alderney Festival continues to be so popular and so successful in attracting anglers to the island.

Specimen Fish Hunt

As we have already seen, the late 1980's and early 1990's saw a strong trend in Bailiwick angling towards judging competitions both at club level and in open events on specimen fish rather than heaviest bags. In fact, a number of clubs including the Guernsey Bass Anglers Sportfishing Society, the Bailiwick Bass Club, the Guernsey Mullet Club, the Guernsey Shore Anglers Premier Pursuers and the Sarnia Specimen Club all based their championships on specimen fish alone.

The Bass Festival that started in 1981 and the Guernsey Mullet Club Open that began in 1986 were the first opens to adopt the specimen fish principle, although, as we have seen, the GMC judged their open on heaviest bags for the first few years.

The Alderney Festival was the first annual open that used specimen fish as the criteria for awards where different species of fish were involved.

However, up to 1990 there was no annual specimen fish open that covered all the different species for Guernsey-based anglers.

This situation was resolved in 1991 when one of the local dealers, Peter Perrio of Tackle and Accessories, introduced the Specimen Fish Hunt, which would be open to all anglers including juniors, women and visitors.

The winner of the new event would be the angler that caught the greatest number of different species over the competition's qualifying weights. He (or she) would become the Specimen Hunter of the Year. If more than one angler ended up with the same number of species, it would go to the angler whose catch attained the highest aggregate percentage, all the fish being compared with the Bailiwick shore record.

The format of the new event took a little time to settle down. In the first year it was organised on similar lines to the Alderney Festival. It ran for a week from Saturday to Saturday.

In the following year it ran for five days from Thursday through to Tuesday, while from 1993 to 1995 it was held over a series of four week-ends each running 48 hours from Friday evening to Sunday evening. Finally in 1996 it settled down to a three week-end event, one being held in September, October and November respectively.

The top prize in the competition has been £500 of fishing tackle with subsidiary prizes for second and third place. In the early days there were awards for the top fish in selected species, similar to the Alderney Festival, but in more recent years this was changed into a cash pool of £1,000. The pool would be shared between the captors of the best fish of each species of each weekend, and the best over the complete Fish Hunt. The most landed in one year being 18 in 1996. In addition there was a special prize of £3,000 which would go to any angler breaking a Bailiwick shore record during the competition, although in more recent years this has been reduced to £1,000.

Sam Robins, picture here with a bull huss, the angler who has dominated the Specimen Fish Hunt, winning on five occasions and in 2003 landing 11 different species, a record for the event.

The event was an instant hit with Guernsey's specimen hunting anglers with first year attracting 131 anglers. The highest attendance was 165 in 1993 and the lowest 91 in 2003 with the average number of entrance being 114.

The first winner was Simon Newton, who caught five species over the qualifying weights: mackerel, garfish, bass, black bream and lesser-spotted dogfish.

Up to 2010, two anglers had dominated the event, Sam Robins and Marc Eppelein both winning on five occasions, Sam's successes included three wins in consecutive years from 2002 to 2004.

The most species landed by an individual angler, was the 11 caught by Sam Robins in the 2003 competition.

The Fish Hunt was to provide probably the most exciting competition ever seen in any Bailiwick open event.

In the first leg of the three week-end contest in 1996 Sam Robins caught a 3-11-7 smooth hound. Sam's catch was a Bailiwick shore record but would it qualify for the £3,000? The problem was that it didn't actually break a Bailiwick record. There wasn't a smooth hound on the record list, so Sam's fish would merely fill the vacant spot.

Obviously the organisers of the Fish Hunt had taken out insurance cover against the possible payment of such a big prize, so the matter was referred to the insurance company for their consideration.

By the end of the first week-end the leader in the competition was Mark Thomson who had four species, while Sam was in second place with three.

The second week-end saw little changed, Mark remained on four, Sam on three, but three other anglers came up to join Sam in second place.

It was all to come to an unbelievable climax on the third and last week-end.

On the first weigh-in Mark returned with more qualifying fish to bring his species tally up to six. His catch included a new British and Bailiwick shore record Couch's sea bream of 2-0-7, which meant he was now in the running for the £3,000!

However, Sam returned with two qualifying fish of his own to bring his total up to five species.

The two anglers were now locked in a fantastic battle. Both had claims in for the £3,000 and they were separated by just one species for the main £500 prize.

All rested on the very last weigh-in late on the Sunday evening. Mark returned with his seventh qualifier, a 5-14-9 grey mullet, the heaviest of the competition. Surely this was the clincher?

Not to be outdone Sam returned with two qualifiers, a 2-11-13 red mullet and a 1-7-1 red gurnard to bring him level on seven species with Mark. It now came down to the best aggregate percentage, which gave Sam victory by 447.09% to 398%.

The big question remained, what about the £3,000? Sadly for Sam it had been decided that his smooth hound did not comply with rule 10 of the competition which stated that 'any fish breaking a Guernsey record will be eligible for the special cash prize'.

So it was Mark Thomson who followed Jonathan Reeves into the local angling history as only the second Bailiwick angler to win such a major special award. Mark didn't have to wait so long as Jonathan for his money, as the Bailiwick of Guernsey Record (Rod-Caught) Fish Committee met just two months later and ratified the record. Amazingly a third angler was to win the £3,000, two years later in 1998.

Keith Quertier, who was participating in the Specimen Fish Hunt, won the big pay-out for catching a new Bailiwick shore record trigger fish that weighed 3-10-6.

There was to be further big payouts in later years. In 2002 Dave Saunders won the £1000 in the Specimen Fish Hunt when he achieved the almost unbelievable feat of landing two Bailiwick records, a 5-0-13 salmon and a 1-0-1 shore rockling.

A £1000 also went to Mark Le Page in 2004 for a 2-13-11 Bailiwick record lesser spotted dogfish, Lynton Carre in 2006 for a 2-7-0 record Couch's sea bream and Sam Robins in 2008 for a 1-12-12 twaite shad.

Keith Quertier with his Bailiwick of Guernsey 3-10-6 shore record trigger fish, which won him a prize of £3000 in the 1998 Specimen Fish Hunt

However the biggest ever payout for any Channel Island angler went to Jersey man Steve Mullins.

In 2004 he landed a 50-14-13 tope whilst fishing in the Alderney Angling Festival. It gave him the £2000 prize for breaking a Channel Island record, and he also won the £10,000 award in the Guernsey Autumn Angling Challenge, a competition that was run for a couple of years by Visit Guernsey (the States Tourist Board). If you add the £150 for winning the best fish in the over 5-0-0 other species category in the festival, his total winnings came to a staggering £12,150!!

The two unluckiest anglers must be Simon Rowe who had an 18-6-5 record bass in 1999, and Paul Carre who landed a massive

Mark Le Page with the 2-13-11 record lesser spotted dogfish that won him £1000 in the 2004 Specimen Fish Hunt.

65-14-10 record conger in 2000. Both should have won at least £1000 prize, but sadly in those two years such an award was not included in the Specimen Fish Hunt Prize list.

243

The majority of Bailiwick anglers consider that Alderney is the top island as far as angling potential is concerned. They point to the results of the Alderney Festival as confirmation.

Some argue that if a similar competition was held in Guernsey, the results would be on a par and confirm that Guernsey's potential is at least equal to that of the northern isle as far as shore fishing was concerned.

The Specimen Fish Hunt has given an opportunity for such a comparison to be made. It's not possible to compare exactly like with like. Records of the Alderney Festival came from a 20 year period 1986 to 2006, while the Fish Hunt only covered 16 years from 1991 to 2006. In addition the average number of anglers entering the two competitions flucuate considerably. Nevertheless they are held at the same time of the year and are roughly fished for the same total length of time.

Even allowing for the differences in the number of anglers and the number of years the competitions have been running, the results leave no doubt, Alderney catches are far superior and Guernsey comes off an extremely poor second.

As we have already noted Alderney had 35 ballan wrasse over 7-0-0, biggest 8-5-10, Guernsey had 14, biggest 8-1-6 by Trevor Ferbrache in 1999. It's a similar story for other species. Alderney recorded those 24 conger over 40-0-0, biggest 57-0-0, Guernsey had 2, the biggest being the 65-14-10 specimen caught by Paul Carre in 2000.

Guernsey had nine black bream over 3-8-0, the heaviest being the 4-4-7 fish, caught by Shane Huxster in 2003 at Bec du Nez; Alderney had 45, heaviest 4-12-6. It was no better for Guernsey as far as bass was concerned. Alderney had 19 over 10-0-0 topped by a 16-3-12 fish, while Guernsey produced 10, the biggest 18-6-5 by Simon Rowe in 1999.

It's the same story for plaice: Alderney 11 over 4-0-0, best 5-11-0, Guernsey two, heaviest 4-13-0 by Terry Dodd in 1992.

Surprisingly, bearing in mind Alderney's long tradition for big mullet, Guernsey does not lag too far behind. The score for mullet over 5-0-0 is Alderney 34, Guernsey 22, with Guernsey's biggest fish being the 7-0-8 specimen caught by Steve Elliott in 1995, which almost equalled Alderney's top fish of 7-1-14.

The only species where Guernsey comes out on top is red mullet. They have had 26 over 2-0-0, well up on Alderney, and Guernsey's best, 3-9-13 by Ian Torode in 1996, easily beats the 2-12-4 top specimen from Alderney. The trend has continued over the years 2007 - 2010.

Sark has one open each year held in conjuction with their Water Carnival in August. There used to be another event on Boxing Day but that was discontinued due to declining support.

The open is run to raise money for charity, proceeds usually going to the Sark Medical Fund.

In Guernsey there used to be an open angling competition at the Rocquaine Regattas which was held during the summer months. It tended to be a rather low key affair and due to the rather poor support from the angling fraternity, its occurrence has become a little spasmodic!

An unusual catch in the 2006 Specimem Fish Hunt - Mark P. Fletcher with his 5-5-13 small eyed ray

Father and son, Steve (left) and Shane Huxster with their catch of conger in the 2006 Specimen Fish Hunt, fish of 33-14-0 and 23-0-0

Kayak Open

In the early 2000's angling from kayaks had become increasingly popular. Consequently in 2009, local tackle dealers Quayside organised the first open kayak competition. It was a huge success attracting 31 anglers including four from the UK. The top prizes worth £200 were won by Paul Clark who had the most species and and the best fish. In all he caught six bass and four ballan wrasse. It was a catch and release match but a quick weigh in on his kayak confirmed that his top bass weighed 8-1-0 and the best wrasse 4-0-0. The event was repeated in 2010 organised by the West Coast Sea Angling Club in association with Quayside. The competition was for the most species over the qualifying weights. Jaime Falla won with a 1-1-3 cuckoo wrasse, Paul Clark second with a 3-11-0 bass and third Tim King 2-8-0 pollack. Although the entry of 18 anglers was a little disapointing it is almost certain that this new event will become a permanent fixture on the local angling calandar.

Miscellaneous Open Events

In addition to the open competitions that have become annual events there have been a number held that have been organised for a special one-off occasion, or have attracted so little support they they have not been repeated.

In 1984, one of the tackle dealers organised a Go for Gold Open Competition. It was so-called because the first prize was a gold plated Abu 6500 multiplier reel. The 12-hour roving shore event was a specimen fish contest with prize reels going to the captors of the top three fish of the day, as compared with the Bailiwick shore record. It attracted 138 anglers and was to produce the closest result ever seen in an open Bailiwick competition.

Mick Smith returned with a 2-6-0 common eel which was worth 82.608%, while Alan Drillot came back with a 6-15-0 ballan wrasse which scored 82.605%. Yes, it was an incredible result, Mick had won by 0.003%, or if you prefer, three thousandth of one per cent! Richard Seager took third spot with a 5-10-8 ballan wrasse worth 67.348%.

The competition was repeated in 1985 when it was called Go for Carbon with prizes of carbon rods.

Once again a common eel won the event, Simon Newton taking top place with a 2-5-0 fish worth 80.43%. John Rothwell was second with a 5-15-8 ballan wrasse and Geoff Hicks third with a 1-13-0 common eel.

The match only attracted 54 anglers and probably as a result the series of competitions was discontinued.

In 1986 a local travel agent organised a fishing race in Herm, a competition where prizes were awarded for the angler catching the most different species.

This unique competition was won by Peter Frise who landed four species, plaice, garfish, ballan wrasse and black bream. His prize was a week's fishing in the Isle of Man. Dave Phillippe and Geoff Hicks each had three species and both won two tickets to London. Rodney Le Moigne had the heaviest fish of the day, a 6-11-2 ballan wrasse which won him two tickets to either Jersey or Alderney.

Unfortunately Peter's prize was never honoured and he finally accepted a cash prize in lieu. There was speculation at the time that the competition would become an annual event, but it was never repeated.

In 1988 the Guernsey Sea Anglers Club held a one-off four-day long Open Festival to celebrate their 50th anniversary. It was a shore contest with a very comprehensive prize list and based on specimen fish. Sponsorship was obtained from an electrical goods company and as a result the prizes consisted of a hi-fi system, a microwave oven, deep fat fryers, car radios, steam irons and many other household goods.

The GSAC was delighted by the friendship shown by other local clubs on the occasion, for prizes were donated by the Guernsey Federation of Sea Anglers, the Guernsey Mullet Club and the Guernsey Bass Anglers Sportfishing Society.

The Festival attracted 141 anglers including some from the Jersey Sea Fishing Club. It was JSFC member Dennis Megaw who was to win the top award for the best fish, his winning catch being a 9-10-7 pollack which scored 321.74% when judged against the Festival's qualifying weight. Junior Patrick Hanley did exceptionally well, winning the best fish by a junior award with a 10-0-0 bass, the best bass prize, the most fish over the Festival qualifying weights and one of the daily prizes.

The club ended the celebrations by holding a roving open shore competition on the Sunday. This was won by Richard Seager with 21 ballan wrasse for a weight of 41-5-0, a superb catch for a five- hour competition.

In the 1990's there was a resurgence of interest in spinning with artificial lures. Following requests from a number of anglers, one of the local tackle dealers organised an Open Spinning Shore Competition in 1995. It was run over a week-end with a top prize of £1,000 for the heaviest fish over the Bailiwick shore record, as well as prizes for the heaviest bass, pollack, ballan wrasse, garfish and mackerel.

It was not a success. In spite of the apparent interest and enthusiasm shown by the anglers prior to the event only 38 actually entered the competition. Shaun Fallaize won the bass category with a 9-4-14 fish and Anthony Cohu the mackerel prize with a 1-10-4 specimen. All the other prizes remained unclaimed. Needless to say the competition was not repeated in the following years.

No doubt encouraged by the success of the shore-based Specimen Fish Hunt that started in 1991, the WCSAC decided to introduce a Boat Specimen Fish Hunt in 1996. It was due to be run over a week-end in June, but bad weather caused a postponement until July. It was won by Adrian Exall who landed the most different species over the competition's qualifying weights. His winning fish were a 1-11-0 mackerel, a 2-6-0 lesser-spotted dogfish and a 2-4-0 black bream.

It was however, an extremely disappointing event particularly from the organiser's point of view. The Fish Hunt was run using the same popular format as the shore-based competition, with a similar comprehensive prize list, including the big cash award for an angler breaking a Bailiwick boat record. In spite of this attractive range of awards and perfect weather on the event's rearranged date, it only attracted 31 competitors, the smallest entry ever recorded for a major Bailiwick angling open.

The reasons for the almost complete lack of interest by the island's anglers is a mystery. As a consequence, it can be no surprise that the competition joined the "one-off event" list!

During the period 1969 to 1973 the Guernsey Sea Anglers Club ran an annual individual knock-out competition. The first contest attracted 64 anglers and was won by John Oakley.

It was fairly popular with an average entry of 66 over its fiveyear history. Nevertheless in 1974 the club discontinued the knockout as an open competition and made it an event for club members only.

Current Open Events

It's very apparent that the history of Bailiwick open angling competitions has been a very busy and dynamic one and will no doubt continue to be so in the future.

Anglers, particularly visitors and newcomers to the sport, may well be somewhat confused, as to which competitions are currently being held.

Although further changes will almost certainly occur in the future, the following lists the open events held in 2010, each of which was planned to continue in the following years. Each is open to all anglers including women and juniors.

1. **Bailiwick Bass Challenge**
   Organisers – Bailiwick Bass Club.
   Specimen bass competition.
   Held in June or July.
   Duration – 72 hours, Friday evening to Monday evening.
   Boat and shore sections.
   Awards up to a value of £400 for the best bass in both the boat and shore sections. Special prizes for women and juniors.
   Special cash prizes for the angler(s) who beat the Bailiwick boat or shore records by the greatest margin (£1000 in 2010).

2. **Kayak Open**
   Organisers – Quayside / WCSAC.
   Fishing Race (Most Species)
   Held in July/August
   Duration – Saturday/Sunday
   Award up to £300 for most species.

3. **Open Bass Festival**
   Organisers – Guernsey Bass Anglers Sportfishing Society.
   Specimen bass competition.
   Held in August or early September.
   Duration – 96 hours, Thursday evening to Monday evening.
   Boat and shore sections.
   Awards up to a value of £500 for the best bass in both the boat and shore sections. Special prizes for women and juniors.
   Special cash prizes for the angler(s) who beat the Bailiwick boat or shore records by the greatest margin (£5000 in 2010).

4. **Open Spring Bass Festival**
   Organisers - Bailiwick Bass Club on behalf of The Piriou Family
   Held in May.
   Duration – Friday evening to Sunday evening.
   Shore section only
   Cash and fishing tackle awards.
   All proceeds to go to a charity selected by the Piriou family.

5. **Sark Water Carnival**
   Organiser – Glyn Williams
   Specimen fish and heaviest bag competition.
   Held in July or August.
   Duration – 8 hours on a Saturday. Boat and shore sections.
   Prizes of fishing tackle, pottery etc., depending on donated awards.
   (Proceeds of competition go to the Sark Medical Fund).
   Special prizes for women and juniors.

6. **Alderney Angling Festival**
    Organisers – Alderney Festival Committee.
    Specimen fish competition.
    Held in October
    Duration – 7 days, Saturday to Saturday.
    Shore fishing only.
    Awards up to a value of £150 for the top UK and Channel Island anglers and up to £150 for the top five fish in a number of selected different species. Special prizes for women and juniors.
    Special cash prizes for the angler who beats the British shore record (£2000 in 2010) and for the angler who beats an Alderney record (£500 in 2010).

7. **Open Mullet Competition**
    Organisers – Guernsey Mullet Club.
    Specimen mullet competition.
    Held in February, March or April.
    Duration – two weekends each from Friday evening to Sunday evening.
    Shore fishing only.
    Prizes of fishing tackle including rod and reels, for the best fish.
    Special prizes for women and juniors.

8. **Specimen Fish Hunt**
    Organisers – West Coast Sea Angling Club
    Specimen fish competition.
    Held in September, October and November.
    Duration – 3 weekends (each 52 hours, Friday evening to Sunday evening).
    Shore fishing only.
    Awards of cash and fishing tackle up to a value of £500 for the anglers catching the most different species over the competition's qualifying weights and cash prizes for the captor of the best fish of each species. Special cash prize for the angler who beats the Bailiwick shore record by the greatest margin (£1000 in 2010).

9. **Fur and Feather**
    Organisers – Guernsey Sea Anglers Club.
    Specimen fish and most species competition.
    Held in late November or early December.
    Duration – 7 hours on a Sunday.
    Shore fishing only.
    Prizes of Christmas Fare including turkeys, chickens, wine, etc. for best overall fish and the best fish of each species. Special prizes for women and juniors.

Two children's Open events were held each year. Noel Rive, a member of the GSAPP club was very keen to see more juniors interested in angling, so much so that following his untimely death in 1999, the club decided to organise an annual open competition for juniors to honour his memory. It was held for the first time in 2000 at the White Rock. The top award in the open is the Noel Rive Memorial Trophy, but there are numerous other prizes for the runners up. The event normally attracted an average of 25 youngsters. Any profits from the event were donated to a local charity. In spite of the demise of GSAPP in 2006, volunteers hoped to continue to organise and hold the annual event, but sadly interest waned and the competition had to be discontinued.

At about the same time the Bailiwick Bass Club started their annual Children's Open which attracts a similar number of juniors. Initially it was held at Vazon, but was later switched to St Peter Port Harbour. Although run by a bass club, all species of fish are accepted. It is usually held in September.

Gladstone/Players Gold Leaf Competitions

When Bob Pagett from the Guernsey Tobacco Company and Peter Witterick from the Guernsey Press had a conversation in 1966, they could never have anticipated the far reaching effects it would have on the future of Bailiwick angling. As a result of that conversation, an agreement was reached for angling to receive sponsorship from the Tobacco Company.

It was decided to run two events that would be open to all anglers in the Bailiwick. The Gladstone competition would be for the best specimen fish, as judged against the British Record, while the Players Gold Leaf would be for the best shark or tope. Both competitions would run from 1May to 31 October.

The inaugural Gladstone event in 1966 attracted 29 entries. The winner was Max Fitzgerald with a 24-4-0 turbot, worth 83.621%.

There were 14 prizes, the winner received a trophy, the top four received vouchers valued between £20 and £5 and all 14 received 200 Gladstone cigarettes.

There were only three entries in the Players Gold Leaf competition, the winner being Bill Sylvester with a 162-0-0 porbeagle shark. All three received cash prizes and 200 Players Gold Leaf cigarettes.

In 1967 the Gladstone attracted 24 entries, the winner being Mike Dew with a 29-0-0 blonde ray worth 100.432%, while 1968 had 36 entries, the winner being Richard Payne with a 0-6-14 common topknot worth 104.76% (there was not a 1-0-0 lower limit in the competition).

The Players Gold Leaf attracted just one entry in 1967, the winning fish being an 84-0-0 porbeagle shark caught by your author!

Neither of the competitions had a long history. Probably due to the lack of entries, the Players Gold leaf was discontinued after the 1967 competition. The Gladstone lasted one more year, but as sponsorship was withdrawn, the 1968 competition was to prove to be the last.

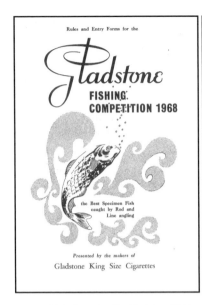

Entry forms for the Gladstone Fishing Competition and the Player Gold Leaf
the forerunners of the Fish of the Month Competition.

Fish of the Month Competition

The ad-hoc committee that had run the two competitions consisted of Bob Pagett (Guernsey Tobacco Co.), Ernie Baker (GSAC President), Steve Falla (30 Fathom Club Chairman), Terry Rowe (TAC Secretary), John Newton (non-club rep.) and Peter Witterick (Guernsey Press Angling Columnist).

At a meeting held on 21 November 1968 at L'Auberge Divette (now the L'Auberge Restaurant) the committee decided that as the Gladstone competition had been such a great success they would not disband, but stay together and try to introduce a new similar competition.

As a result the Fish of the Month was born!

As the name suggests, it would be a specimen fish competition with a prize each month for the captor of the best fish, as compared with the Bailiwick record. Only fish over 1-0-0- would be eligible.

There were initial doubts whether enough support would be found to fund the new competition. It would need a continuous stream of awards if it was to meet its target of a prize every month. The worries were quickly dispelled. Sponsorship was soon forthcoming from local businesses, angling clubs and even individual anglers.

The committee could not have known at the time just how far reaching and successful the new competition would be.

An early meeting of the Guernsey Anglers Competition Committe, (left to right) Peter Witterick, Bob Pagett, Tony Bougourd, Peter Franks, John Newton, Terry Rowe and Ernie Baker. (Peter Franks was Bass Charrington's representative, he was not a member of the committee)

It was to become a Bailiwick institution and is still running 43 years later.

Obviously the members of the organising body, which is known as the Guernsey Anglers Competition Committee, have changed over the years. However, it is unique in that it was self appointed and has always been self perpetuating! No annual general meetings or elections have ever been held to decide the membership of the committee. If a member resigns an invitation is extended to a suitable angler to fill the vacancy. This has worked well and the outstanding success of this unique long-running competition, which is the envy of other angling centres, is a testimony to the hard work and enthusiasm of its founder members and those that have followed over the years.

In the beginning it was decided that the monthly prize would be a suitably engraved tankard, which still remains the top award. However, the prize list has expanded quite considerably.

As from March 1983 separate awards were introduced for the best boat and shore-caught fish during the summer months, and this was extended to the whole year as from November 2001.

Two runner-up prizes were added to the prize list. These have usually been bottles of whisky, vodka or a crate of beer. As from 1995 the list was further enhanced when a tackle company added a prize for the best overall fish each month.

A monthly award for the best fish by a junior was added in 2005, and finally one of the local tackle dealers donated a monthly spot prize.

Over the years the most consistent and much appreciated supporter or the FOM contest has been the building firm, J Meerveld and Sons. They have sponsored the shore-caught tankard for over 24 years, commencing in January 1987 and up to the end of December 2010 they had donated no fewer than 289!

Once a year, the entries for the previous year are evaluated and at a presentation evening, trophies are presented to the captors of the top overall fish of the year, the best summer and winter-caught specimens and the best fish by a junior.

The competition had a modest start. The first contest in February 1969 attracted just one entry! It was from Alderney angler Bert Pike who submitted a shore-caught 1-11-8 golden grey mullet which scored 100.011% and ensured that he won the Ernie Baker Tankard.

After the first month entries increased. There were seven in March, and by the end of 1969 the total number of entries had reached 75. Although interest in the competition has wavered a little at times it has continued to be a popular contest and by December 2010 the total number of entries received from local anglers had reached 4788! Over the same period over 750 tankards had been awarded.

The greatest number of entries received in one year was 166 in 1982, while the lowest was 67 both in 1970 and 1978.

The highest monthly total was 29 in September 1980 and the lowest, just one, in February 1969, February 1978 and January 2010.

No fewer than 54 different species of fish have won tankards. Ballan wrasse have been by far the most successful species accounting for 94 tankards, with bass in second place with 56 and lesser-spotted dogfish third with 39. At the other end of the scale some species,including thornback ray, spotted ray, bogue and hake have accounted for just one tankard each.

Bearing in mind Alderney's fishing potential, it will be no surprise that an angler from the northern isle tops the list for the most tankards won by an individual. The legendary Bert Pike won eight, six with golden grey mullet, one with a ballan wrasse and one with a gilthead bream. Alderney angler Roddy Hays and Tony de la Haye from Guernsey have won seven, while Anthony Le Prevost, Leroy le Gallais and Fred Ferbrache are just some of the anglers with six.

Des Bougourd has the honour of recording the highest ever percentage in the competition's history. A 36-0-0 boat-caught monkfish that he caught in May 1972 scored a massive 411.40%.

Junior angler Toby Patch has the doubtful privilege of recording the lowest winning percentage, his 4-12-15 shore caught bass that he landed in August 2005 scoring a modest 26.14%!

The heaviest fish to win a tankard was Jamie Allen's 295-8-6 porbeagle shark caught in August 2007 and the smallest a 1-0-4 shore-caught shore rockling entered by Shane Huxster in June 2006. Women anglers have had their moments

Diana Bougourd, the first woman to win a Fish of the Month Tankard, in October 1970 for a 2-7-12 red gurnard, pictured here with a brill in 1971

Eight year old Jill Sheppard in 1974, with her 3-10-3 trigger fish caught off Belvoir, Herm. It scored 187.32% in the Fish of the Month, the best ever entry by a women or junior angler!

of glory and up to January 2011, 15 have won tankards. The first was Diana Bougourd in October 1970, when her winning catch was a 2-7-12 boat caught red gurnard which was worth 116.30%.

Jill Sheppard's 3-10-3 trigger fish caught in August 1974 scored 187.32%, the best ever entry by a woman angler. As Jill was only eight when she made her catch it is also the best ever fish entered by a junior angler!

If you are a visitor to the Bailiwick you can join in the fun of the Fish of the Month with a chance of winning an engraved tankard which would be a wonderful souvenir of your holiday. If you catch a fish that you think would be worth an entry, consult one of the tackle dealers, who will give you friendly advice and be able to supply you with an entry form.

The visitor's section of the Fish of the Month started only four months after the opening of the competition in February 1969. Following the offer of sponsorship from Ernie Baker who was one of the local tackle dealers at the time, the committee decided to run a special separate section for visiting anglers.

This commenced in June 1969 and was still running in 2010. In the early years there was a visitor's tankard for each of the four main summer months, this increased to seven, fell back to four then went up to six!

It has been well supported with 561 entries up to the end of 2010. The best year was 1995 with 25 entries, and the best month 13 in August 1981.

There have been many great fish caught by visitors including British and local records. The highest scoring fish entered by a visitor was the 38-0-0 Bailiwick shore-caught record angler fish, landed at St Peter Port Breakwater by Christopher Geaves in August 1974, which scored 198.68%.

The heaviest fish was the 108-0-6 boat-caught Bailiwick record conger caught by Dutch angler Victor Kroon over a wreck mark in August 1991, which was worth 110.157%.

Bass Competition

Peter Witterick and Bob Pagett, who had been so instrumental in the introduction of the Fish of the Month competition in 1969 were to come up with another exciting innovation before the year was over.

They held informal discussions with Peter Franks from the Bass Charrington Company in Jersey about the possibility of sponsorship.

To their delight this was quickly offered. The implications of the company

name were obvious and it should be no surprise that a bass competition was introduced.

The Guernsey Anglers Competition Committee agreed to run the new contest in parallel with the Fish of the Month and the Bass Charrington Bass Competiton came into being.

It was decided that the new competiton would be a simple one. It would be open to both local and visiting anglers and as it only covered one species, it would be decided on weight alone.

After consultation with the sponsors it was agreed to run two competitions a year, one running through the winter from November to April, and the other May to October. The awards would be suitably engraved tankards for the top three fish and crates of the company's ale for the winners and runners-up.

The highest scoring fish ever entered in the visitor's Fish of the Month. Christopher Geaves with his 38-0-0 angler fish in 1974, which scored 198.68%. It still stood as the Bailiwick shore record in July 2011.

At the end of each competition the company hosted a presentation night which was also used as an occasion to present Fish of the Month awards.

The first competition ran from November 1969 to April 1970 and attracted 10 entries. The honour of being the first winner fell to Ted Callaway who won with a 10-4-0 fish.

The competition was to continue in this format until the end of 1982. From 1983 it became an annual contest, running over the calendar year from January to December.

Bass Charrington were to be the sponsors for a period of 20 years until December 1989. From 1990 to 1992 the sponsorship was taken over by Bass Guernsey.

As from 1993 the competition's connection with the 'Bass Company' ceased and there were real concerns the competition would have to come to an end.

It was the Phoenix Fish Company that came to the rescue and ensured that the competition would continue. Although the contact with the "brewery trade" had been severed, the Phoenix Fish Bass Competition, as it was now known, maintained the tradition of tankards and cases of beer as prizes!

Up to December 2010, 26 half year and 29 full year competitions had been held. The 55 contests produced 1255 entries which gives a good indication of its popularity.

Esther Hatton with her 13-7-10 bass in 2009

However, the real story of the competition is the amazing quality of the entries. No fewer than 503 bass, or 40.07% of the total entries have been fish of 10-0-0 or over. The list of "double figure" bass is really quite remarkable. There were 195 over 10-0-0, 148 over 11-0-0, 83 over 12-0-0, 30 over 13-0-0, 19 over 14-0-0, four over 15-0-0, 13 over 16-0-0 , eight over 17-0-0 and three over 18-0-0. The best ever entry was the 18-6-12 boat-caught fish which won the 2005 competition for visiting angler Brett Adams, obviously the best catch ever by a visitor. The top shore-caught fish was the 18-6-5 bass landed by Simon Rowe in 1999. (see pages 223 and 224)

Only two women anglers have won the top prize. Miss B. Piriou won the summer 1973 contest with a 10-9-4 fish, while Jocelyn Gavey's 13-0-4 bass won the 1990 competition. However the heaviest bass entered by a woman was the 13-7-10 fish caught by Esther Hatton in 2009, which gave her second prize. The top bass by a junior was the 12-15-0 fish by Brandon La Touche in 2009 which gave him fourth place.

Fish that weighed less than 10-0-0 have only won the competition on four occasions, with the lightest being the 8-10-8 fish that gave Dave Brouard victory in the 1971/1972 winter contest.

The smallest ever entered was a 1-9-2 fish in the summer of 1973. In 1974 the committee introduced a 3-0-0 lower limit.

Only four anglers have won the competition twice, Martyn Bourgaise's brace of wins was the most remarkable. He won the summer 1974 event with a fish of 11-0-0 when he was still a junior. Up to the end of December 2010, he remained the only junior to have won the competition. His next win was 17 years later in 1991, when his winning entry weighed 12-14-15. Bert Pike won the 1974/1975 and the 1975/1976 winter competitions with specimens of 8-10-12 and 10-12-4 caught in Alderney, while Max Gaudion won the 1972/1973 winter competition and the 1988 contest with fish weighing 13-3-12 and 13-6-6. Mick Maurice had back to back wins in 2001 and 2002 with fish of 14-8-10 and 16-3-12. The most entries received for one competition was 94 for the summer 1977 event. The least was seven for the winter 1974/1975 contest.

The most fish over 10-0-0 entered in one competition was 29 in 2002.

One of the most interesting facets of the competition has been the amazing increase in the quality of the bass entries in recent years.

Up to 1997, 965 entries were made of which 279 or 28.9% were 10-0-0 or over. However, for 1998-2010 290 entries were received of which 225 or 78.36% were over the 10-0-0 mark. Surprisingly in 2010

Dave Brouard (left) receives the Bass Charrington tankard from Peter Franks in 1972. His 8-10-8 bass was the lightest ever to win the competition!

and 2011 interest in both the FOM and Phoenix Fish started to fall. It follows that the future of the competitions will be dependant on anglers continued support.

Miscellaneous Competitions

If anglers fishing in the Bailiwick are fortunate to catch a specimen fish they are not restricted to the Fish of the Month and Phoenix Fish Bass Competitions. Nearly all the national angling publications and even a few Sunday newspapers run the best fish of the month or week contests.

In addition, if the angler belongs to a club, or is a member of the Angling Trust they can also enter their specimen competitions.

It is appreciated that the formalities and form filling that is necessary to make entries in all these competitions, can be time consuming and rather irksome.

So much so that one angler considered that if he was lucky enough to catch a steady stream of good fish, he would need his own secretary!

Nevertheless, it is worthwhile making the effort. The captor of a really outstanding fish could win many hundreds, if not thousands of pounds worth of prizes.

A good example is the awards won by your author in 1970. A 19-6-13 boat-caught undulate ray, that was a Bailiwick and British record, won no fewer than 14 prizes, ranging from a five-day angling holiday in Cobh, Southern Ireland, to a 50p fish of the month tackle voucher from the Telephone Angling Club!

With so many good prizes there to be won, it really is a mystery that many anglers say "I just can't be bothered". Two excuses made by anglers are, "I can't get the entry forms" or "I don't know if the fish is worth entering". A good idea is to obtain a supply of forms beforehand. Cut out and keep the entry forms from the various publications and get some Fish of the Month and Phoenix Fish Bass

TABLE OF OUNCES AND DRAM'S EXPRESSED AS DECIMALS OF A POUND (CORRECT TO FOUR DECIMAL PLACES)

Ozs	Dms	Decimals	Ozs	Dms	Decimals	Ozs	Dms	Decimals	Ozs	Dms	Decimals
			4	0	0.2500	8	0	0.5000	12	0	0.7500
0	1	0.0039	4	1	0.2539	8	1	0.5039	12	1	0.7539
0	2	0.0078	4	2	0.2578	8	2	0.5078	12	2	0.7578
0	3	0.0117	4	3	0.2617	8	3	0.5117	12	3	0.7617
0	4	0.0156	4	4	0.2656	8	4	0.5156	12	4	0.7656
0	5	0.0195	4	5	0.2695	8	5	0.5195	12	5	0.7695
0	6	0.0234	4	6	0.2734	8	6	0.5234	12	6	0.7734
0	7	0.0273	4	7	0.2773	8	7	0.5273	12	7	0.7773
0	8	0.0312	4	8	0.2812	8	8	0.5312	12	8	0.7812
0	9	0.0351	4	9	0.2851	8	9	0.5351	12	9	0.7851
0	10	0.0390	4	10	0.2890	8	10	0.5390	12	10	0.7890
0	11	0.0429	4	11	0.2930	8	11	0.5430	12	11	0.7929
0	12	0.0469	4	12	0.2969	8	12	0.5469	12	12	0.7969
0	13	0.0508	4	13	0.3008	8	13	0.5508	12	13	0.8008
0	14	0.0547	4	14	0.3047	8	14	0.5547	12	14	0.8047
0	15	0.0586	4	15	0.3086	8	15	0.5586	12	15	0.8086
1	0	0.0625	5	0	0.3125	9	0	0.5625	13	0	0.8125
1	1	0.0664	5	1	0.3164	9	1	0.5664	13	1	0.8164
1	2	0.0703	5	2	0.3203	9	2	0.5703	13	2	0.8203
1	3	0.0742	5	3	0.3242	9	3	0.5742	13	3	0.8242
1	4	0.0781	5	4	0.3281	9	4	0.5781	13	4	0.8281
1	5	0.0820	5	5	0.3320	9	5	0.5820	13	5	0.8320
1	6	0.0859	5	6	0.3359	9	6	0.5859	13	6	0.8359
1	7	0.0898	5	7	0.3398	9	7	0.5898	13	7	0.8398
1	8	0.0937	5	8	0.3437	9	8	0.5937	13	8	0.8437
1	9	0.0976	5	9	0.3476	9	9	0.5976	13	9	0.8476
1	10	0.1016	5	10	0.3515	9	10	0.6015	13	10	0.8515
1	11	0.1055	5	11	0.3555	9	11	0.6055	13	11	0.8554
1	12	0.1094	5	12	0.3594	9	12	0.6094	13	12	0.8593
1	13	0.1133	5	13	0.3633	9	13	0.6133	13	13	0.8633
1	14	0.1172	5	14	0.3672	9	14	0.6172	13	14	0.8672
1	15	0.1211	5	15	0.3711	9	15	0.6211	13	15	0.8711
2	0	0.1250	6	0	0.3750	10	0	0.6250	14	0	0.8750
2	1	0.1289	6	1	0.3789	10	1	0.6289	14	1	0.8789
2	2	0.1328	6	2	0.3828	10	2	0.6328	14	2	0.8828
2	3	0.1367	6	3	0.3867	10	3	0.6367	14	3	0.8867
2	4	0.1406	6	4	0.3906	10	4	0.6406	14	4	0.8906
2	5	0.1445	6	5	0.3945	10	5	0.6445	14	5	0.8945
2	6	0.1484	6	6	0.3984	10	6	0.6484	14	6	0.8984
2	7	0.1523	6	7	0.4023	10	7	0.6523	14	7	0.9023
2	8	0.1562	6	8	0.4062	10	8	0.6562	14	8	0.9062
2	9	0.1601	6	9	0.4101	10	9	0.6601	14	9	0.9101
2	10	0.1641	6	10	0.4140	10	10	0.6640	14	10	0.9140
2	11	0.1680	6	11	0.4180	10	11	0.6680	14	11	0.9179
2	12	0.1719	6	12	0.4219	10	12	0.6719	14	12	0.9219
2	13	0.1758	6	13	0.4258	10	13	0.6758	14	13	0.9258
2	14	0.1797	6	14	0.4297	10	14	0.6797	14	14	0.9297
2	15	0.1836	6	15	0.4336	10	15	0.6836	14	15	0.9336
3	0	0.1875	7	0	0.4375	11	0	0.6875	15	0	0.9375
3	1	0.1914	7	1	0.4414	11	1	0.6914	15	1	0.9414
3	2	0.1953	7	2	0.4453	11	2	0.6953	15	2	0.9453
3	3	0.1992	7	3	0.4492	11	3	0.6992	15	3	0.9492
3	4	0.2031	7	4	0.4531	11	4	0.7031	15	4	0.9531
3	5	0.2070	7	5	0.4570	11	5	0.7070	15	5	0.9570
3	6	0.2109	7	6	0.4609	11	6	0.7109	15	6	0.9609
3	7	0.2148	7	7	0.4648	11	7	0.7148	15	7	0.9648
3	8	0.2187	7	8	0.4687	11	8	0.7187	15	8	0.9687
3	9	0.2226	7	9	0.4726	11	9	0.7226	15	9	0.9726
3	10	0.2265	7	10	0.4765	11	10	0.7265	15	10	0.9765
3	11	0.2305	7	11	0.4805	11	11	0.7304	15	11	0.9804
3	12	0.2344	7	12	0.4844	11	12	0.7344	15	12	0.9844
3	13	0.2383	7	13	0.4883	11	13	0.7383	15	13	0.9883
3	14	0.2422	7	14	0.4922	11	14	0.7422	15	14	0.9922
3	15	0.2461	7	15	0.4961	11	15	0.7461	15	15	0.9961
									16	0	1.0000

forms. If you don't know where from, seek the help of your tackle dealer. Keep these in your kit so they are available the moment that great fish comes your way. You will be able to obtain witnesses' signatures before they disperse and you will be ready to record all the details when weighing formalities are being completed.

What fish to enter? The majority of the competitions are run on a percentage basis, the prize going to the best fish as judged against the club, Bailiwick or British record. Usually any fish over 50% is worth considering, unless you know the percentage of the fish in the bottom prize winning position, for obviously it would not be worth entering a fish of a lesser value.

If you want to calculate the percentage value of your catch, or alternatively the value of the other entries you are up against, you may find the table on page 259 to be a help. It lists ounces and drams up to a pound in decimal fractions. This removes the need to reduce all the weights down to ounces or drams. One example. What is the percentage of a 7-13-7 ballan wrasse as compared with the 8-10-13 record? Using the table you can confirm that the weight of your fish as 7.8398lbs when expressed as a decimal fraction and the record as 8.6758lbs. Using a calculator is then easy to work out the necessary calculation

$$\frac{7.8398 \times 100}{8.6758} = 90.36\%$$

More and more fish are being weighed on metric scales. The table can also be used when a conversion to avoirdupois weight is needed. The conversion factor kilos to pounds is 2.2046. To work out the conversion of an 11.321 kilo fish, multiply by 2.2046 which gives 24.9582lbs. The table would confirm that the weight is 24-15-5, which is given by the nearest listed decimal fraction under the calculated weight. The nearest decimal fraction over the calculation cannot be used, as that would give a result over the fish's true weight.

Casting Competitions

On October 1965 the Guernsey Sea Angler's Club held the first casting competition ever held in the Bailiwick. The distance and target contests took place on Vazon beach and were only open to club members. The under 10ft rod class was won by Nick Machon with a cast of 94yds 1ft 7in, while Peter Witterick came top in the over 10ft rod class with a length of 114yds 2ft 6inches.

In the following year the short rod class was won by Roy Priest with 102yds 1ft, while your author won the over 10ft class with 99yds.

Anglers may well be surprised by the modest distances achieved. However, it must be borne in mind that these were very much fun events with the competitors using their normal rods and reels that they had regularly been using in fishing competitions. In addition it must be remembered that rod and reel technology in the 1960's was not what it is today.

After those initial two years the club dropped the event from their calendar and although the Jamaica Inn Angling club included some casting competitions in their programme, very little casting was done on a competitive basis until 1982.

The Sea Angler magazine had started to organise casting competitions countrywide and presented sew-on badges to all participants which denoted the

Caster Tom Ozanne in action. In December 2010 he held the record for the longest cast by a Bailiwick angler; 254 yards

standard they had reached.

In 1982 Richard Browning, from the local company Sarnia Custom Rods organised a Sea Angler event in Guernsey which attracted 17 anglers. Richard himself won the contest with a new Bailiwick best cast of 167yds 2ft.

In 1983 the event was repeated, with Mike Toomer from Sea Angler coming over for the occasion. Mike gave a number of demonstration casts, including one of 219yds 2ft which still remained in 2010 as the Bailiwick all comers record! The best cast by a local angler on the day was 141yds by Charlie Greenslade.

For the next three years 1984 to 1986 the contest was organised by Ron Harris from the Channel Islands Rod Co. Richard Seager won in 1984 and 1985 achieving casts of 155 yards and 159 yards respectively.

In 1986 Alan Drillot won with the best ever cast by a local angler, 179yds.

In 1987 the venue used for the competition became unavailable and due to the difficulty of finding an alternative suitable site the event was discontinued.

However in 1987 the Guernsey Shore Anglers Premier Pursuers held a club event, which was won by Alan Drillot with a cast of 184yds 2ft, the longest ever measured cast achieved by a local angler at an event held in the Bailiwick.

In 1991 Guernsey angler Dave Saunders entered a casting competition in Norfolk where he became the first Bailiwick angler, to officially break the 200yds mark, his cast measuring 204yds 2ft 9 inches.

Although he was delighted with his achievement, the standard of local casting was put into perspective by the fact that he was the last of the 28 competitors, with the winner on the day casting 278yds.

Dave Saunders record was to stand until November 2005 when Tom Ozanne cast a length of 245yds in a tournament held in Jersey.

He was to further improve on this record when he attended the 2006 Jersey event and achieved a distance of 254yds (231.85 meters).

If a casting tournament was held in Guernsey, there is no doubt the Bailiwick all-comers record of 219yds 2ft, and the best cast of 184yds 2 ft by a local angler in Guernsey, would both be easily beaten.

Guernsey Anglers Team Knock-Out Competition
As we have already noted the Guernsey Federation of Sea Anglers was formed in 1981 following the deliberations of an ad-hoc committee formed in the later 1970's to investigate the need and feasibility of such a body.

There had however, been some informal discussions in the early years of the 1970's on the need for Bailiwick anglers to get together and as an indirect result of those conversations the Guernsey Anglers Team Knock Out Competition was born in 1972.

Its object was to promote friendly competitive angling between teams in Guernsey. It was run on the heaviest aggregate weight principle.

Its first committee was Chairman Bill Tabel, secretary Mick Le Sauvage and Treasurer Dave Sebire.

The six-a-side competition encouraged entries from all anglers, not just those from angling clubs.

This policy was to prove very successful and teams have taken part representing companies, public houses, States Departments and banks, while many were formed from just groups of angling friends.

As the teams did not usually officially represent a formal angling club the names of the teams were quite imaginative and sometimes quite hilarious.

The Perelle Pirates, Ebbs and Flows, Cod Row, Screeching Clutches, Piscatorial Artists, Shirvy Throwers, Otto's Danglers, Rodbenders, Last Post Hookers, Trott's Lot and Hot Rods being just a few examples.

GATKOC's committee from its inception in 1972 to 1988, Bill Tabel (left) Mick Le Sauvage (centre) and Dave Sebire

The number of entries varied year by year, reaching a high of 21 teams in 1979 and 1980 and a low of seven in 1997 and 1999.

Although the matches could be fished afloat or ashore, almost 100% of the teams opted to fish from boats.

The results were obviously dependent on the length of time the two teams agreed to fish and the venue chosen. Catches of over 600-0-0 for a match have been recorded when it has been an all day match fished over wrecks or deep water marks, down to under 20-0-0, for a short evening match on inshore marks.

The first ever winners were the Herons, captained by Bill Tabel, the team's title being the name of Bills boat!

Although it was a six-a-side tournament, teams were allowed to register up to eight. The remainder of the Herons team squad were Mark Tabel, Terry and Tony Bougourd, Roy Priest, John Oakley and Dennis Lempriere.

The Herons dominated the first years of the competitions, winning on three occasions in the first four competitions, their sequence of four straight possible wins being broken by Houmet Odds and Sods who won in 1974.

The Herons, the first ever winners of the GATKOC in 1972. Back row (left to right) Tony Bougourd, Roy Priest, Denis Lempriere. Front row (left to right) John Oakley, Mark Tabel, Bill Tabel and Terry Bougourd.

Each year the format of the teams changed, often with anglers swapping their allegiance to another team. It was therefore difficult for one team to dominate for a long period.

One exception was Les Boucanniers, which was mainly made up by anglers from the Jamaica Inn Angling Club. They were the most successful team, winning it on five occasions during the period 1982 to 1988.

The competition broadened a little since its inception, for in addition to the team championship shield there was a runner-up trophy, individual awards for the heaviest bag, best pollack, bass and flattie and thanks to sponsorship from one of the tackle dealers, prizes of fishing tackle.

The competition's success was largely due to its dedicated committee. Bill Tabel, Mick le Sauvage and Dave Sebire were to stay together in office for 17 years, almost certainly the longest unchanged committee ever in local angling history.

In 1988 Bill Tabel retired from his chairman's post which was filled by Harold Bewey. Following Harold's untimely death in 1993 Brett Shepperd took over the post.

In 1998, the 27th year of the competition, Mick Le Sauvage and Dave Sebire still filled the secretary and treasurer's posts, a unique and dedicated record of service to the angling community, and achievement of which they can be justly proud.

Sadly in the late 1990's it became clear that the support for the competition was starting to dwindle. Team entries slumped to less than 10, and in 2002 the event was not held for only three teams registered their intention to take part.

There was a mini-revival in 2003 when 10 teams took part, but it proved to be the last competition. The Black Sea Horses, a team representing Lloyds TSB Bank had the honour of being the last winners.

A very sad end to a competition that had run for over 30 years and had provided so much fun and enjoyment.

National Competition Finals

It's not just the local anglers who have enjoyed competition fishing in Bailiwick waters. As news of the excellent fishing in local waters filtered out beyond the shores of the Channel Islands, individual anglers began to come over and take part in open competitions. In addition as angling administrators elsewhere became aware of its potential they arranged for many prestigious events to take place in the Bailiwick.

NFSA Shore Championship Final competiitors pose on Herm Breakwater.
Two anglers kneeling in front are Joe Gomez (left) and Peter Frise, locals who have acted as guides, ghillies and shirvy suppliers in each year the event was held in Herm. Fourth from right in back row is Alan Yates, an English international who won the final on four occasions. Fifth from left is David Rowe Development Officer in the NFSA, and organiser of the event

It all started in 1988 when the National Federation of Sea Anglers decided to fish their shore championship finals in Herm. It proved so successful they came over every year, with 2008 being the 20th year that the 10 finalists out of the hundreds who enter the heats held throughout the United Kingdom were brought over by David Rowe, who was the NSFA Development Officer, to battle it out in a two-day match on Herm to decide who will be the NFSA shore champion. There was a break in 2006 when the final was not held, but it was fished in 2007 along with that years final. The most successful angler in the championships has been English International Alan Yates who has won it on four occasions – an incredible feat.

Changes in the format of angling organisations in the UK including the end of the NFSA and the formation of the Angling Trust proved to be the death knell for the competition with the last one being held in 2008.

1988 was to prove quite a year for the TV South/NFSA boat championship final and the TV South West/NFSA champion of champions final were also held locally.

In 1989 over 100 anglers and friends came to Guernsey for the European Federation of Sea Anglers (Netherlands Division) boat championship finals, while in 1991 the TV South/NFSA boat finals returned to the Bailiwick but on this occasion to fish the waters around Alderney.

In 1993 and 1994 there were more visitors from the NFSA, for their Wessex Division fished their shore and boat championship finals in Guernsey.

There were many other such visits, including the British Police Angling Championships, teams of anglers from the British Prison Service and the final of the Suzuki National Boat League.

Bailiwick Entry into International Competitions

Bailiwick anglers are much more insular in their views and seem very reticent to travel overseas to fish competitions. Possibly this is due to the excellent local fishing. Why go elsewhere when it's all there on your own doorstep?

As we have already noted, one exception was the West Coast Sea Angling Club (formerly the JIAC) who used to travel to Devon on a biannual basis.

However, on two occasions, Guernsey anglers did venture abroad and with some success!

In 1979 and 1980, a Guernsey team of five anglers, along with team manager, Harold Bewey, entered the Irish Federation of Sea Anglers/Tylers International Angling Championships at Cobh in Eire.

This was a top event which attracted national teams from all over Europe. They were made up of their country's top sea anglers, who had all been carefully selected for their experience and proven competitive ability at the very top level.

There had been no such selection process to decide the Guernsey team. It consisted purely of anglers who expressed in interest in taking part and who were prepared to pay all of their own, quite considerable expenses.

In 1979 the Guernsey contingent did not know what to expect and were largely unprepared for such an occasion. They were not disgraced, finishing 11th of the 13 national teams taking part, while Guernsey's top individual angler was John Clark who finished in 14th place.

The Guernsey team went over to Cobh again in the following year. It was largely unchanged with four of the 1979 squad taking part again. The team, which consisted of Ron Harris, John Rothwell, John Clark, Cedric Bayles and your author had phenomenal success. They took the prize for winning on the first day of the four-day competition and went on to finally finish second out of the 10 teams, being very narrowly beaten by Scotland for first place.

Ron Harris led for the individual championship for the first three days and although a disappointing catch on the fourth day dropped him down to third it was a very credible performance, especially bearing in mind the standard of the anglers taking part. In addition, team members accounted for two best catch of the day awards, and won two prizes for the second best fish of the day.

It was very exciting and also a lot of fun. On one evening each of the teams was expected to provide an item for the evening's entertainment. Most teams chose to sing one of their national songs or play a musical instrument. Ron Harris and John Rothwell were to prove the stars of the week! They dressed up in drag, including false breasts and did a hilarious strip routine that really brought the house down!

There is no doubt that a correctly managed and selected team consisting of the Bailiwick's top anglers would do incredibly well in both national and international competition. The talent, expertise and experience exist, it just needs the interest and enthusiasm to bring it all together.

Ron Harris (left) and John Rothwell as you've never seen them before - all dressed up for their strip act at the IFSA/Tyler Championships in Cobh, Eire in 1980!

The Guernsey team that did so well in IFSA/Tyler International Angling Championship in Cobh, Eire in 1980. Back row (left to right) Your author, Cedric Bayles, John Clark, John Rothwell, Ron Harris and front, team manager Harold Bewey

Chapter 9 - Records

Some anglers regard record fish as an irrelevance, having no interest in claiming at club, Bailiwick or British level and often not even bothering to record their own catches.

However, This only seems to apply to a small minority. Most have a keen interest in formal records and fully realise the value of a system that ensures that outstanding fish of all species are chronologically and historically recorded, providing an official record that is accepted and recognised by everyone.

Records have become an essential tool in angling administration, for both British and Bailiwick records are now used as a yardstick for many club and open specimen fish competitions, the anglers catch being judged against the local or national best.

For individuals they have become a target. Anglers feel a real sense of achievement, if they can catch a fish that ensures that their name appears on the record list.

We take record lists for granted nowadays, but prior to 1966, formal record lists were almost non-existent.

The long established Guernsey Sea Anglers Club maintained separate boat and shore club record lists, but that was it!

A British record list had been in existence since 1957 but no local anglers had even considered claiming a national record.

The only list in the Bailiwick was kept by Peter Witterick, a feature writer and columnist at the Guernsey Press. Peter, who was later to become the paper's Features Editor, wrote the weekly angling column and kept his own list of heaviest fish as reported to him by local anglers.

He would have been the first to agree that the list was very unsatisfactory. It merely listed the specimens he became aware of while obtaining news for his column. If an angler rang up and said "I've caught a 3-8-0 garfish at Grandes Rocques," that was jotted down and included.

There was no procedure for ensuring that the fish had been fairly caught on rod and line, weighed on accurate scales or that it had been

One of the original unofficial records compiled by Peter Witterick. Bob Elliott with his 15-7-0 bass in 1962

correctly identified by a competent independant person. This was all to change. At a committee meeting of the Guernsey Sea Anglers Club held on 10 August,1966 at the Dorset Arms it was decided that a formal Bailiwick fish record list should be created.

Peter Witterick was asked to organise the formation of the Bailiwick's first record fish committee.

The next move took place on 24 November, 1966 at L'Auberge Divette. Peter, Ernie Baker, (who was then the GSAC president), and I met to discuss the initial moves necessary to form the committee.

A number of fundamental points were quickly agreed. The committee would be completely independent and would have no affiliation to any club or organisation. It would be as widely representative of island anglers as possible, and would include delegates from angling clubs, independent anglers who were not members of any club, and a consultant marine biologist.

The inaugural meeting of the Bailiwick of Guernsey Record (Rod-Caught) Fish Committee was held at the Dorset Arms on 1 December, 1966.

Present on that auspicious occasion were Reg Elliott and Pip Le Blancq from the GSAC, Ken Seager and Terry Rowe from the Telephone Angling Club, Les Bougourd and Mike Dew from the 30 Fathom Club, Peter Sirett and Joe Guerin from the Tektronix Angling Club, Peter Witterick, Ernie Baker and myself.

At the meeting the committee's first officers were elected: Peter Witterick, chairman, treasurer/assistant recorder Mike Dew, and myself as secretary/recorder. Roger Brehaut had been approached and asked to become the committee's consultant marine biologist and he had accepted.

By 2011, 45 years on from the committee's formation, only Roger and myself remain from that original committee.

Peter Witterick was to be the committee's chairman for 14 years, and it was due to his leadership and wise counsel that the committee was steered successfully through its difficult and busy early years.

Under his guidance the committee's constitution, aims and objects and rules were compiled, claim forms and record certificates designed and printed and sponsorship obtained from the Guernsey Press.

Peter Witterick, the first chairman of the Bailiwick Record Committee, Pictured with an 8-2-4 pollack in July, 1965.

One early problem was the creation of the first record list. A proposal to throw the list open to all claims was quickly rejected. An angler could have submitted a 4 oz pollack to start the ball rolling, to be followed by a 7 oz fish from another angler followed by a 1-2-0 specimen, followed by . . . . !?

Such a scenario was unthinkable.

It was finally decided to use fish that had been entered in the Players Gold Leaf and Gladstone competitions of the previous year. It was accepted that entries in these competitions, which were the forerunners of the present Fish of the Month contest, had been weighed accurately and seen by independent witnesses.

The result was an overall list which contained 19 species. Most were quickly beaten and it is interesting to note that none of those initial records still stand today. The record weights were only quoted in pounds, ounces and drams. The inclusion of the equivalent metric weights did not appear on the record lists until 1990.

The first ever Bailiwick Record Fish list

Bailiwick of Guernsy Record (Rod-caught) Fish Committee RECORD LIST AS AT JANUARY 11, 1967.					
	Fish Weight				
	lb.	oz.	drms.	Captor Place	Date
BASS	12	0	0	B. Burton	Les Amarreurs	16.10.66
"	12	0	0	R. F, Denning	Perelle Bay	25. 9.66
BREAM, BLACK	4	3	0	D. Fergus Ferguson	S. of La Cachalière Alderney	21. 8.66
BRILL	7	10	0	R. Jehan	Great Bank	9. 7.66
COD	14	14	0	C. W. Bragg	Longy Bay, Alderney	31.10.66
CONGER	28	0	0	E. J. Pawley	St Sampson's Breakwater	6. 7.66
DAB	1	5	4	J. Pommier	Pembroke	17.10.66
GARFISH	2	0	0	H. S. Goodison	St Martin's Point	15. 8.66
"	2	0	0	J. K. Porter	St Martin's Point	19. 8.66
GURNARD, RED		1	11	0 Mrs. I. Jehan	Great Bank	16. 8.66
MACKEREL ...	2	7	0	L. R. Le Page	S. of Hanois	19. 6.66
MULLET, GREY	4	7	0	B. C. Le Feuvre	Belle Greve Bay	16. 9.66
MULLET, RED ..	1	9	8	R. King	Pembroke	2.10.66
POLLACK	6	13	0	R. Hockey	Pembroke	2.10.66
SHARK, BLUE .	63	0	0	B. Bertrand	S. of Guernsey	21. 8.66
SHARK, PORBEAGLE ..	162	0	0	W. Sylvester	S. of Guernsey	10. 9.66
SOLE	2	5	0	R. M. Luxton	Pembroke	30. 7.66
THREE BEARDED ROCKLING	1	8	12	A. Mudge	Terres Point	3. 7.66
TOPE	30	4	0	L. R. Le Page	S. of Hanois	3. 7.66
TURBOT	24	4	0	M. L. Fitzgerald	Great Bank	18. 6.66
WRASSE, BALLAN	6	2	0	R.J. Quesnel	Pembroke	30. 7.66

There was considerable concern in the first committee that it would not be accepted by Bailiwick anglers as the record authority, as it was self-appointed.

The fears were to prove groundless. Claims started to roll in almost immediately.

Henry Neville had the distinction of being the first record claimant, submitting a 12-6-0 bass caught off the shore at Bordeaux on 29 January, 1967.

Henry Neville with his 12-6-0 shore-caught bass, the first ever Bailiwick record claim on 29 January, 1967.

By the end of the first year no fewer than 56 claims had been processed, followed by 70 in the next two years.

By the end of May 2011, 704 claims had been made and the committee had met on 154 occasions.

The heaviest fish out of that huge list of claims was the current porbeagle shark record of 295-8-6 caught by Jamie Allen in August 2007. The lightest was the greater pipefish of 0-1-7 caught by David Sheath in June 1969 and the 0-1-7 goldsinny wrasse caught by Tracey Bougourd in August 1973.

Some species started off with a big fish, which has stood as the record for some time. The oldest on the lists is a case in point. Pip Le Blancq landed a 13-14-0 greater spotted dogfish (or bull huss) on the shore in Herm on 10 June, 1967, which still stood 44 years later in June 2011.

Other species were beaten with almost monotonous regularity and taking into account both the boat and shore-caught lists the coalfish record changed hands 22 times. Red bream, bass and pollack were other examples with a high turn over, each seeing 20 changes. Couch's sea bream were just one behind with 19.

Some records stood for less than a day! Five anglers share this doubtful privilege.

George Jennings with the 3-6-3 shore caught common eel landed on the Albert Pier in St Peter Port Harbour on 10 August 1986

Dave Rabey with a 2-2-2 lesser spotted dogfish in 1968, Dave Brouard 17-9-9 pollack in 1972, Steve Huxster 3-15-0 black bream in 1976, Noel Rive 4-9-12 gilthead bream in 1980 and Bob Bannister 14-15-10 bull huss 2006.

Your author has made the most individual claims with 19, followed by Alderney angler Bert Pike with 10 and John (Tiny) Rogers with eight. Many of these claims were from the early days when records were easier to beat, and consequently it is unlikely that these individual totals will ever be beaten.

Obviously, that early rush of claims could not be sustained and it soon came down approximately 20 a year as the list settled.

John (Tiny) Rogers, who had a total of eight Bailiwick records in his time, pictured with two good pollack

271

However, in 1976 the Bailiwick committee followed the British committee's lead and split the overall lists into three separate ones, boat-caught, shore-caught and a mini-list for fish under a pound in weight.

An explosion of claims followed as anglers rushed to fill vacant spots on the three lists. No fewer than 85 claims were received over the next two years.

The trend can be seen on the graph.

BAILIWICK OF GUERNSEY
RECORD (ROD-CAUGHT) FISH COMMITTEE
RECORD OF CLAIMS RECEIVED

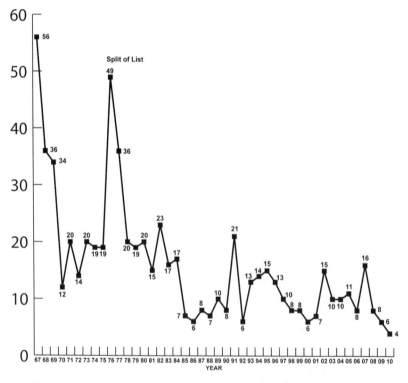

The number of claims received included a small number of freshwater fish.

As we have already seen, early on there was very little freshwater fishing done in the Bailiwick. The Guernsey Trout Society fished the reservoir, but have a policy not to submit record claims.

Consequently the few claims came from the extremely small number of anglers who had access to private quarries. As a result a small freshwater list was maintained which did not relate to the hidden potential of local freshwater fishing.

Things changed considerably once the Guernsey Freshwater Angling Society was formed. In their early years they did not allow their members to make record claims, but once this restriction was removed the number of claims received dramatically increased. As a result the Bailiwick Freshwater record list did, at last, begin to reflect the standard of the local freshwater fishing, although, to date, the owner of the two recently created ponds, do not permit record claims to be made for fish caught in their water.

Bailiwick of Guernsey (rod caught) record fish – FRESHWATER

As at 24 June, 2011

SPECIES	DATE	CAPTOR	LOCATION	kilos gms	lb	oz	dms
Bream	30.7.07	D. Copperwaite	Ville Baudu II Quarry	2 092	4	9	13
Carp	3.9.06	J. Rosbrook	La Lande Quarry	17 321	38	3	0
Carp, Grass	20.7.08	S. G. Le Cloarec	Grand Mare Pond	7 626	16	13	0
Catfish	30.7.03	N. Carter	Carteret Quarry	2 438	5	6	0
Chub	12.3.04	T. Cotterill	La Lande Quarry	2 597	5	11	10
Eel. Common	26.5.11	G. Whitehead	La Lande Quarry	2 760	6	1	6
Perch	17.10.05	P. Clark	La Lande Quarry	1 247	2	12	0
Rudd	29.7.07	C. Byng	Les Rouvets Lake	0 489	1	1	4
Tench	14.5.11	P. Berryman	Ville Baudu II Quarry	2 665	5	14	0
Trout, brown	25.2.90	L. R. Le Page	Lucksall Quarry	4 582	10	1	10

C.I. Records

An early aim of the committee was to see the formation of a Channel Island Record List. There was a Jersey Record Committee with similar aims and standards, so the issue of a joint list should not have posed a problem. Protracted and sometimes difficult negotiations ensued with the Jersey Record (Rod-Caught) Fish Committee and it wasn't until 1971 that a Channel Island overall record list finally came into being. In 1976 the list followed the Bailiwick and British list by splitting into boat, shore and mini sections.

The C.I. lists are published each year in January or February after the two island committees have agreed the updates to the lists following the scrutiny of the record claims received and approved during the previous year in both Bailiwicks. Channel Island record certificates are issued to all record holders.

Unfortunately, to date, there is no Channel Island Freshwater record list. Unlike in the Guernsey Bailiwick, the Jersey Record committee do not process freshwater claims. The only freshwater records held in Jersey are maintained by the freshwater club. An approach from a representative of the Guernsey record committee to the Jersey Freshwater organisation met with a very disappointing response. The Jersey freshwater anglers do not seem to be interested in a Channel Island list, and until their attitude changes no further progress will be made.

273

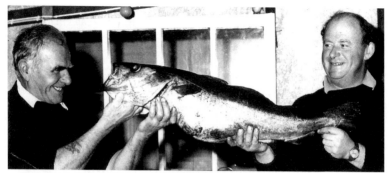

Eddie Plevin (left) and Chippy Corbet with the 17-6-7 Bailiwick record pollack caught by Eddie north of Guernsey in December 1971

British Records

Without doubt the most satisfying and exciting success story due to the formation of the Bailiwick Record committee has been the incredible number of British Record claims made on behalf of Bailiwick-caught fish.

Dave Sebire set the ball rolling with a 0-4-1 common topknot almost immediately after the committee was formed. It was only the third claim received by the committee on 28 February, 1967. When it was decided to make the claim, it was soon realised it would create a precedent.

At that time there were no mini species (fish below 1-0-0) on the British list, and there were real concerns on the possibility of an adverse reaction from the national body. Nothing daunted, the committee submitted a claim to the national committee on behalf of Dave. The worries proved unfounded for the claim was approved without comment.

The local committee's involvement in the claim was unique for normally the angler concerned would contact the British committee directly. It was not usual for a second party to act on behalf of the angler making the claim. Nevertheless, the procedure worked smoothly on that occasion and it became the 'norm' for future claims.

In fact a friendly rapport soon built up with the national body as they realised that claims from the Bailiwick were quickly and accurately processed and submitted on the angler's behalf.

Expressions of their appreciation were received on a number of occasions, both when the British Records Committee came under the wing of the now defunct National Anglers Council and more recently through the National Federation of Sea Anglers which is now part of the Angling Trust.

To date the local committee have submitted no fewer than 119 claims to the British committee. This represents approximately one in six of the total claims received by the local body. This really is a quite staggering statistic! It underlines the quality of the fishing in the Bailiwick area. Out of the 119 claims made only 10 were unsuccessful, these mainly being due to larger fish of the same species

Andy Loveridge with his 5-6-13 Bailiwick shore-caught record flounder - landed n St Peter Port Harbour in December 1998. It was only three drams under the British record.

being submitted simultaneously from elsewhere in the UK, thereby ruling out the locally based claim. This problem was very much in evidence in 1976 when the British list was split. It was inevitable that some claims would clash with other similar submissions from elsewhere.

The 119 claims cover 40 different species. Although Couch's sea bream did not appear in local waters until 1993 they top the claims list with 15 submissions, followed by golden grey mullet with nine, cuckoo wrasse with eight, and black bream with six.

In January 2011 the Bailiwick held four boat, 10 shore and five mini British records.

For the majority of anglers, to catch a British record is a lifelong ambition. The Bailiwick must be unique in providing so many anglers who have achieved that goal, and yet incredibly, there are six local anglers who have gained more than one national record!

Pride of place goes to the legendary Bert Pike who has had no fewer than five British shore caught records in his time! They were golden grey mullet of 1-11-8 and 1-12-6, gilthead bream of 3-5-14, black bream of 4-2-11 and sole of 4-8-0.

John Maurice actually made four claims but one failed due to a larger fish being landed elsewhere. His three successful claims for shore-caught records were plaice 6-9-12, small eyed ray 13-4-1, and sole 4-5-0.

Your author also had three national records, a 19-6-13 boat-caught undulate ray, a 1-6-11 boat-caught

John Martel with the 3-10-0 red mullet which held the British and Bailiwck shore records from 22 October, 1967 to 30 September, 1996!

275

cuckoo wrasse and an 0-7-0 Baillon's wrasse.

Anglers with two records, all shore caught were Fred Odoire with 2-8-4 and 2-10-4 golden grey mullet, Jonathan Reeves with 2-12-12 and 3-0-4 golden grey mullet and Mark Hooper with 1-12-10 cuckoo wrasse and 2-4-8 Couch's sea bream.

Ironically, the most outstanding fish dealt with by the Bailiwick Record Committee wasn't even caught in Bailiwick waters!!

In late June 1969 members of the Guernsey 30 Fathom Club travelled on Graham Cowley's "Storm Drift" down to Jersey, and on to the Pipette rocks, on the north edge of the enormous Minquiers reef.

Shaun Savident with the Bailiwick boat-caught record 5-4-0 whiting caught on Godine Bank in February 1998.

The 29 June was to prove to be a momentous day. The object of the long trip was to fish for shark, which were known to frequent the area.

Des Bougourd, using tackle more suitable for tope rather than large shark hooked an enormous fish. After a titanic struggle he finally boated a 430-0-0 porbeagle shark.   (see page 221)

The "Storm Drift" brought the shark and its delighted captor directly back to Guernsey, where on behalf of Des, the record committee successfully claimed the British record, and following submissions to the International Game Fishing Association in Florida, the World All Tackle and 80lb line class records.

Up to June 2011, it remains the only world claim processed by the Bailiwick committee.

There was no doubt at the time that the shark could not qualify as a Bailiwick of Guernsey record, but it would become a Jersey record, as it was caught in Jersey waters.

In later years the question of which record fish belonged to whom, was a problem that was to cause some discussion. It was caused in part by anglers using faster boats to travel much further afield and fish the more distant wrecks and marks.

The question arose, "How far out can you go, and how long can you stay out before your catch fails to be a Bailiwick fish?"

The committee looked to the national body's procedures for guidance and after much deliberation, the following standard was agreed.

"Claims will only be considered if the boat concerned has left and returned to a port in the Channel Islands within a 24 hour period, without calling at any port outside the Channel Islands.

Fish taken in waters that are the responsibility of other countries (including the Bailiwick of Jersey) will not be considered.

Fish must be caught within the area bounded by the median line with other countries fishing areas, the 12 mile limit from other countries, and to a maximum limit of 30 miles from the nearest land in the Bailiwick."

To ensure that this was clear and understood, in 1984 the committee issued an illustrative chartlet. (See next page)

Over the years the committee has faced many challenges but the standards and principles laid down in the early years has held the committee in good stead to cope with the problems and come to the right decisions.

The committee's mandate from the beginning was to make it was representative of all island anglers as possible, and there is no doubt that this aim has been met.

Alderney legend Bert Pike with his 7-9-8 Bailiwick shore-caught record plaice, landed on 28 October, 1977 at Houmet Herbe.

As the number of clubs multiplied, so did the number of delegates to the committee, which meant that, at one stage, it had 25 members!

The expansion included a delegate from the Guernsey Freshwater Angling Society, as well as from Alderney and Sark.

Over the years no fewer than 126 different anglers have attended committee meetings.

Following Peter Witterick's retirement form his post in 1980 the committee has been led, in turn, by Pip Le Blancq, Harold Bewey and Mike Weysom.

They and all the committee members continue to strive to maintain the record lists with impartiality, and to ensure the integrity of the lists is upheld even if at times, they have had to make unpopular decisions and reject claims.

In spite of the fact that the sea fish record lists are continually updated, all three bailiwick record lists and the three Channel Island lists are included on the following pages.

They provide a snapshot of the state of the record lists on the dates quoted and give a good illustration of how far things have progressed since 1966.

They are reproduced with the kind permission of the Bailiwick of Guernsey Record (Rod-Caught) Fish Committee.

BAILIWICK OF GUERNSEY
RECORD (ROD-CAUGHT) FISH COMMITTEE

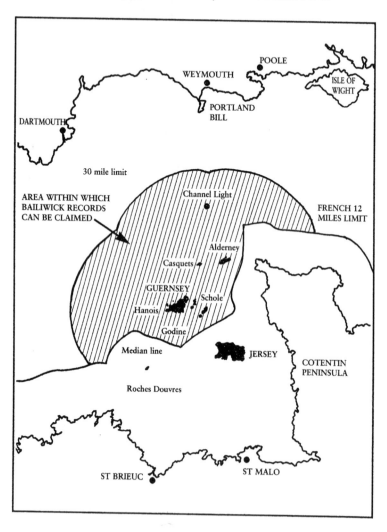

Bailiwick of Guernsey (rod caught) record fish – BOAT

As at 24 June, 2011

SPECIES	DATE	CAPTOR	LOCATION	kilos	gms	lb	oz	dms
Almaco Jack	29.8.07	C. Torode	Grande Rocques	0	673	1	7	12
Amberjack, Guinean	7.9.00	G. A. Staples	Noir Pute	0	641	1	6	10*
Angler Fish	20.6.95	P. Kennedy	W. of Guernsey	33	100	72	15	9
Bass	20.9.05	B. Adams	Alderney Race	8	356	18	6	12
Bogue	19.8.85	S. P. Martel	Grand Havre	0	754	1	10	10
Bream, Black	24.7.99	D. Reid	NW. of Guernsey	3	019	6	10	8
Bream, Couch's Sea	28.4.07	R. J. Fallaize	Susanne	2	989	6	9	7*
Bream, Gilthead	14.9.03	S. Rowe	Gate rock, Herm	2	344	5	2	11
Bream, Pandora	3.9.98	C. Shrigley	Belgrave Bay	1	270	2	12	13
Bream, Red	21.9.95	P. de Jersey	NW. of Guernsey	3	100	6	13	5
Brill	5.4.86	R. Seager	Banc au Nord	6	151	13	9	0
Coalfish	30.3.97	N. Reid	W. of Hanois	11	900	26	3	12
Cod	29.7.87	E. Carter	W. of Hanois	17	690	39	0	0
Conger	19.8.91	V. Kroon	W. of Guernsey	49	000	108	0	6
Dab	6.8.68	S. Falla	Off Fort Doyle	0	767	1	11	1
Dogfish, Greater-Spotted (Bull Huss)	5.6.06	J. Beck	East of Sark	7	399	16	5	0
Dogfish, Lesser-Spotted	28.8.78	A. Ogier	W. Coast Guernsey	1	436	3	2	11
Dogfish, Spur	23.5.91	P. A. Shannan	W. of Guernsey	5	712	12	9	8
Eel, Common	26.8.87	C. Bale	St Peter Port Harbour	1	686	3	11	8
Flounder	10.9.77	A. H. Corbet	Nr Beaucette Marina	0	772	1	11	4
Garfish	12.5.02	A. Gibbons	Banc de la Schole	1	256	2	12	5
Gurnard, Grey	24.7.99	W. Gough	Godine Bank	0	600	1	5	3
Gurnard, Red	31.8.95	B. Le Noury	Havre Gosselin	1	295	2	13	11
Gurnard, Tub	10.7.10	L. Le Poidevin	Godine Bank	3	632	8	0	2
Haddock	24.6.82	S. P. Martel	Great Bank	0	992	2	3	0
Hake	17.7.87	G. A. Siddall	W of Guernsey	6	998	15	6	14
John Dory	15.5.01	J. Cataroche	Great Bank	5	000	11	0	5
Ling	4.7.79	Mrs A. Wright	W of Alderney	16	726	36	14	0
Lumpsucker	9.5.71	C. Browning	Anfre	2	500	5	8	3
Mackerel	7.7.92	P. M. Walsh	Great Bank	1	888	4	2	10
Mackerel, Spanish	25.7.08	K. Beausire	Banc Au Nord	0	609	1	5	8*
Megrim	15.4.11	M. Le Sauvage	Godine Bank	0	772	1	11	4
Monkfish	13.5.72	D. Bougourd	Great Bank	16	329	36	0	0
Mullet, Grey, Golden	18.7.03	M. Bourgaize	Grande Havre	1	139	2	8	3
Mullet, Grey, Thick-Lipped	21.12.08	R. Smith	Longy Bay, Alderney	4	008	8	7	6
Mullet, Red	10.11.81	M. T. Hamel	Petils Bay, Bordeaux	1	559	3	7	0*
Plaice	16.9.78	C. F. Merrien	S. of Guernsey	3	956	8	11	9
Pollack	20.1.01	P. Berry	NW. of Guernsey	11	680	25	12	0
Pout	15.6.08	F. J. Van Zyl	SW of Guernsey	1	610	3	8	13
Ray, Blonde	29.6.05	P. Williams	Alderney Swinge	16	398	36	2	7
Ray, Marbled Electric	15.10.10	G. Crane	East of Sark	4	952	10	14	11*
Ray, Small-Eyed	14.7.82	R. Hays	Off Platte Saline	5	832	12	13	12
Ray, Spotted	9.7.82	D. J. Sebire	Off Perelle	2	300	5	1	8
Ray, Sting	19.9.70	L. E. Hall	Vermerette	18	483	40	12	0
Ray, Thornback	14.6.09	W. Calladine	SE of Sark	8	278	18	4	0
Ray, Undulate	1.11.70	L. R. Le Page	Amfroque	8	811	19	6	13
Rockling, Three-Bearded	2.9.91	A. N. Dunglinson	Nr Beaucette Marina	0	799	1	11	8
Scad	9.9.07	M. Giles	Petites Canupes	0	958	2	1	13
Sea Trout	14.8.96	P. B. Prout	off Les Tielles	2	657	5	13	12
Shad, Twaite	24.2.82	G. A. Staples	Godine Bank	0	857	1	14	4
Shark, Blue	3.8.02	P. Priaulx	W. of Guernsey	60	248	132	13	3
Shark, Porbeagle	10.8.07	J. J. Allen	Off Hanois	134	050	295	8	6
Smooth Hound, Starry	8.10.08	R. Seager	East of Sark	6	435	14	3	0
Sole, Common	19.6.93	M. Eppelein	Great Bank	1	864	4	1	12
Sunfish	14.8.84	S. J. Davies	Off Alderney Breakwater	13	380	29	8	0
Sunfish	14.9.85	K. Thomson	Brehon Tower	13	380	29	8	0
Tope	25.9.83	R. Hays	Alderney South Banks	25	287	55	12	0
Trigger Fish	26.8.74	Miss J. Sheppard	Herm	1	649	3	10	3
Turbot	29.4.05	J. Robert	Banc Au Nord	13	721	30	4	0
Weever, Greater	20.7.04	P. Berry	Casquets S.W. Bank	0	464	1	0	5
Whiting	7.2.98	S. Savident	Godine Bank	2	381	5	4	0
Wrasse, Ballan	5.11.88	G. D. Pallot	Petites Canupes	3	657	8	1	0
Wrasse, Cuckoo	14.1.07	P. Broe Bougourd	Anfre	0	955	2	1	11

*British Rod-Caught Record.

Bailiwick of Guernsey (rod caught) record fish – SHORE

As at 24 June, 2011

SPECIES	DATE	CAPTOR	LOCATION	kilos	gms	lb	oz	dms
Angler Fish	5.7.74	C. Geaves	St Peter Port Breakwater	17	236	38	0	0
Bass	23.10.99	S. Rowe	Pembroke	8	343	18	6	5
Bogue	19.11.78	S. G. Torode	Pembroke	0	885	1	15	4*
Bream, Black	31.10.01	Miss R. E. Guille	Creux Harbour, Sark	2	958	6	8	6*
Bream, Couch's Sea	16.7.08	S. J. Newton	Belgrave Bay	1	486	3	4	7*
Bream, Gilthead	25.7.09	C. Tranter	Near Beaucette Marina	4	064	8	15	6
Bream, Red	19.9.79	A. Salmon	Alderney Lighthouse	2	012	4	7	0*
Brill	7.11.84	N. Loving	Mannez, Alderney	2	197	4	13	8
Coalfish	7.1.95	R. Le Ray	St Peter Port Breakwater	5	228	11	8	10
Cod	28.12.81	N. P. du Jardin	L'Ancresse	13	154	29	0	0
Conger	29.9.00	P. R. Carre	Bec Du Nez	29	900	65	14	10
Dab	9.8.81	C. McClean	Fort Doyle	0	710	1	9	1
Dogfish, Greater-Spotted (Bull Huss)	10.6.67	P. Le Blancq	Herm	6	293	13	14	0
Dogfish, Lesser-Spotted	1.10.04	M. Le Page	St Peter Port Breakwater	1	295	2	13	11
Eel, Common	11.9.87	G. C. Jennings	Albert Pier	1	793	3	15	4
Flounder	23.12.98	A. Loveridge	St Peter Port Harbour	2	461	5	6	13
Garfish	1.12.02	J. Rothwell	Crown Pier	1	238	2	11	11
Gurnard, Red	6.8.00	A. Loveridge	L'Ancresse Bay	1	031	2	4	6
Gurnard, Tub	26.6.05	O. Bailey	Chouet	2	524	5	9	1
John Dory	18.8.67	B. G. Horsepool	St Peter Port Breakwater	1	452	3	3	4
Ling	18.12.88	L. Le Gallais	St Peter Port Breakwater	6	421	14	2	8
Lumpsucker	24.1.76	H. Froome	St Peter Port Breakwater	5	273	11	10	0
Mackerel	3.8.77	D. Jones	White Rock	1	275	2	13	0
Mullet, Grey, Golden	11.10.91	J. R. Reeves	Cats Bay, Alderney	1	369	3	0	4
Mullet, Grey, Thick-Lipped	24.3.85	R. L. Simonet	Longy, Alderney	5	397	11	14	6
Mullet, Grey, Thin-Lipped	21.2.10	M. Weysom	St Peter Port Breakwater	1	506	3	5	2
Mullet, Red	1.10.96	T. Wright	Longy, Alderney	1	796	3	15	0*
Plaice	8.12.85	R. V. Holland	Bordeaux	3	720	8	3	4
Pollack	21.12.98	N. Jouault	Alderney Lighthouse	7	296	16	1	6
Pout	7.7.91	R. Andrews	Pembroke	2	069	4	9	0*
Ray, Blonde	7.12.86	C. Reeves	Mannez, Alderney	14	740	32	8	0*
Ray, Marbled Electric	27.10.95	D. Rose	Alderney Breakwater	5	611	12	5	14
Ray, Small-Eyed	4.12.93	J. Maurice	Corblets, Alderney	6	566	14	7	10
Ray, Spotted	4.7.82	M. J. Le Sauvage	Herm	2	140	4	11	8
Ray, Sting	18.10.09	R. Torode	Vermerette	26	762	59	0	0
Ray, Undulate	5.12.96	C. Reeves	Alderney, South Coast	8	639	19	0	12
Rockling, Shore	24.2.11	T. Froome	Fort Doyle	0	497	1	1	9
Rockling, Three-Bearded	4.8.07	S. V. Huxster	St Peter Port Breakwater	1	389	3	1	0
Salmon	13.2.07	J. Holdaway	St Sampsons Harbour	2	390	5	4	5
Salmon, Coho	21.7.77	R. J. McCracken	Petit Port	0	681	1	8	1*
Scad	4.7.85	H. Felbabel	St Peter Port Breakwater	1	070	2	5	12
Sea Trout	17.4.99	R. C. Bott	Salerie	2	129	4	11	2
Shad Twaite	5.10.08	S. J. Robins	QEII Marina	0	815	1	12	12
Smooth Hound	29.1.05	S. Fletcher	St Peter Port Breakwater	2	866	6	5	2
Smooth Hound, Starry	2.2.06	S. Ace	Alderney Breakwater	6	609	14	9	2
Sole, Common	13.9.91	N. Guilmoto	Alderney, South Coast	2	996	6	8	10*
Sunfish	17.9.94	J. Maurice	Volta, Alderney	14	783	32	10	0
Tope	18.10.04	S. Mullins	Platte Saline, Alderney	23	099	50	14	13
Trigger Fish	22.8.04	P. Guille	Hog's Back, Sark	1	665	3	10	12
Turbot	25.8.68	L. Benoist	St Sampson's Breakwater	10	064	22	3	0
Whiting	25.1.92	L. Le Gallais	St Peter Port Breakwater	1	013	2	3	12
Wrasse, Ballan	27.3.93	J. P. Le Noury	St Peter Port Harbour	3	935	8	10	13
Wrasse, Cuckoo	17.10.99	M. Hooper	Rosaire, Herm	0	809	1	12	9*

*British Rod-Caught Record.

280

Bailiwick of Guernsey (rod caught) record fish – MINI
(for fish up to 1lb, BOAT or SHORE)
As at 24 June, 2011

SPECIES	DATE	CAPTOR	LOCATION	Grammes	oz	dms
Atherine Smelt	30.11.75	A. D. Laws	New Jetty	72	2	9*
Blenny, Tompot	16.9.05	A. J. Leaman	Creux Harbour, Sark	149	5	4
Bream Axilliary	15.10.95	J. Breedijk	S. W. of Guernsey	237	8	5*
Bream, White	19.7.09	A. Marquis	Salerie	65	2	5
Comber	30.7.78	L. Gallienne	S. of Guernsey	400	14	1
Dragonet	17.8.81	J. K. Taylor	Nr Beaucette Marina	117	4	2
Goby, Giant	2.11.94	A. M. Carre	Beaucette Marina	262	9	4*
Gurnard, Streaked	6.8.93	J. West	Banc de la Schole	290	10	4
Herring	15.6.90	R. Langlois	Great Bank	363	12	13
Long-spined Sea Scorpion	16.7.95	M. E. Bewey	Castle Emplacement	229	8	1
Pilchard	1.7.79	N. J. Barritt	Great Bank	181	6	6
Pipefish, Greater	1.6.69	D. J. Sheath	St Sampson's Breakwater	40	1	7
Poor Cod	29.6.88	L. R. Le Page	Off St Peter Port Harbour	170	6	0
Rockling, Five-bearded	22.2.82	A. Aitken	St Sampson's Harbour	177	6	3
Sandeel, Greater	23.6.79	B. K. Le Breton	Amfroque	239	8	7*
Saury Pike	12.9.07	R. Wheatland	Hurd Deep	72	2	8
Shanny	28.5.77	K. J. Woolfe	St Martin's Point	65	2	4
Tadpole Fish	1.6.95	L. Bearder	St Peter Port Breakwater	439	15	8
Topknot, Common	10.8.98	R. Thomson	Grandes Rocques	382	13	8*
Weever, Lesser	9.7.94	C. Druce	Banc de la Schole	67	2	6
Whiting, Blue	28.5.80	S. Clyde	Great Bank	114	4	0
Wrasse, Baillon's	22.11.01	L. R. Le Page	St Peter Port Breakwater	198	7	0
Wrasse, Corkwing	17.10.77	M. P. Smith	St Peter Port Breakwater	286	10	1
Wrasse Goldsinny	11.9.77	A. L. C. de Guerin	St Peter Port Breakwater	56	1	15
Wrasse, Rock Cook	13.9.77	A. L. C. de Guerin	St Peter Port Breakwater	72	2	8

*British Rod-Caught Record.

Mark Giles with the 2-1-13 boat record scad caught at the Petites Canupes in September 2007.

Channel Islands (rod caught) records, 2011
SHORE

SPECIES	DATE	CAPTOR	LOCATION	kilos	gms	lb	oz	dms
Angler Fish	1974	C. Geaves	Guernsey	17	236	38	0	0
Bass	1999	S. Rowe	Guernsey	8	343	18	6	5
Bogue	1978	S. G. Torode	Guernsey	0	885	1	15	4*
Bream, Black	2001	Miss R. Guille	Sark	2	958	6	8	6*
Bream, Couch's Sea	2008	S. J. Newton	Guernsey	1	486	3	4	7*
Bream, Gilthead	2009	C. Tranter	Guernsey	4	064	8	15	6
Bream, Red	1979	A. Salmon	Alderney	2	012	4	7	0*
Bream, White	2007	R. Allen	Jersey	0	756	1	10	11
Brill	1984	N. Loving	Alderney	2	197	4	13	8
Coalfish	1995	R. Le Ray	Guernsey	5	228	11	8	10
Cod	1981	N. du Jardin	Guernsey	13	154	29	0	0
Conger	2000	P. Carre	Guernsey	29	900	65	14	10
Dab	1981	C. McClean	Guernsey	0	710	1	9	1
Dogfish, Greater-Spotted	1967	P. Le Blancq	Herm	6	293	13	14	0
Dogfish, Lesser-Spotted	2002	S. Santos	Jersey	1	495	3	4	12
Dogfish, Spur	1980	J. Rault	Jersey	0	846	1	13	14
Eel, Common	1998	F. W. Pickett	Jersey	2	041	4	8	0
Flounder	1998	A. Loveridge	Guernsey	2	461	5	6	13
Garfish	2002	J. Rothwell	Guernsey	1	238	2	11	11
Gurnard, Red	2000	A. Loveridge	Guernsey	1	031	2	4	6
Gurnard, Tub	2005	O. Bailey	Guernsey	2	524	5	9	1
John Dory	1961	F. Scar	Jersey	2	721	6	0	0
Ling	1981	D. Rogan	Jersey	8	731	19	4	0
Lumpsucker	1977	R. E. Clarke	Jersey	6	102	13	7	4
Mackerel	1977	D. Jones	Guernsey	1	275	2	13	0
Mullet, Grey, Golden	1991	J. Reeves	Alderney	1	367	3	0	4
Mullet, Grey, Thick-Lipped	1985	R. L. Simonet	Alderney	5	397	11	14	6
Mullet, Grey, Thin-Lipped	2010	D Le Merrer	Jersey	2	792	6	2	8
Mullet, Red	1996	T. Wright	Alderney	1	786	3	15	0*
Plaice	1985	R. Holland	Guernsey	3	720	8	3	4
Pollack	1998	N. Jouault	Alderney	7	296	16	1	6
Pout	1991	R. Andrews	Guernsey	2	069	4	9	0*
Ray, Blonde	1994	K. Fraine	Jersey	14	740	32	8	0*
Ray, Blonde	1986	C. Reeves	Alderney	14	740	32	8	0*
Ray, Electric	1963	G. Clarke	Jersey	3	685	8	2	0
Ray, Marbled Electric	1990	M. Porter	Jersey	6	334	13	15	11*
Ray, Small-Eyed	1993	J. Maurice	Alderney	6	566	14	7	10
Ray, Spotted	1982	M. Le Sauvage	Herm	2	140	4	11	8
Ray, Sting	2009	R. Torode	Herm	26	762	59	0	0
Ray, Thornback	1997	L. Vibert	Jersey	8	164	18	0	0
Ray, Undulate	1983	K. Skinner	Jersey	9	638	21	4	0*
Rockling, Shore	2009	D. Vaudin	Guernsey	0	487	1	1	3
Rockling, Three-Bearded	2007	S. V. Huxster	Guernsey	1	389	3	1	0
Salmon	1971	R. Lawrence	Jersey	3	903	8	9	11
Salmon, Coho	1977	R. J. McCracken	Guernsey	0	681	1	8	1*
Scad	1985	H. Felbabel	Guernsey	1	070	2	5	12
Sea Trout	1987	E. Read	Jersey	5	453	12	0	6
Shad, Allis	1977	K. Swanton	Jersey	0	829	1	13	4
Shad, Twaite	1960	E. Tricot	Jersey	1	119	2	7	8
Skate, Common	1967	B. Poutney	Jersey	7	711	17	0	0
Smooth Hound	2009	C. Renouf	Jersey	7	229	15	15	0
Smooth Hound, Starry	2007	L. Guyoncort	Jersey	8	731	19	4	0
Sole, Common	1991	N. Guilmoto	Alderney	2	996	6	8	10*
Sunfish	1994	J. Maurice	Alderney	14	798	32	10	0
Tope	2004	S. Mullins	Alderney	23	099	50	14	13
Trigger Fish	1999	J. Gavey	Jersey	1	702	3	12	1
Trout, Rainbow (Steelhead)	1989	B. Swain	Jersey	0	784	1	11	11
Turbot	1968	L. Benoist	Guernsey	10	064	22	3	0
Whiting	1992	L. Le Gallais	Guernsey	1	013	2	3	12
Wrasse, Ballan	1994	S. Gavey	Jersey	4	000	8	13	2
Wrasse, Cuckoo	1999	M. Hooper	Herm	0	809	1	12	9*

*British Rod-Caught Record.

Channel Islands (rod caught) records, 2011
BOAT

SPECIES	DATE	CAPTOR	LOCATION	kilos	gms	lb	oz	dms
Almaco Jack	2007	C. Torode	Guernsey	0	673	1	7	12
Amberjack, Guinean	2000	G. Staples	Guernsey	0	641	1	6	10*
Angler Fish	1995	P. Kennedy	Guernsey	33	100	72	15	9
Bass	2005	B. Adams	Alderney	8	356	18	6	12
Bogue	1985	S. P. Martel	Guernsey	0	754	1	10	10
Bream, Black	1997	P. Bisson	Jersey	3	075	6	12	8
Bream, Couch's Sea	2007	R. J. Fallaize	Guernsey	2	989	6	9	7*
Bream, Gilthead	2003	S. Rowe	Herm	2	344	5	2	11
Bream, Pandora	1998	C. Shrigley	Guernsey	1	270	2	12	13
Bream, Red	1995	P. De Jersey	Guernsey	3	100	6	13	5
Brill	1986	R. Seager	Sark	6	151	13	9	0
Coalfish	1997	N. Reid	Guernsey	11	900	26	3	12
Cod	1987	E. Carter	Guernsey	17	690	39	0	0
Conger	1991	V. Kroon	Guernsey	49	000	108	0	6
Dab	1968	S. Falla	Guernsey	0	767	1	11	1
Dogfish, Greater-Spotted	1990	G. Blaby	Jersey	8	524	18	13	0
Dogfish, Lesser-Spotted	2003	R. Bailey	Jersey	1	445	3	3	0
Dogfish, Spur	1994	W. Latham	Jersey	6	793	14	15	10
Eel, Common	1987	C. Bale	Guernsey	1	686	3	11	8
Flounder	1989	D. Kane	Jersey	1	190	2	10	0
Garfish	2002	A. Gibbons	Guernsey	1	256	2	12	5
Gurnard, Grey	1999	W. Gough	Sark	0	600	1	5	3
Gurnard, Red	1995	B. Le Noury	Sark	1	295	2	13	11
Gurnard, Tub	2010	L. Le Poidevin	Sark	3	632	8	0	2
Haddock	1982	S. Martel	Guernsey	0	992	2	3	0
Hake	1984	S. Arthurs	Jersey	7	030	15	8	0
John Dory	2001	J. Cataroche	Guernsey	5	000	11	0	5
Ling	1979	Mrs A. Wright	Alderney	16	726	36	14	0
Lumpsucker	1971	C. Browning	Guernsey	2	500	5	8	3
Mackerel	1992	P. M. Walsh	Guernsey	1	888	4	2	10
Mackerel, Spanish	2008	K. Beausire	Sark	0	609	1	5	8*
Megrim	1991	A. Savident	Guernsey	0	655	1	7	2
Monkfish	1971	R. Weafer	Jersey	18	540	40	14	0
Mullet, Grey, Golden	2003	M. Bourgaize	Guernsey	1	139	2	8	3
Mullet, Grey, Thick-Lipped	2008	R. Smith	Alderney	4	008	8	7	6
Mullet, Grey, Thin-Lipped	2010	D. Kane	Jersey	2	987	6	9	6*
Mullet, Red	1981	M. J. Hamel	Guernsey	1	559	3	7	0*
Plaice	1978	C. Merrien	Guernsey	3	956	8	11	9
Pollack	2001	P. Berry	Guernsey	11	680	25	12	0
Pout	1998	P. McMullen	Jersey	1	817	4	0	2
Ray, Blonde	1993	W. Latham	Jersey	16	442	36	4	0
Ray, Bottlenose	1975	E. Buesnel	Jersey	9	071	20	0	0
Ray, Eagle	1971	M. Goddard	Jersey	22	226	49	0	0
Ray, Marbled Electric	1990	A. Thomas	Jersey	6	542	14	7	0
Ray, Small-Eyed	1986	I. Nuttall	Jersey	6	917	15	4	0
Ray, Spotted	1982	D. Sebire	Guernsey	2	310	5	1	8
Ray, Sting	1983	R. Pallot	Jersey	25	911	57	2	0
Ray, Thornback	1969	E. Le Rossignol	Jersey	10	234	22	9	0
Ray, Undulate	1986	D. Taylor	Jersey	9	752	21	8	0
Rockling, Three-bearded	1991	A. Dunglinson	Guernsey	0	779	1	11	8
Salmon	1984	K. Crowhurst	Jersey	2	147	4	11	12
Scad	2007	M. Giles	Guernsey	0	958	2	1	13
Sea Trout	1998	P. Pratesi	Jersey	4	695	10	5	10
Shad, Twaite	1982	G. Staples	Sark	0	857	1	14	4
Shad, Allis	1985	W. Latham	Jersey	0	405	0	14	5
Shark, Blue	2001	T. Phillips	Jersey	62	596	138	0	0
Shark, Porbeagle	1969	D. Bougourd	Jersey	195	044	430	0	0
Shark, Thresher	1961	R. Varcoe	Jersey	71	667	158	0	0
Skate, Common	1968	Mrs N. Alexandre	Jersey	10	120	22	5	0
Smooth Hound	2008	D. Kane	Jersey	5	503	12	2	2
Smooth Hound, Starry	2006	P. Wheaton	Jersey	9	865	21	12	0
Sole, Common	1993	M. S. Eppelein	Guernsey	1	864	4	1	12
Sunfish	1989	D. Kane	Jersey	24	720	54	8	0
Tope	1983	R. Hays	Alderney	25	287	55	12	0
Trigger Fish	1991	M. Le Riche	Jersey	2	195	4	13	7
Turbot	2005	J. Robert	Sark	13	721	30	4	0
Weever, Greater	2004	P. Berry	Alderney	0	464	1	0	5
Whiting	1998	S. Savident	Sark	2	381	5	4	0
Wrasse, Ballan	1999	T. Heart	Jersey	4	302	9	7	12*
Wrasse, Cuckoo	2007	P. Broe Bougourd	Guernsey	0	955	2	1	11

*British Rod-Caught Record.

283

Channel Islands (rod caught) Mini records, 2011

SPECIES	DATE	CAPTOR	LOCATION	Grammes	oz	dms
Atherine Smelt	1975	A. Laws	Guernsey	72	2	9*
Blenny, Tompot	2005	A. J. Leaman	Sark	149	5	4
Bream, Axillary	1995	J. Breedijk	Guernsey	237	8	5*
Comber	1978	L. Gallienne	Guernsey	400	14	1
Dragonet	1981	J. K. Taylor	Guernsey	117	4	2
Goby, Black	1982	P. Rondel	Jersey	29	1	0
Goby, Giant	1994	A. M. Carre	Guernsey	262	9	4*
Goby, Rock	1979	K. Skinner	Jersey	17	0	9
Gurnard, Streaked	1993	J. West	Guernsey	290	10	4
Herring	1990	R. Langlois	Guernsey	363	12	13
Pilchard	1990	M. Pirouet	Jersey	204	7	3
Pipefish, Greater	1969	D. Sheath	Guernsey	40	1	7
Poor Cod	1988	L. R. Le Page	Guernsey	170	6	0
Rockling, Five-bearded	1992	A. Letto	Jersey	184	6	8
Sandeel, Corbins	1978	S. Carter	Jersey	128	4	9*
Sandeel, Greater	1979	B. K. Le Breton	Herm	239	8	7*
Saury Pike	2007	R. Wheatland	Alderney	76	2	8
Sea Scorpion, Long-Spined	1995	M. E. Bewey	Guernsey	229	8	1
Shanny	1977	K. J. Woolfe	Guernsey	65	2	4
Tadpole Fish	1995	L. F. Bearder	Guernsey	439	15	8
Topknot, Common	1998	R. Thomson	Guernsey	382	13	8*
Weever, Lesser	1994	C. D. Druce	Guernsey	67	2	6
Whiting, Blue	1980	S. Clyde	Guernsey	114	4	0
Wrasse, Baillon's	2001	L. R. Le Page	Guernsey	198	7	0
Wrasse, Corkwing	1977	M. P. Smith	Guernsey	286	10	1
Wrasse, Goldsinny	1977	A. de Guerin	Guernsey	56	1	15
Wrasse, Rock Cook	1977	A. de Guerin	Guernsey	72	2	8

*British Rod-Caught Record.

The angler's quest for beating records gets harder each year as the standard of the Bailiwick record lists continues to rise.

There are, however, other targets, particularly for anglers who belong to one of the local clubs.

Nearly all clubs keep records of their own. They are generally of a high standard, the club insisting that the fish are weighed on club or commercial scales and that there is a check on the correct identification.

The quality of the list reflects, to a degree, the age of the club. The older the organisation, the better and more settled the record list.

As in the case of Bailiwick records, the clubs often use their own records as a yardstick for club specimen fish competitions, and present awards to members who improve on the club's best fish.

Then there are personal records, which differ from all other records in that the angler can compile them in any form that he or she wishes. Some anglers don't bother, they look upon it was a lot of boring and unnecessary paper work.

Some merely keep a list of their best fish of each species while others keep a comprehensive dossier of all their angling exploits.

With such a variety of fishing venues both ashore and afloat, the extreme range and strengths of the tides and the varying climatic conditions, detailed records can be a great aid to future planning.

Records which list the venue fished, the time of the year, the state of the tide, the time of the day (or night) the prevailing weather conditions, the bait used, and details of the catch, can confirm a pattern of fish habits and can make all the difference between success and failure on future fishing trips. Keeping clear accurate personal records, in what ever form, adds great interest to the angler's sport, and is highly recommended.

Bailiwick anglers are fortunate in having such a unique and comprehensive range of records at which to aim their sights.

The ongoing success of the record lists rests in anglers' hands. If they take the trouble to submit claims it will ensure that the Bailiwick's best fish continue to be accurately and historically recorded at British, Channel Island, Bailiwick, club and who knows even at world level!

It's certainly an interesting task to be involved in the administration of the record process. If anglers get the chance to take their turn on the Record Committee they will find it a very rewarding experience.

Many British and Bailiwick records have been caught in local waters by visiting anglers.

If you are a visitor and catch a superb fish during your stay you may not know who to contact.

In that happy situation see any one of the local tackle dealers. In such a small and close knit community as the Bailiwick, they will know who you should see and will usually ensure that the relevant person is contacted.

If any angler believes that they have caught a record fish they must observe the following guidelines. Obtain the names and addresses of two witnesses to the capture whenever possible or, in the event of no witnesses to the actual capture being available, the names and addresses of some reliable persons who have actually seen the fish at the earliest possible time after capture.

Weigh the fish on modern tested scales, the weighing to be verified by two independent witnesses who should not be relations of the claimant. Fish must be weighed ashore, claims for record fish weighed on a boat will not be accepted.

Preserve your fish intact. This is important until the fish has been positively identified. In the event of a delay occurring between the capture of the fish and the formal identification of it by a Record Committee representative, arrange for it to be placed in a refrigerator, but have it accurately weighed and witnessed first. Fish may also be kept alive in a keep-net or container.

Contact any of the Record Committee members.

Complete the official claim form, obtaining witnesses' signatures where required.

Wherever possible, support your claim with photographs. These should be large and in focus, showing as many of the specific characteristics of the species as possible.

Unless these simple procedures are followed it is possible that a record claim could be unsuccessful.

The following account of one claim, clearly illustrates the problems that can arise, leading to a probable disappointing outcome.

In October 2004 a 10-3-0 ballan wrasse was landed at Cobo. The shore-caught specimen would have smashed the 8-10-13 Bailiwick record, the 8-13-2 Channel Island record and the 9-1-0 British record. However, the young captor and his family had recently taken up residence in Guernsey after moving from abroad, and consequently had no knowledge of what the fish was, it's record potential, the procedure necessary to claim the records or who to contact for advice.

It was only weighed on unreliable domestic scales and was cut up and eaten before the record committee representative had the opportunity to see the fish and complete the necessary formal identification. Needless to say, the chance of pursuing a successful record claim was impossible. As a result the young angler's opportunity to become a national and local record holder was lost.

The story of local records cannot be closed without expressing gratitude to the Guernsey Press. They have sponsored the committee since its inception for its day-to-day running costs and have regularly published angling news in their sports pages.

The support given by the Press has not only helped the committee to fulfil its mandate by removing any financial worries, but has also ensured that since 1966 anglers have always been kept fully informed on up-to-date record information.

For over 35 years the Press published its updated record lists in the angling column, which appeared in their sports section.

A problem arose when the Press changed its format from broadsheet to tabloid for the comparatively large space that was needed to publish the lists was not always available. As a consequence the Record Committee decided to produce a booklet containing all the Bailiwick and Channel Island lists. The first issue appeared in August 2004 and has become an annual publication that comes out in January / February of each year.

As from issue four in February 2006 it was enlarged to include not just the lists but also the committee rules, aims and objectives, notes for the guidance of claimants, a list of the current members, and a claim form. The booklet can be obtained from local tackle dealers at a very modest sum a charge that is necessary to cover printing and distribution costs.

Chapter 10 - Conclusions

The Bailiwick of Guernsey is not blessed with the big game fishing for exotic species that can be found in the warmer seas and oceans of the world, but it is fortunate to have a dynamic environment that supports a great variety of different, if more modest species.

The small size of the islands allows the local anglers to enjoy the area's great potential, literally 'on their doorstep' so it's not surprising that angling is so popular.

It's a fact that the angling infrastructure in the Bailiwick is almost out of all proportion for the size of the community.

In September 2009 it was estimated that the islands of the Bailiwick had a total population of approximately 65,000 and yet there are 10 tackle dealers, eight angling clubs including The Guernsey Freshwater Angling Society, 10 annual open angling competitions or festivals (including one for children), two continuous running specimen fish competitions and its own 'national' record lists.

A situation that surely is almost unique, and one that would be the envy of many other angling centres.

All this has not happened by chance. It has been achieved by the hard work of dedicated angling administrators, who have put in many hours of their own time, that has ensured that new ideas have been introduced, and that clubs and open competitions have continued to operate successfully.

In most sports the burden of office tends to fall on just a few and angling is no exception.

Every angler who has put in even a few hours on behalf of his sport deserves the profound thanks of all those who "wet a line", for their efforts have helped to ensure the continuing success of the sport to the benefit of all.

There are a few anglers who deserve special recognition. Some were the stalwarts in the early days who had the foresight and imagination to introduce many new activities and facilities that are taken for granted today. Others are those who have put in very many years of service not just to one club or committee, but across a wide spectrum of angling administration.

Peter Witterick was one of those early stalwarts who fully deserves the greatest accolade from the Bailiwick angling fraternity His efforts on behalf of angling were quite remarkable and it's not surprising that his achievements have already been mentioned in this publication.

He was the Guernsey Press angling columnist for over 30 years and in 1957 he wrote the only book on local angling that was published prior to the first edition of this book.

In the early days he used the weekly angling column to try and encourage anglers to think positively about their sport and try to correct many of the anomalies and prejudices that existed at the time. There is no doubt that the steady progress of Bailiwick angling towards a more dynamic and modern approach was largely down to his influence.

As a member of the Guernsey Sea Anglers Club committee, he was the main architect of the competition points system which is now widely used by angling clubs throughout the islands.

He was a founder member and the first secretary of the 30 Fathom Club and one of the prime movers in the formation and setting up of the Bailiwick of Guernsey Record (Rod-Caught) Fish Committee and became its first chairman, remaining in the post for 14 years.

He was responsible for the start of the Gladstone Specimen Fish Competition which soon became the Fish of the Month, and the Bass Charrington Bass Competition which was one of the forerunners of the present day Phoenix Fish Bass Competition. He became the first secretary of the Guernsey Anglers Competition Committee, a post he was to hold for over 10 years.

As the angling activity in the Bailiwick expanded with an increasing number of clubs and organisations, anglers were needed who were prepared to give a lot of their time in administration work.

There is no better example of dedication in this regard than the much respected Harold Bewey. His range of accepted responsibilities must be almost unique.

He served for 14 years on the GSAC Committee, 12 years as the club's vice-president. He was the chairman of the Bailiwick of Guernsey Record (Rod-Caught) Fish Committee and the chairman of the Guernsey Anglers Team Knock-Out Competition. He was the first president of the now defunct Guernsey Federation of Sea Anglers and served a period as president of the Guernsey Bass Anglers Sportfishing Society. He also spent many years on the Guernsey Anglers Competition Committee.

He was greatly in favour of more contact between Bailiwick anglers and those elsewhere.

In both 1979 and 1980 he was the manager of the Guernsey teams which took part in International Team Angling Competitions in Cobh, Eire. Under his guidance the teams did exceptionally well, particularly in 1980, returning with many awards. He also organised an international festival in Guernsey, but sadly this did not find enough support to make it a success, although no fault can be attributed to Harold in this regard.

There have of course been many other dedicated anglers, many of whom have put in over 20 years of work for the angling community.

These include Ernie Baker, tackle dealer, GSAC President, 30 Fathom Club President and Guernsey Anglers Competition Committee Member. Mick Le Sauvage 27 years Guernsey Anglers Team Knock-Out Committee Secretary, 18 years Jamaica Inn Angling Club Secretary and Bill Tabel, 17 years GATKOC Chairman, secretary of the Telephone Angling Club and a period on the GSAC committee including a term as the club's vice-president.

There was the quiet man of angling administration, Dave Sebire who completed 27 years as GATKOC Treasurer and 15 years on GACC and was a member of the Bailiwick Record Committee for a number of years. Others include John Petit who served the 30 Fathom Club and more recently the Royal

Fathomers AC for over 25 years, filling various posts including chairman, secretary, treasurer and trip organiser. Pip Le Blancq who was on the GSAC committee for well over 20 years as treasurer and vice-president as well as serving many years on the Record Committee including a five year spell as its chairman.

Other dedicated administrators were Steve Elliott, ex Telephone Angling Club Chairman, recorder of GACC and Record Committee Member. Joe Gomez, President of the Guernsey Mullet Club, vice-president of the GSAC and treasurer/assistant recorder of the Record Committee, Mike Weysom, who has filled various positions on the GSAC committee including junior section secretary, competition secretary and President, was competition secretary of the Guernsey Freshwater Angling Society, secretary of the Guernsey Mullet Club, Vice President and President of the Guernsey Trout Society, and was secretary of the now defunct Guernsey Association of Angling Clubs. Peter Frise vice-president of the Guernsey Mullet Club and GSAC boat organiser, Len Hall from the GSAC and GACC and Len Benoist ex POAC president and GACC member. Some anglers restrict their loyalty and hard work to support just one organisation, a good example being Dave Copperwaite who has been chairman of the Guernsey Freshwater Angling Society for over 30 years.

Boat skipper Roy Taylor with a gaffed ling.

Thankfully there is a continuing stream of anglers who are prepared to put something into their sport as well as taking things out! Maybe when the next Bailiwick angling book is compiled it will include angling administrators of more recent times, those who have filled a number of different posts.

Commercial angling boat skippers have also played their part in the success of Bailiwick angling, both as regards competitive fishing and in more recent years the exploitation of the more distant marks, especially the wrecks.

Almost certainly the longest serving boat skipper and the most flamboyant was Roy Taylor. For a period of 25 years, at first with the Highland Laddie and then with the Belle de Serk catamaran he took out not just the locals but many thousands of visitors.

One of the earliest skippers was Louis Marella. He was soon followed by Graham Cowley, Frank Le Page and Bill Ogier, who took out the then fledgling 30 Fathom Club on shark and deep sea trips.

Other skippers have included Arnie Brehaut, Dave Langlois, Dougal Lane, Alf

Taylor, Tim Morris, Brian Blondel, Richard Keen, Graham Eker and Richard Seager.

Sponsorship has become an increasing factor in Bailiwick angling. The Fish of the Month and Bass competitions, open angling festivals and individual clubs have all benefited from the financial and sometimes practical support that has been given, not just from tackle dealers but from companies across a wide spectrum of the local business community.

Compared with other sports the amounts concerned are extremely small, but it has helped clubs to cover their expenses and greatly enhanced the number and value of prizes awarded in the many competitions. The sport owes all those who support angling a great debt of gratitude.

The best way for anglers to show their appreciation to both sponsors and the sport's administrators is to continue to give active support to the competitions.

Visitors to the Bailiwick and indeed local residents may well gain the impression that local angling is a very successful, thriving sport. This would be a logical assumption, bearing in mind its comprehensive infrastructure, its level of activity, and the considerable support it enjoys.

Paradoxically this is not the case. It is probably the highest participant sport in the islands and yet in spite of the successes and achievments of the angling clubs, including the numerous open events, it remains without doubt the Bailiwick's Cinderella sport!

It suffers from a number of fundamental problems.

(a)   A lack of respect for the sport from the community.

Anglers are usually treated with disdain or complete disinterest. In spite of its enormous popularity it does not enjoy the recognition that is given to other sports such as football, cricket or golf.

Anglers have to put up with indifference, particularly by other sea-users to the point where at times their sport and enjoyment becomes adversely affected.

Crabpots, trots and nets are often laid very close inshore, at known popular shore angling marks. Boats, including yachts and sailing dinghies will cut across anglers lines even when there is ample space to avoid such incidents. Commercial fishing boats will often work so close inshore they will break anglers tackle and there have even been instances where rod and reels have been dragged into the sea.

Sadly it seems that anglers have no recourse in such incidents, they have to be accepted as hazards over which the angler has apparently no control.

(b)   An appalling lack of recognition by the establishment, including the Bailiwick's politicians.

They don't seem to realise angling's value to the island's economy either regarding jobs or tourism. Even though many recent comprehesive studies in the UK have proved that recreational angling is of great benefit both in monetary and social terms to the local community. In many cases these benefits outweigh those that arise from commercial fishing activities.

All would agree that support from both the government and the community, to ensure the futures of the professional fishermen is essential.

However, the enormous contribution made by recreational angling cannot be ignored and should be given a much higher profile when any new policies are being considered.

Decisions that affect angling are made quite unilaterally without any consultation or any effort to seek anglers' views. The need to close parts of the docks to anglers might be justified for safety or security reasons, but no contact is made to explain or discuss the situation with the anglers who may have been fishing the areas in question for years.

Boat moorings have been allowed to cover many of the traditional bait digging grounds with anglers being warned off by boat owners or parish authorities from areas where bait has been dug for decades.

Conservation areas have been discussed so will these be the next parts of the shore-line where bait collection and angling will be banned? — and will the anglers' points of view be sought at the time? As things currently stand that's very doubtful.

(c)   There is the complete lack of facilities that has already been discussed in an earlier chapter.

(d)   In 2006/2007 the question of bag limits was raised by the authorities for the first time.

They were concerned over the activities of the large number of English charter boats that came over to enjoy the excellent fishing around Alderney.

Large catches of turbot, brill, bass and pollack were made and there were allegations that some of the fish were being sold by boat skippers who did not have a license to sell their catch.

The Guernsey Sea Fisheries decided to overcome this perceived problem by proposing that bag limits be set for these charter boats. Each angler would be restricted to just two fish each of the following species, turbot, brill, bass, pollack, rays and black bream.

Many visiting anglers indicated that if this ruling was introduced they could boycott such trips, which would not only be of great detriment to the livelihood of the boat skippers, but also to Alderney itself, whose economy greatly benefited from so many anglers visiting the northern isle.

The Sea Fisheries sent out a consulation document to all parties that could be affected by such a ruling, including the angling fraternity.

The bag limit proposal generally had a hostile and critical reception. A flood of replies, many containing alternative ideas in how the problem could be solved.

291

Many anglers feared that this introduction of bag limits would be the thin edge of the wedge, and rules brought in for the visiting charter boats would soon spread and be applied to all local angling activities, including private boats, although any such intention was emphatically denied by the authorities.

At that time the matter was not brought to a conclusion.

However in 2010 the subject was raised again up in Alderney, where it was part of a Sea Fisheries consultation paper dealing with future fishing policy in the northern isle.

It follows that there is still a possibilty of bag limits being introduced at some time in the future.

(e)   Every other leading sport caters for its juniors. They are considered to be the sports future and are given training, help and encouragement. This doesn't happen in Bailiwick angling organisations. The GSAC have a junior section, and other clubs have the odd youngster but that's all. There is no coordinated effort to encourage juniors in to the sport or to provide tuition for the youngsters.

Further problems will soon arise. All of which could have adverse and far reaching effects on future angling activities.

Anglers could be banned from certain areas both afloat and on shore. They have already lost access to many parts if the harbour as well as the east side of Beaucette Marina. Matters could get worse with the probable introduction of marine conservation areas and the installation of tide and/or wind turbines.

The angling fraternity have never made requests to the community for anything! Unlike other sports they do not require large tracts of land to provide playing areas, they do not need large buildings, they do not need to close off roads, or take over large areas of the harbour to run their activities.

The majority of anglers just wish to quietly pursue their sport. This may well be the main reason that anglers are largely ignored. It has such a low profile that they are forgotten when issues arise that will affect them.

What must be done to overcome the growing list of problems and unsatis-actory situations? Anglers must shake off the complacency and appalling apathy that currently exists and start to be in control of it's own destiny.

It is essential that it must start by putting it's own house in order. It must have strong leadership and an elected central organisation consisting of dedicated positive thinking anglers.

Past failures in this regard must be forgotten, and the sport must look to the future.

Its purpose would be to raise the level of awareness about angling throughout the community and to raise its profile particularly with the politicians at both States and Parish level. Its prime object would be to change people's perception and place angling where it belongs, on a par with the other popular Bailiwick sports. It would also need to find solutions to the anglers' increasing number of problems that cause so much frustration.

Such a committee would need to take an active role by ensuring that the anglers views are taken into account when new policies, rules or restrictions are being considered by the authorities.

Although there are a number of excellent club or "privately run" websites that quickly disseminates news of anglers catches and activities there would need to be an "official" website which would ensure that news and all the important matters that could affect their sport is readily available to all anglers.

Anglers have everything to enjoy in the Bailiwick, good fishing, adequate bait supplies and a wonderful marine environment. All it needs is positive action to secure its future and ensure its rightful place within the community.

If nothing is done there will certainly be long term problems that could adversly affect the wonderful sport that we all enjoy. A central body to organise and protect the sport for the good of all anglers is absolutely essential. However its creation is very unlikely bearing in mind the current apathy that bedevils our sport.

The famous civil rights leader Martin Luther King once said 'I have a dream'. Well your humble author has one as well!

He sees a well designed palatial waterfront angling headquarters at St. Peter Port Harbour. It has its own slipway pier and steps where charter and private boats can leave and return with their catches.

It has areas where competition weigh-ins are held and the results can be displayed. It has specially equipped facilities where fish can be gutted, cleaned and filleted. It has storage areas for tackle and equipment.

There are bars, lounges and a restaurant where anglers and their friends can meet socially and where members of a Bailiwick Sea Anglers Federation Committee can entertain visiting anglers, members of the media and local politicians. Committee rooms that would be used not just by the Federation but also the island's individual clubs and other angling organisations such as the Record Committee.

Sadly Martin Luther King never saw his dream on civil rights fulfilled in his lifetime and it is extremely doubtful that your author will be any more fortunate!

Finally.... more pictures from yesteryear.

Above: A general view of the GSAC individual KO's final stages held at Fontenelle Bay in February 1972.

Right: Roy Smith and Danny Inder with a modest ballan wrasse caught in the final.

A catch that pre-dates the record lists, George Le Blond with a 12-8-0 bass caught at Lancresse in March 1964.

Peter Fletcher with his 10-7-2 John Dory caught on the Great Bank. It held the Bailiwick boat record from the 30th June 1993 until 15th May 2001.

Colin Brown with the 8-7-0 plaice which held the boat record from 14th November 1976 until 15th September 1978.

295

Bernie Martel with 3-9-12 red bream which held the boat record from 7th October 1972 until 30th July 1974.

14 year old Alan Woodnutt caught this 34-15-8 record blonde ray on his first ever boat trip on 2nd January 1978. It was boated at Cocq Lihou off Alderney. The record was to stand for 27 years until 29th June 2005.

Brian England with a 20-14-0 cod caught at the Hoffets in November 1968.

The 3-13-4 gilthead bream which held the shore record from 17 October 1977 until 19th July 1980. Peter Salmon landed it at the White Rock.

Yet another record caught on The Great Bank. Martyn Torode with 12-7-6 starry smoothhound that was the boat record from 28th April 1979 until 8th October 2008.

The 22-0-0 pollack boat record caught on the 23rd July 1977 by Richard Exall. It was to hold the title until 20th January 2001.

Your author (left), Pip Le Blancq & Alf Bridel fishing a Guernsey Sea Anglers Club competition at St Martins Point in the late 1960's.